THE OXFORDSHIRE RECORD SOCIETY

The Society was founded in 1919. Its objectives are to publish transcripts, abstracts and lists of primary sources for the history of the county of Oxfordshire, and to extend awareness and understanding of archives relating to Oxfordshire. The Society welcomes proposals for volumes for publication. There are no restrictions on time period or topic.

The publication programme of the Society is overseen by an Editorial Committee, established in 2017. Its members are:

Elizabeth Gemmill, BA, MA, PhD, FRHistS
Deborah Hayter, MA
Adrienne Rosen, MA, DPhil
Kate Tiller, OBE, DL, MA, PhD, FSA, FRHistS
Simon Townley, BA, PGCE, DPhil, FSA
Arabella St John Parker (Secretary, ORS, *ex officio*)

Information about the Society, its publications and how to make a proposal for a publication may be found on its website

https://oxrecsoc.org

From Country House Catholicism to City Church

The Registers of the Oxford Catholic Mission 1700–1875

Edited by Tony Hadland

The Boydell Press
Oxfordshire Record Society
Volume 75

© Oxfordshire Record Society 2023

All rights reserved. Except as permitted under current legislation no part of this work may be photocopied, stored in a retrieval system, published, performed in public, adapted, broadcast, transmitted, recorded or reproduced in any form or by any means, without the prior permission of the copyright owner

First published 2023

An Oxfordshire Record Society publication
Published by Boydell & Brewer Ltd
PO Box 9, Woodbridge, Suffolk IP12 3DF, UK
and Boydell & Brewer Inc.
668 Mt Hope Avenue, Rochester, NY 14620–2731, USA
website: www.boydellandbrewer.com

ISBN 978-0-902509-77-1

A CIP catalogue record for this book is available
from the British Library

The publisher has no responsibility for the continued existence or accuracy of URLs for external or third-party internet websites referred to in this book, and does not guarantee that any content on such websites is, or will remain, accurate or appropriate

This publication is printed on acid-free paper

Printed and bound in Great Britain by
TJ Books Limited, Padstow, Cornwall

Contents

List of maps and illustrations	vii
Foreword	ix
Acknowledgements	xi
Abbreviations and conventions	xiii
Introduction	1
The national and local historical context	2
The legal status of Catholics	16
Locations of the Oxford Mission	29
Local timeline	47
The registers: editorial method and description of their contents	50
Commentary on entries in the registers	52
Themes found in the registers	70
The Registers: transcribed, translated, and tabulated	77
Baptisms	78
Confirmations	160
Marriages	166
Deaths and burials	175
Conversions	187
Appendices	
A: Priests of the Oxford Mission 1700–1875	191
B: The Catholic Mission at Bampton	195
Select bibliography	197
Index to the Introduction	201
Index to the Registers	207

List of maps and illustrations

Maps

Map 1. The Oxford Catholic Mission and Roman Catholicism in Oxfordshire. (Map by Giles Darkes, adapted from K. Tiller and G. Darkes (eds), *An Historical Atlas of Oxfordshire* (ORS 67, 2010), p. 85) — 27

Map 2. Post-Reformation Roman Catholic centres in Oxford. (Map by Giles Darkes) — 28

Figures

Fig. 1. Holywell Manor, Oxford. Photograph © Edward Rokita, reproduced by permission. — 30

Fig. 2. Waterperry House in 1787: engraving by Richard Corbould and John Roberts. Image © Oxfordshire History Centre, reference POX0505482. — 34

Fig. 3. The chapel of St Ignatius at St Clement's, Oxford: undated lithograph in Bodleian Library, G.A. Oxon. a.69, p. 116. Reproduced by courtesy of The Bodleian Libraries, University of Oxford. — 42

Fig. 4. The nave of St Ignatius's chapel in 1906: photograph by Henry Taunt, © Oxfordshire History Centre, reference POX0108019. — 43

Fig. 5. The sanctuary of St Ignatius's chapel in 1906: photograph by Henry Taunt, © Oxfordshire History Centre, reference POX0108030. — 43

Fig. 6. The interior of the church of St Aloysius Gonzaga on Woodstock Road, Oxford: photograph (1906) by Henry Taunt, © Oxfordshire History Centre, reference POX0107858. — 45

Fig. 7. The west front of the church of St Aloysius Gonzaga: photograph by Henry Taunt, © Oxfordshire History Centre, reference POX0107814. — 46

Fig. 8.	List of those confirmed at Waterperry 20 May 1753, from the 1700–1800 Waterperry Register: image kindly supplied by The Oxford Oratory.	54
Fig. 9.	List of death anniversaries kept at Waterperry in the late 18th century, from the 1700–1800 Waterperry Register: image kindly supplied by The Oxford Oratory.	55
Fig. 10.	First page of the burials list for St Ignatius's chapel, from the 1700–1800 Waterperry Register: image kindly supplied by The Oxford Oratory.	56
Fig. 11.	The earliest entries for marriages at Waterperry, from the 1700–1800 Waterperry Register: image kindly supplied by The Oxford Oratory.	58
Fig. 12.	First baptism entries in the St Ignatius register started in 1854: image kindly supplied by The Oxford Oratory.	63

The editor, contributors and publisher are grateful to all the institutions and persons listed for permission to reproduce the materials in which they hold copyright. Every effort has been made to trace the copyright holders; apologies are offered for any omission, and the publisher will be pleased to add any necessary acknowledgement in subsequent editions.

Foreword

This volume breaks new ground for the Oxfordshire Record Society. It is the first of its publications to make available records of post-reformation Roman Catholicism in the county.

The registers, here carefully transcribed, translated and tabulated in Tony Hadland's accessible edition, illuminate the sacramental life and rites of passage of Oxfordshire Catholics between 1700 and 1875. It is a telling span, reflecting major shifts in national and local religious life and played out in contrasting settings within the county, from rural Waterperry, to St Clements on the periphery of historic Oxford and finally to suburban Woodstock Road, close to the city centre. The registers begin with small and scattered groups whose religion was still proscribed by the state, then from the later eighteenth century increasingly move towards toleration and legal emancipation (eventually achieved in 1829) and then to a growth in numbers and a prominent presence, securely established in Victorian Oxford.

The records opened up by this volume will be of use and interest to historians of religion, locality and family alike. They throw light on an era of 'country house' Catholicism, when the practice of the faith was largely linked to the presence of local landowners, they illuminate the theory and practice of legal exclusion, the gradual movement to a more public faith, and the emergence of a confident and outward-looking Roman Catholic role. The names and identities recorded in the registers help identify the nature of congregations and how they changed and varied over time.

ORS is delighted to fill this gap in its coverage of Oxfordshire records. It could not have been achieved without the help of many, above all of Tony Hadland as volume editor. The book was brought to publication in the difficult and disrupted days of 2020 and 2021. Particular thanks for their help and advice are due to the members of ORS's Editorial Committee, to Professor Bill Gibson and Dr Colin Haydon, and to colleagues at Boydell & Brewer.

Kate Tiller, Chair, Oxfordshire Record Society

Acknowledgements

The editor gratefully acknowledges the assistance, guidance and support provided by Dr Kate Tiller, the late Fr Jerome Bertram, Dr Colin Haydon, Professor William Gibson, Paul Gaskell, the staff of Oxfordshire History Centre, and Rosemary Hadland. Any errors are entirely the responsibility of the editor.

Abbreviations and conventions

CO	Congregation of the Oratory (Oratorian priest)
CRS	Catholic Record Society
Fr	Father (originally used only for Jesuit priests)
ODNB	*Oxford Dictionary of National Biography* (2004)
ORS	Oxfordshire Record Society
OSB	Order of St Benedict (Benedictine monk)
OSF	Order of St Francis (Franciscan friar)
OSFC	Order of St Francis, Capuchin (Capuchin friar)
SJ	Society of Jesus (Jesuit priest)
Stapleton	Mrs B. Stapleton, *A History of the Post-Reformation Catholic Missions in Oxfordshire* (London, 1906)
VCH	*Victoria County History* (London, 1900–)

Following standard conventions, Acts of Parliament are cited by chapter number, preceded by the year(s) of the reign during which the relevant parliamentary session was held and the monarch's name.

Unless otherwise indicated:
All dates are New Style, with the year beginning on 1 January (rather than 25 March, Lady Day, as was the norm until 1752).
Catholic means Roman Catholic.
Recusant means Catholic recusant.
St Clement's means the Oxford suburb rather than the Anglican parish.

Conversions of historical sums of money to present-day equivalents may be made from L.H. Officer and S.H. Williamson, 'Five ways to compute the relative value of a UK pound amount, 1270 to present', at https://www.measuringworth.com.
In the period covered, a pound (£) was divided into twenty shillings (s), each comprising twelve pence (d).
An English mark was two thirds of a pound, i.e. 13s 4d.

Introduction

This volume presents the contents of the sacramental records known to survive from the Oxford Catholic Mission, 1700–1875. These original registers are held in five volumes in the Archives of the Oxford Oratory. The Oratory's Oxfordshire archive consists of registers from Waterperry House, the chapel of St Clement's, Oxford, and the church of St Aloysius Gonzaga, Oxford. A further brief register from the Catholic chapel of St Mary the Virgin, Bampton, 1856–60 (see Appendix B) found its archival home in this collection although it is not historically linked to the Oxford Mission, and has been included in this volume for completeness. The registers feature much common form and use of Latin, and the contents are made accessible here in transcribed, translated, and tabulated form.

The registers record the sacramental life and rites of passage of what began as a small, thinly spread community of Oxfordshire Catholics. They were drawn from a cross-section of society much like other Oxfordshire people, except that they were Roman Catholics. The documents start in 1700 and go on to span the watershed of Catholic Emancipation in 1829. They record the transition from 'hidden' country house Catholicism to a city church with influential priests and a varied, sometimes international, congregation. In 1700, Catholicism had been proscribed by the state. Over the following two centuries the implementation of anti-Catholic legislation was first eased and then, from 1778, followed by new measures of toleration and eventually emancipation. The Catholic community in the county grew, reflecting general population growth, immigration from Catholic countries and, at some periods, evangelisation and conversion (particularly from the Church of England). The Catholic presence also shifted geographically, from Waterperry to St Clement's to Woodstock Road, from a small, discreet base in the countryside to the fringes of Oxford and then to a respectable suburb close to the city centre. To help understand the national and local background to the registers, this introduction offers an overview of their historical context and a commentary on the register texts as follows:

- The national and local historical context
- The legal status of Catholics
- Locations of the Oxford Mission
- Local timeline
- The registers: editorial method and description of contents
- Commentary on entries in the registers
- Themes found in the registers

The national and local historical context
Elizabethan legacies

In July 1586, nearly two decades after Queen Elizabeth I rejected the Pope's authority over the English Church, a secret conference was held at Harleyford Manor in Buckinghamshire, seven miles downstream from Henley-on-Thames. The conference attendees included the only members of the Society of Jesus then in England: the Jesuit superior William Weston, the poet Robert Southwell, and Henry Garnet. The conference lasted a week, discussing how to maintain Catholicism in England and how best to try to reconvert the country, now that the religion was proscribed, its adherents persecuted and its priests threatened with death. The answer was a strategy whereby Catholic clergy would be distributed about the country, living in the houses of sympathetic gentlemen. Each priest would be responsible for ministering not only to his host's household but also to a surrounding area, and would pass as his host's friend, relative, tutor or steward. Thus, for the next two hundred years, most Catholic missions were chaplaincies based in country houses. One of these was Waterperry House in Oxfordshire.[1]

Terms used to describe Catholics in this period include 'recusants', those who refused to attend Church of England services as required by law (from the Latin verb *recusare*, to refuse). Recusancy could result in heavy fines, sequestration of property and imprisonment. Most recusants were Catholics, referred to by the authorities as 'popish recusants'. In this volume, unless otherwise indicated, the term 'recusant' denotes Catholic dissenters. The word 'papist' was a widely used and deliberately pejorative term for Catholics, stressing their supposed loyalty to the Pope rather than to the monarch. The term 'Roman Catholic' was rarely used before the early seventeenth century.

Some Catholics, especially male heads of gentry families during the reign of Elizabeth, conformed outwardly to the Church of England while maintaining a Catholic chaplain and household. They were known as 'church papists' because they attended the parish church and thus, avoided the punishments inflicted on recusants. Church papists were regarded as neither fish nor fowl by popish recusants and Protestants alike. However, without church papistry, Catholicism in England would not have survived as it did.[2] During Elizabeth's reign, up to a third of Oxfordshire gentry were identified as loyal to Catholicism. As many as 171 Oxfordshire parishes have some history of recusancy.[3]

---

1   M. Hodgetts, *Secret Hiding Places* (Dublin, 1989), pp. 9–12, 143.
2   A. Walsham, *Church Papists* (Woodbridge, 1993).
3   M. Hodges, 'Roman Catholic Recusants 1558–1800', in K. Tiller and G. Darkes (eds), *An Historical Atlas of Oxfordshire* (ORS 67, 2010), pp. 84–5, 172.

James II and the 'Glorious Revolution'

In 1685 James, Duke of York, was already an enthusiastic Catholic convert when he acceded to the throne as King James II and shortly after his coronation, the Vatican reinstated the role of Vicar Apostolic (missionary bishop) in England. John Leyburn, formerly President of the English College at Douai in northern France, was appointed to the position in 1685 and set up headquarters in Lincoln's Inn Fields, London. The king funded him to the considerable sum of £1,000 per annum and approved the appointment of three other Vicars Apostolic.[4]

James embarked on a rapid and insensitive programme of positive discrimination in favour of Catholics and Catholicism. He set up a Catholic royal chapel in London and thereafter many other Catholic chapels opened across the country. In the spring of 1687, the king issued a Declaration of Indulgence, suspending anti-Catholic legislation and giving rights of public worship to Catholics and Protestant Nonconformists alike. A year later, the Declaration having been widely ignored, he reissued it with the comment that 'we cannot but heartily wish, as it will easily be believed, that all the people of our dominions were members of the Catholic Church; yet … conscience ought not to be constrained nor people forced in matters of mere religion'.[5]

Although clearly favouring Catholicism, this was the most liberal official stance on religious plurality in England's history up to that time.[6] Moreover, the king also provided support for Huguenot refugees fleeing Catholic France. But he was a strong believer in royal power, and tried to implement major shifts of policy against the will of Parliament. Seven Anglican bishops, including the Archbishop of Canterbury, presented a petition seeking relief from the requirement to read the Declaration of Indulgence in Anglican churches; they were tried for seditious libel but acquitted. The King's positive discrimination in favour of Catholics was too much, too soon. Many Protestants had already been disturbed by his harsh treatment of the Monmouth rebels. The triumphalist attitude of some Catholics, following the reissue of the Declaration of Indulgence, did not help their cause.

In 1688, James was removed in what became known as the Glorious Revolution, characterised by a recent historian as the 'first modern revolution'. With support from some English Protestant nobility and gentry, James's Dutch Protestant nephew and son-in-law, William of Orange, landed in Devon with an estimated 15,000 to 21,000 troops.[7] As the Dutch army advanced across Wessex towards London,

---

4   J.A. Hilton (ed.), *Bishop Leyburn's Confirmation Register of 1687* (Wigan, 1987), p. 2.
5   H. Bettenson, *Documents of the Christian Church* (Oxford, 1967), p. 298.
6   Though many regarded the policy as a feint to permit Catholicisation, after which Protestantism would be proscribed. Lord Halifax's *A Letter to a Dissenter* (London, 1687) commented (p. 3) that 'You are therefore to be hugged now, only that you may be the better squeezed at another time'.
7   E. Vallance, *The Glorious Revolution* (London, 2007), pp. 113, 123; see also W. Gibson, *James II and the Trial of the Seven Bishops* (Basingstoke, 2009) and S. Pincus, *1688, The First Modern Revolution* (New Haven, 2009) for recent accounts of these events.

James retreated and eventually went into exile in France. William of Orange entered London and, after a convention of former MPs and peers, Parliament recognised him and his wife Mary as joint monarchs. Three of the four Vicars Apostolic, including Bishop Leyburn, were arrested and held for two years without trial.[8] Inflammatory anti-Protestant comments by the Catholic landlord of the Mitre Inn at Oxford led to the mob smashing the windows of Catholic houses in the city.[9]

The 1689 Bill of Rights prescribed the line of succession to the monarchy to ensure that no Catholic could succeed to the throne in the foreseeable future. This was reinforced by the 1701 Act of Settlement, which stated that no Catholic, nor anyone married to a Catholic, could be monarch. Moreover, the sovereign had to swear to uphold the Church of England. To crush Catholicism, the new regime used social engineering and the fear of long prison sentences, rather than the threat of torture and execution. Various measures were put in place in 1689 immediately following the accession of William and Mary. Other anti-Catholic legislation was enacted over the following seventeen years.[10]

The possession of landed property by the Catholic gentry and nobility was an important factor in the survival of Catholicism. The government therefore introduced several measures to penalise Catholic landowners and thereby encourage them to abandon their religion. There was to be none of the inspirational glamour of martyrdom, with its attendant bad publicity for the English regime abroad (though the treatment of Ireland was deplored in Catholic states). Instead, Catholics were to be ground down by a sort of internal exile based on economic disadvantage, diminished status and loss of political and social freedom. It was a remarkably effective strategy.

Jacobitism

Throughout the history of Catholic recusancy in England, enforcement of anti-Catholic legislation was sporadic and half-hearted. Government clampdowns tended to be reactions to specific perceived threats. Sometimes these threats were imaginary but usually there was enough evidence to justify the action. A major reason for the actions instigated against Catholics by the regime of William and Mary and their successors was the Jacobite threat to restore James II and his successors to the British throne. Jacobitism was not confined to Catholics (supporters included Scottish Episcopalians, dispossessed Irish landowners and some Anglican Tories) but English Catholics were well represented among their numbers. Between 1689 and 1693, the exiled Stuart court commissioned more than forty English Catholic officers into six regiments; and between 1694 and 1701 about forty English Catholics

---

8   J.C.H. Aveling, *The Handle and the Axe* (Colchester, 1976), p. 240.
9   Mrs B. Stapleton, *A History of the Post-Reformation Catholic Missions in Oxfordshire* (London, 1906) [hereafter Stapleton], p. 217.
10 See pp. 16–25.

and their families, including half the Catholic peerage, were in residence at the court in exile.[11]

While the government found little evidence of enduring active Jacobite support among Catholics in Oxfordshire, Jacobite sympathies lingered in some quarters. A few recusants raising the occasional toast to 'the little gentleman in black velvet'[12] did not pose a great menace. But what if such sentiment led to an armed rising? Toryism was strong in Oxfordshire and a Jacobite alliance between Tories and the Catholic gentry was a possibility. An example of an Oxfordshire Anglican Tory Jacobite was Sir James Dashwood (1715–79) of Kirtlington Park, who was sympathetic to the lifting of legal restrictions on Catholics and helped at least one Catholic friend get round them. Dashwood was a candidate in the Oxfordshire parliamentary election of 1754, 'one of the most notorious of the eighteenth century for bribery and chicanery'. The result was fiercely contested. Whig accusations of 'popery' featured strongly, including an attempt to associate the Tories with the Rag Plot, in which a Carfax grocer's wife had allegedly discovered treasonable Jacobite verses in a bundle of rags outside the shop.[13]

The Jacobite risings of 1715, 1719 and 1745 proved that there was a real threat, especially in Scotland and northern England. However, the failure of the '45 demonstrated the decline of English support for the cause, even in formerly strong Jacobite areas of the north. The refusal thereafter of the Pope to recognise Charles Edward Stuart as Charles III considerably weakened the Jacobite threat. In 1759, without the involvement of Charles Edward Stuart, the French attempted to harness Jacobitism in a final unsuccessful attempt to invade Scotland, when the French fleet was defeated by the Royal Navy at Quiberon Bay off the west coast of France. Thereafter, there was no common political stance among recusant Catholic gentry and nobility. As Glickman points out:

> Recusant lay leaders adopted a variety of political postures in engagement with the Hanoverian kingdom. Catholic stances could range from the loyalist Toryism of the Welds, as friends of George III, to the Whig grandeur of the house of Norfolk, to the radical spirit that rose among the Swinburnes of Capheaton, who 'scandalised' the ageing Jacobites of their county with histrionic displays of support for the revolution in France.[14]

---

11 G. Glickman, *The English Catholic Community, 1688–1745: Politics, Culture and Ideology* (Woodbridge, 2009), pp. 259–61.
12 An allusion to the mole whose hole caused the death of William III by tripping his horse.
13 R.J. Robson, *The Oxfordshire Election of 1754* (1949); W.R. Ward, *Georgian Oxford* (Oxford, 1958), p. 195; G.H. Dannatt, *The Oxfordshire Election of 1754* (Oxfordshire County Council Record Publication no. 6, 1970).
14 Glickman, *English Catholic Community*, p. 254.

Later eighteenth-century Catholicism

The repressive anti-Catholic legislation had impinged considerably on religious practice in the Catholic missions. Hidden worship usually had to be in places with a legitimate secular use, such as attics, bedrooms, storerooms or workshops, and this encouraged simplicity and minimalism. There was little scope for statues, votive candles or any form of specifically Catholic religious ornamentation. However, by the eighteenth century, as enforcement of the penal code became increasingly rare, it was not difficult for a Catholic stranger to gain access to a family chapel, either through an acquaintance or by production of documentary evidence of Catholicism, such as a certificate signed by a Catholic priest. Moreover, domestic chaplains might sometimes make missionary excursions into the surrounding area.[15]

The experience of Catholics and the perceptions others had of Catholicism varied socially, locally and at different times. As Alexandra Walsham has observed of the seventeenth and eighteenth centuries, persecution was at times a side effect and by-product of toleration and vice versa, as demonstrated by the reaction to the Declarations of Indulgence of Charles II and James II. As she puts it, 'separation and assimilation, introversion and integration, were similarly interwoven features of social experience, cross-currents that constantly muddled and muddied the waters of interpersonal and interdenominational relations'.[16]

The influence of cisalpine ideas

English Catholicism at this time had no conventional parish structure: England was missionary territory. The gentry and noble families who provided most of the local bases for Catholic clergy were well aware of their own importance in keeping the faith alive and what this cost them. They, not the clergy nor any other part of the institutional Church – least of all the Pope – were the ones who took the greatest risk in conserving a Catholic presence in England. It was they who, in so doing, suffered the most disadvantage, social and financial. Some of their ancestors had endured imprisonment, fines, sequestrations, dispossession, exile, torture and even martyrdom for the cause. On paper the threat of these penalties still hung over them, although with the exception of the double land tax there was little to fear after 1746. Not surprisingly many of the Catholic gentry and nobility had a distrust of papal authority, which by some of its manifestations (such as the attempted deposition of Queen Elizabeth I) had made their lives very difficult, especially in the matter of perceived divided loyalty. There was the huge question of oath taking. Could Catholics give credible assurances that they would live peaceably under Protestant governments? Protestants maintained that Catholics could be absolved from any oath and that Catholics were not obliged to keep faith with those they viewed as heretics.

---

15   J. Bossy, *The English Catholic Community, 1570–1850* (London, 1975), p. 260.
16   A. Walsham, *Charitable Hatred: Tolerance and Intolerance in England, 1500–1700* (Manchester, 2006), p. 322.

Moreover, the Catholic gentry tended to regard themselves as more English than the English. In their view they were maintaining the true form of the traditional English religion, as practised by their forefathers for a millennium or more. It was not they who had relatively recently espoused new foreign (and in their view heretical) religious ideas from Germany, Switzerland and France and brought them into English parish churches built by their English Catholic ancestors for Catholic worship. In stressing their traditional Englishness, English Catholics tended to avoid devotional practices that might appear superstitious or southern European to their Protestant peers, particularly in the Age of Reason. They also wanted to emphasise this because of the propaganda that the exiled Stuarts were 'foreign', living in France or Rome, and with the Pretenders buried in St Peter's.

Thus, the Catholic gentry increasingly held cisalpine[17] views, playing down papal influence in matters of discipline and practice, and being as English in church matters as possible while still in communion with Rome.[18] In the last three decades of the eighteenth century, one of the most influential cisalpines was Joseph Berington (1743–1827), who had taught philosophy at the English College at Douai until he was expelled in 1771. In 1792, he became chaplain to Sir Robert Throckmorton of Buckland.[19] Berington met Throckmorton through the Catholic Committee, which campaigned for the revocation of anti-Catholic legislation and included a group known as the Protesting Catholic Dissenters, who denied that the Pope had any temporal powers.[20] Berington was deprived of his priestly faculties twice by the Vicar Apostolic. He enjoyed friendly relations with Protestant clergy such as John Wesley and Joseph Priestley. He attacked Catholic religious orders as not fit for purpose and criticised traditional Italian and Spanish religious practices. He wrote that 'Catholic is an old family name which we have never forfeited … I am no Papist nor is my religion Popery'. There is an appreciative memorial to Joseph Berington in the Anglican parish church of St Mary in Buckland.[21]

Not all English Catholic gentry were as cisalpine or radical in outlook as Berington. The more conservative elements were led by Bishop Richard Challoner (1691–1781), Vicar Apostolic of the London District and the most revered English Catholic of his time. But although he regularly worshipped at the Sardinian embassy chapel in London, he too was opposed to devotional practices that might be seen as superstitious. He was also a keen advocate and author of prayers in English.

---

17 Cisalpine means 'on this side of the Alps'. In contrast, views described as ultramontane, meaning 'on the other side of the Alps', emphasised supreme papal authority, not only in matters of faith but also in church discipline and practice.
18 D. Mathew, *Catholicism in England: Portrait of a Minority, its Culture and Tradition* (London, 1936), pp. 146–8.
19 Then in Berkshire, now Oxfordshire.
20 P. Marshall and G. Scott (eds), *Catholic Gentry in English Society: The Throckmortons of Coughton from Reformation to Emancipation* (Farnham, 2009), pp. 20–1.
21 A.S.N. Wright, *The History of Buckland* (Oxford, 1966), pp. 50–1.

Challoner stressed the importance of the Bible and was personally responsible for a revision of the Catholic Douai-Rheims translation.[22] His body was interred in the family vault of his friend Bryant Barrett, the king's lacemaker, in the crypt of the Anglican parish church at Milton near Abingdon.[23]

Towards emancipation?

In the second half of the eighteenth century, with Jacobitism no longer a threat and Catholics now required by the Pope to pray for the Hanoverian monarch, neither the government nor the judiciary nor the leaders of the Church of England had any desire for enforcement of anti-Catholic legislation. The political theorist and philosopher Edmund Burke described the penal laws as 'the bigotry of a free country in an enlightened age'.[24] Some Catholics felt it best to let sleeping dogs lie rather than press for repeal, but in 1778 the Papists Act (generally known as the First Catholic Relief Act) was introduced to Parliament by Sir George Savile. It is noteworthy that the Act resulted from government negotiations with a committee of lay Catholics headed by Lord Petre. The Catholic clergy were not involved and a leading member of the committee, William Sheldon, stated that the 'English Roman Catholic Gentlemen' were 'quite able to judge and act for themselves in these affairs'.[25]

Ever since 1600 there had been sporadic efforts by English Catholic gentry and nobility to identify an oath that would demonstrate their loyalty to the crown while enabling them to practise their religion freely. The new Act introduced an oath that denounced Stuart claims to the throne, denied the civil jurisdiction of the Pope in England, and rejected the power of Rome to release Catholics from their oaths:[26]

> I A.B. do sincerely promise and swear, That I will be faithful and bear true Allegiance to His Majesty King George the Third, and Him will defend, to the utmost of my Power, against all Conspiracies and Attempts whatever that shall be made against His Person, Crown, or Dignity; and I will do my utmost Endeavour to disclose and make known to His Majesty, His Heirs and Successors, all Treasons and traiterous Conspiracies which may be formed against Him or them; and I do faithfully promise to maintain, support and defend, to the utmost of my Power, the Succession of the Crown in His Majesty's Family, against any Person or Persons whatsoever; hereby utterly renouncing and abjuring any Obedience or Allegiance unto the Person taking upon himself the Stile and Title of Prince of Wales, in the Life-time of his Father, and who, since his Death, is said to have assumed the Stile and Title of King of Great Britain, by the name of Charles the Third, and to any other Person claiming or pretending a Right to the Crown of these Realms; and I do swear, that I do reject and detest, as an unchristian and impious Position, That

---

22   E. Norman, *Roman Catholicism in England: From the Elizabethan Settlement to the Second Vatican Council* (Oxford, 1985), pp. 46, 52–5.
23   Milton, not to be confused with Great Milton or Little Milton, was then in Berkshire but became part of Oxfordshire in 1974.
24   Norman, *Roman Catholicism in England*, p. 55.
25   Ibid. p. 65.
26   Ibid. p. 55.

it is lawful to murder or destroy any Person or Persons whatsoever, for or under Pretence of their being Hereticks; and also that unchristian and impious Principle, That no faith is to be kept with Hereticks: I further declare, that it is no Article of my Faith, and that I do renounce, reject, and abjure, the Opinion, That Princes excommunicated by the Pope and Council, or by any Authority of the See of Rome, or by any Authority whatsoever, may be deposed or murdered by their Subjects, or any Person whatsoever: And I do declare, that I do not believe that the Pope of Rome, or any other foreign Prince, Prelate, State, or Potentate, hath, or ought to have, any temporal or civil Jurisdiction, Power, Superiority, Pre-eminence, directly or indirectly, within this Realm. And I do solemnly, in the Presence of God, profess, testify, and declare, That I do make this Declaration, and every Part thereof, in the plain and ordinary Sense of the Words of this Oath; without any Evasion, Equivocation, or mental Reservation whatever, and without any Dispensation already granted by the Pope, or any Authority of the See of Rome, or any Person whatever; and without thinking that I am or can be acquitted before God or Man, or absolved of this Declaration, or any Part thereof, although the Pope, or any other Persons or Authority whatsoever, shall dispense with or annul the same, or declare that it was null or void.[27]

The practical effect of taking the oath was that a Catholic could now purchase and inherit real estate legally, without the risk of an Anglican claimant taking over his estate. No longer was there the need to create complex trusts involving Protestant collaboration to minimise such risks. The oath also enabled Catholics to serve legally as officers in the British armed forces. It ended the prosecution of Catholic clergy by bounty hunters and lifted the threat of life imprisonment for running a Catholic school. Only after the oath was agreed did the committee show it to Bishop Challoner. He endorsed it nonetheless.[28]

The First Catholic Relief Act sparked a violent reaction in 1779 and 1780. John Wesley published a leaflet attacking the advance of Rome's 'purple power' and Lord George Gordon's Protestant Association petitioned for repeal of the Act. This led to the Gordon Riots which, in London, caused damage or destruction to a dozen public buildings and over a hundred other properties.[29] Two hundred and eighty-five people were killed and more than 156 injured, mostly by regular soldiers and militia attempting to restore order in the capital. Twenty-one people were executed in the aftermath.[30] There was also some damage in other towns, such as Bath, where the Catholic chapel was burned down.

A further breakthrough for Catholics came in 1791. The Second Catholic Relief Act legalised Catholic worship by giving legal existence to registered places of worship, provided that the officiating clergy took an oath of allegiance.[31] The Act

---

27 E.H. Burton, *The Life and Times of Bishop Challoner*, ii (London, 1909), p. 292.
28 Norman, *Roman Catholicism in England*, p. 55.
29 The most recent treatment of the riots is I. Haywood and J. Seed (eds), *The Gordon Riots: Politics, Culture and Insurrection in Late Eighteenth-Century Britain* (Cambridge, 2012).
30 Norman, *Roman Catholicism in England*, pp. 55–6.
31 Mathew, *Catholicism in England*, p. 156.

also re-opened the professions to Catholics. Three years later a separate measure abolished double land tax, to the great relief of Catholic landowners.

The Catholic Emancipation Act 1829

In 1813, 1821 and 1825, emancipation bills were introduced but rejected by Parliament. The source of much opposition to Catholic emancipation was the perceived threat to the union of the British state with the Anglican Church – the so-called 'Protestant Constitution'.[32] There was a fear that if the Irish Catholics were to gain influence in Parliament, the Church of England, the British constitution and all that they stood for would be under threat.[33] In 1829 the Duke of Wellington was Prime Minister. He and Home Secretary Robert Peel feared that civil war might break out in Ireland if Catholic emancipation were further delayed. Hitherto George IV had opposed any such legislation lest he contravene his coronation oath to maintain the established religion, but now he allowed a new bill to proceed.

The resulting Catholic Emancipation Act prescribed a new parliamentary oath for MPs and Lords, denying the Pope any non-spiritual jurisdiction and undertaking not to subvert the position of the Anglican Church. Catholic priests were forbidden to be Members of Parliament. Catholic bishops were not to use titles adopted since the Reformation by Anglican bishops. Catholic clergy were not to officiate except in Catholic places of worship. Catholics could become members of corporations and most public offices were now open to them. Some anti-Catholic laws remained but no serious attempt was made to enforce them.[34]

In reaction to the emancipation campaign, militant Protestant societies known as Brunswick clubs were founded in 1828. There was a perceived threat to the University of Oxford's role as a great Anglican seminary; at least two Anglican parishes in Oxford petitioned against the 1829 act, as did the Oxford city council. Considerable Protestant hostility was directed at Peel who was seen as having betrayed the Tories.

Leading Catholic families rapidly moved back into public life. In 1832, Michael Henry Blount of Mapledurham became High Sheriff of Oxfordshire. The following year, Thomas Stonor was elected Member of Parliament for Oxford and in 1836, he became High Sheriff. Stonor was a friend of W.E. Gladstone and a founder of the Henley Royal Regatta. He also instigated an annual meeting of the Royal Buckhounds at Stonor, became the third Lord Camoys and was Lord-in-Waiting to Queen Victoria under five Liberal administrations.[35]

---

32 J.C.D. Clark, in *English Society 1688–1832* (Cambridge, 1985), argued that from 1688 until 1832 England was a 'confessional state', i.e. an Anglican state regarding political power.
33 Norman, *Roman Catholicism in England*, pp. 62–3.
34 Ibid. p. 64.
35 T. Hadland, *Thames Valley Papists: From Reformation to Emancipation* (2nd edn. Mapledurham, 2004), pp. 194–5.

However, there had been a decline in the number of Catholic gentry families. Previous financial strictures had eroded the fortunes of some. A significant minority of gentry offspring who might otherwise have married became nuns or priests, and produced no children for the next generation. Some Catholic gentry had gone into exile on the Continent and lived and died abroad. There was also the natural tendency of male lines eventually to fail, in which case the estate might be inherited by a Protestant relative. Catholic gentry sons were encouraged by legislation to convert to the Church of England simply to inherit and there was no glory in being an impoverished victim of social exclusion. Joseph Berington, writing in 1781, noted that among the Catholics in the whole country there remained only seven peers, twenty-two baronets and about 150 landed gentry. The Earl of Surrey and Sir Thomas Gasgoigne had recently conformed, leading Berington to comment, 'Within one year alone, we have lost more by the defection of the two mentioned Gentlemen, than we have gained by Proselytes since the revolution'.[36] This was probably more hyperbole than fact but it indicated a widespread perception among the gentry.

We cannot make windows into the souls of the dead. Some of those who, in Catholic eyes, chose apostasy may have been genuine converts to Anglicanism. Others probably accepted it as being the next best thing to remaining Catholic, with the bonus of an end to social exclusion and less land tax to pay (though the tax relief did not take immediate effect). But in the Age of Reason there was much scepticism and cynicism about religion in general, which eased the abandonment of Catholicism. One has only to consider the attitude of the great romantic Catholic hero 'Bonnie Prince Charlie' who secretly converted to Anglicanism to improve his chances of gaining the British throne,[37] and who condemned his former faith as 'the artful system of Roman Infallibility [that] has been the ruin of my family'.[38] Some 'apostates' may have had in mind a reconciliation with Catholicism later in life: Thomas Gage, formerly of Shirburn, Oxfordshire, became a Viscount as a result of conforming but died a Catholic.[39]

The growth of urban Catholicism

As the number and influence of Catholic gentry families declined, the Catholic clergy became more independent of gentry patronage. At the start of the eighteenth century, about two thirds of the clergy were employed by the nobility and gentry; by the end of the century, roughly three-quarters of the clergy were independent,

---

36 J. Berington, *The State and Behaviour of English Catholics, from the Reformation to the Year 1781* (London, 1781).
37 F. McLynn, *Charles Edward Stuart: A Tragedy in Many Acts* (London, 1988), pp. 399, 412.
38 Glickman, *English Catholic Community*, p. 254.
39 Hadland, *Thames Valley Papists*, pp. 146–7.

working in the growing urban Catholic congregations.[40] From the mid-eighteenth century onwards the urban Catholic population had been steadily growing, particularly in centres of industrialisation and Irish immigration. For example, in the Lancashire towns of Liverpool, Manchester, Preston and Wigan between 1767 and 1834, the estimated number of practising Catholics rose twelvefold; just seventeen years later it had more than doubled. In the same group of towns, by 1820 the proportion of practising Catholics who were Irish-born exceeded those who were English. By 1850, immediately after the Great Famine, three-quarters were Irish.[41]

The growth of urban Catholicism can be seen on a smaller scale in Oxfordshire, despite little industrial development. The proportion of Irish immigrants was much lower but there was nonetheless a significant increase during the nineteenth century. There was also immigration from France, Germany and Italy; it was generally easier for skilled self-employed craftsmen to emigrate than for agricultural workers and peasants. Most Catholic immigrants settled in Oxford, where there were better prospects for employment than in rural Oxfordshire.

The returning Catholic presence in urban areas often began with a priest from a gentry mission celebrating Mass in a hired or borrowed room. The next stage might be the establishment of a 'masshouse', a discreet and inconspicuous domestic dwelling with a sympathetic owner or tenant, where arrangements for the regular celebration of Mass could be more secure than in a room hired by the hour. Such places were known to the civil authorities who usually turned a blind eye: in 1767 at Oxford, a congregation of about two dozen attended a masshouse.[42] Then came the construction of simple chapels, such as that of St Ignatius in the St Clement's district of Oxford (built 1793–5). This was greatly facilitated by the Second Catholic Relief Act, which enabled Catholic chapels to operate legally through a registration process.

The congregations of the urban chapels were socially diverse. Many of the mass-goers were poor artisans, craftsmen, labourers and their dependants. Some were descendants of employees in formerly recusant country houses. Some were yeoman families who had moved to the edge of town or who now travelled to hear Mass. Some were first- or second-generation immigrants. Some were recent or potential converts.[43] Others were gentry or nobility visiting the area. Most significantly, there was among them a growing and articulate Catholic middle class.

---

40   Norman, *Roman Catholicism in England*, p. 49.
41   Bossy, *English Catholic Community*, pp. 424, 426–7.
42   M.B. Rowlands (ed.), *English Catholics of Parish and Town, 1558–1778* (CRS Monograph Series 5, 1999), p. 308.
43   Somewhat later, in the 1870s, one such was the young Oscar Wilde, who occasionally attended Mass at the chapel of St Ignatius: see M. Sturgis, 'The importance of being Catholic', *The Tablet*, 29 Sept. 2018, p. 12.

In the second half of the eighteenth century, priests and their chapels grew increasingly financially independent through donations, collections and lay trust funds under their own control. Although not yet formally part of a normal diocesan and parochial structure, the urban missions looked and operated increasingly like parishes.[44] Moreover, the Vicars Apostolic, predecessors of a revived episcopal hierarchy, gained influence at the expense of the religious orders. This was especially so after the Pope suppressed the Jesuits in 1773.[45] Thus, as the gentry and nobility lost influence, the secular clergy, led by the Vicars Apostolic, increasingly took over. Working-class and middle-class urban congregations raised no objections to this.[46]

Exiled French clergy

The French Revolution had an unexpected impact on the development of English Catholicism in the late eighteenth to early nineteenth century. By the autumn of 1792 there were some 1,500 French Catholic priests in England, refugees from the anti-clerical revolutionary regime and its Civil Constitution of the Clergy. Many of them were provided with accommodation by the British government in the Thames Valley region: the King's Arms coaching hotel in Reading accommodated hundreds of Norman priests, while the Mansion House in Thame became home to about a hundred Breton clergy.[47]

The revolutionaries' increasing hostility to Christianity led to a wave of sympathy in England for the exiled French priests, particularly from Anglican clergy, many of whom generously contributed to their upkeep. However, Charles Leslie, struggling to pay for the new chapel of St Ignatius at St Clement's, Oxford, found the appeals for the French clergy detrimental to his own fundraising.[48] Some of the exiled French priests were employed as chaplains and tutors to Catholic gentry and nobility. They included Jean-Baptiste Mortuaire of Rouen, who became chaplain to Thomas Stonor at Stonor Park; and Michel Thoumin des Valpons, archdeacon and Vicar General of Dol in Normandy, who was a guest of William Davey at Overy, near Dorchester. The archdeacon died in 1798 and was buried with honour in Dorchester Abbey, at the expense of the Warden of New College, Oxford.[49]

During the French Revolution, twenty-one of the twenty-three English convents of nuns in France risked returning home to Protestant England, considering it safer than remaining on the Continent. The Poor Clares of Aire in Picardy were imprisoned in their convent for several years but in 1799 were permitted to travel to England. Thomas Simeon Weld, whose sister was one of the nuns, allowed them

---

44   Norman, *Roman Catholicism in England*, p. 48.
45   The English Jesuits were officially revived in 1829 but unofficially in 1803.
46   Norman, *Roman Catholicism in England*, p. 49.
47   Stapleton, pp. 252–3.
48   Ibid. pp. 227–9.
49   Ibid. pp. 247–8.

to stay at Britwell House for fifteen years.[50] Unlike the French clergy, the nuns received no government assistance. Instead, they faced a backlash when the House of Commons passed a bill re-instituting restraints on Catholic education and monasticism. The Lords rejected the bill and communities such as the Poor Clares wisely adopted a low profile.

Increasing ultramontane influences

As already discussed, many leading lay Catholics held cisalpine views, with the objective of minimising the influence of Rome. As the roles of the Vicars Apostolic and secular clergy grew, so did their adoption of the opposing ultramontane position. If the cisalpines endeavoured to be more English than the English, then some ultramontanes gave the impression of trying to be more Italian than the Pope. The emancipation campaign led to more frequent and improved communication between the Vicars Apostolic and the Vatican, which helped increase Roman influence.[51] The influence of the papacy grew following the restoration of the Papal States by the Congress of Vienna in 1815.

There was also an element of 'product differentiation' involved in the rise of ultramontanism. From about 1700 onwards, and particularly in the second half of the eighteenth century, the Catholic Church in England had become ostensibly similar in some respects to dissenting Protestantism:[52] the secular clergy tended to dress in a similar style to nonconformist ministers and the new urban chapels bore a striking architectural resemblance to nonconformist places of worship. But with the rise of emancipated Catholicism, the ultramontane party sought to project an image not merely of Catholicism as yet another denomination but as an altogether different Church. Thus, clerical dress, church architecture, interior decoration and ritual practices – the whole ecclesiology – increasingly followed Roman patterns.

It should be borne in mind that English Catholicism was, as Peter Marshall puts it, 'simultaneously a species of non-conformist sect, and an imagined version of the Church of England itself, with insistent claims to its infrastructure and endowments' and its ancient heritage.[53] This kindled Protestant fears of 'papal aggression', frequently expressed in the nineteenth century, as the Roman Church in England re-established its hierarchy and the Anglican Church emphasised its Catholic past.

Post-emancipation controversies and developments

From the 1830s, the Vicars Apostolic requested that the Pope restore the English Catholic hierarchy. While he was happy to allow the doubling of the number of

---

50   Ibid. pp. 280–1.
51   Norman, *Roman Catholicism in England*, p. 57.
52   Bossy, *English Catholic Community*, p. 129.
53   P. Marshall, 'Confessionalisation and community in the burial of English Catholics, c.1570–1700', in N. Lewycky and A. Morton (eds), *Getting Along? Religious Identities and Confessional Relations in Early Modern England* (Farnham, 2012), p. 75.

vicariates to eight, he held back from re-establishing the hierarchy for fear of goading the Crown into interfering with episcopal appointments. However, in 1850 Pope Pius IX allowed the restoration to take place. At the head of the new hierarchy was the Spanish-born, Irish bishop Nicholas Wiseman, who was raised to the status of Cardinal. He promptly issued a tactlessly exuberant 'Pastoral Letter out of the Flaminian Gate', which was to prove highly inflammatory.[54]

Initially public reaction in England was muted. The British government had been aware of the plan for three years and had raised no objections. The British press reported the matter and there had been little reaction. But then *The Times* started a campaign that invoked the 'No Popery' rhetoric of traditional English anti-Catholicism. Perceived papal aggression, generated by newspaper articles as florid as anything written by Wiseman, led to the Prime Minister, Lord John Russell, condemning the Catholic Church's 'pretension to supremacy over the realm of England'. The Bishop of London denounced the Catholic clergy as 'emissaries of darkness'.[55]

Although the Catholic Emancipation Act already outlawed the adoption by the Catholic Church of territorial titles used by Anglican clergy, the government reacted by passing a new Ecclesiastical Titles Act which also outlawed the appropriation of Anglican titles. In fact, the Catholic Church had already assiduously avoided any such clashes. For example, the Catholics had chosen Westminster rather than Canterbury and Clifton rather than Bristol.[56] Feelings ran high in many parts of the country, and papal aggression and anti-Catholicism were campaigning themes at the 1852 general election.

As always in the Victorian period, Oxford and Oxfordshire as part of Oxford diocese were on the frontline of religious controversies and debates. In order to cope with the fierce feelings amongst his clergy, and the conflicting views of the low and high church parties, Samuel Wilberforce, the Anglican Bishop of Oxford, summoned a special Oxford Diocesan Synod on the papal aggression in November 1850. So many clergy attended that the meeting had to adjourn to the Sheldonian Theatre. A petition to the Queen, whose royal supremacy was considered threatened, was approved.[57] The depth and opposed nature of views on this issue reflected not just the immediate debate but the fact that Oxford was the birthplace and continuing heartland of the Oxford Movement which, since 1833, had been the main driver of Anglo-Catholicism within the Church of England. It was also the training ground of a substantial proportion of the Anglican priests who would serve throughout

---

54   Norman, *Roman Catholicism in England*, pp. 62, 68.
55   Ibid. p. 67.
56   Ibid. p. 69. It did not, however, work the other way round: the Anglicans subsequently established bishoprics in locations such as Birmingham, Liverpool, Portsmouth and Southwark, using names already adopted by the Catholics.
57   K. Tiller, 'Oxford diocese, Bishop Wilberforce and the 1851 religious census', *Oxoniensia*, 83 (2018), p. 95.

the country. Unsurprisingly events in Oxford attracted national attention. By 1850 Anglo-Catholic ideas and clergy were widely diffused, locally and nationally.

In Oxfordshire the number of Roman Catholic churches remained small. The 1851 religious census records eight: Banbury (number in Sunday morning congregation 250); Chipping Norton (127); Dorchester (60); Hethe (150); Heythrop (63); Oxford (50); Radford (53); and Stonor (120). Six of these illustrate the continuing importance after Emancipation of powerful local elites, with Heythrop, Radford and Chipping Norton all the product of the patronage of the Talbots, Earls of Shrewsbury. Although no longer a matter of clandestine country house worship, the influence of dominant families still figured largely in the distribution of Catholic churches. The remaining two were the growing urban Catholic congregations in Banbury and Oxford.[58] By 1876 there were still only nine Roman Catholic churches in Oxfordshire: the chapel at Heythrop had closed, a new chapel had been built at Souldern, and in Oxford St Aloysius had replaced St Ignatius although the latter remained in use as a chapel of ease.[59]

The religious controversies of the mid-1800s continued to have an impact, nationally and locally, throughout the century and into the next. As Catholicism established an increased and wider-spread presence, it became part of a pluralist religious landscape. This stability was still sometimes disturbed by public conflicts and controversies, particularly over styles of worship and building, the provision and funding of primary education, and remaining inequalities such as burial rights.

The legal status of Catholics

The registers of the Oxford Catholic Mission reflect the developing legal context in which Catholicism operated, particularly as regards rites of passage. Although much draconian legislation from earlier times remained on the statute book, the severest penalties were not imposed during the period covered by this volume.[60]

'Popish recusants convicted'

A successfully prosecuted Catholic recusant was termed a 'Popish recusant convicted', liable to the full force of anti-Catholic legislation and to excommunication from the Church of England. He could not hold any public office, nor practise the law, nor serve in the army or navy. Neither could he act as guardian, executor or administrator of an estate. All conveyances of land by such a person could be retrospectively invalidated if they were intended for the support of himself or his

---

58   See K. Tiller (ed.), *Church and Chapel in Oxfordshire 1851* (ORS 55, 1987).
59   *Harrod's Directory of Oxfordshire* (1876).
60   This section draws particularly on the comprehensive account of anti-Catholic legislation in J.A. Williams, *Catholic Recusancy in Wiltshire, 1660–1791* (CRS Monograph Series 1, 1968).

family. Catholics who failed to appear in court to respond to charges of recusancy could automatically be adjudged 'popish recusants convicted'.[61]

Conformity to Anglicanism

Every absence from the Anglican service on Sundays and holy days was punishable by a fine of one shilling[62] collectable by the churchwardens for the relief of the poor of the parish.[63] A fine of £20 could be imposed for each continuous absence of four weeks or more; alternatively, the Crown could seize a recusant's goods and two thirds of his real estate, excluding his main residence. A recusant who could not afford to pay the £20 fine and who lacked an estate or goods of sufficient value to be worth seizing could be made to swear an oath to leave the country for ever and be transported overseas.[64]

A monthly fine of £10 could be imposed on those whose servants or house guests failed to attend the Anglican service.[65] The husband of a persistently recusant woman was liable to a monthly fine of £10 or forfeiture of a third of his property. Alternatively, she could be imprisoned until she conformed.[66] A recusant widow could be deprived of two thirds of her jointure or dower,[67] forfeit all share in her late husband's goods and be disqualified from acting as executrix or administratrix.[68]

Celebrating or attending Mass was illegal: the priest was liable to imprisonment for a year and a fine of 200 marks; members of the congregation also faced a year in gaol and a fine of 100 marks.[69]

Catholic rites of passage

Baptisms, marriages and burials other than according to Anglican rites were illegal until nineteenth-century reforms.[70] A Catholic baptism incurred a £100 fine, a burial £20. Forfeit of property or a £100 fine applied to a Catholic marriage but this was imposed only on 'popish recusants convicted'. However, Anglican church courts could convict any Catholic for what they regarded as a clandestine marriage. This could result in a prison sentence, fine and excommunication, with consequent loss of civil rights. (From 1753, the situation regarding marriage changed.)[71]

---

61 28 & 29 Eliz. I, cap. 6; 3 & 4 Jac. I, cap. 5.
62 The fines specified in the legislation may look small. However, £1 in 1700 was worth approximately £130 in 2018.
63 3 & 4 Jac. I, cap. 4.
64 35 Eliz. I, cap. 2.
65 3 & 4 Jac. I, cap. 4.
66 7 & 8 Jac. I, cap. 6.
67 A dower is a widow's share for life of her husband's estate. A jointure is an estate settled on a wife for the period during which she survives her husband.
68 3 & 4 Jac. I, cap. 5.
69 23 Eliz. I, cap. 2.
70 3 & 4 Jac. I, cap. 5.
71 See below, p. 23.

Apart from reducing the risk of a fine, it was advantageous for Catholics to have their children baptised in the Anglican parish church because it provided an authoritative record of their birth. This could be useful in establishing legitimacy or entitlement to poor relief. Thus, some Catholics had their children baptised twice: first in a private Catholic ceremony and later in the Anglican parish church. Others might simply bribe the vicar to record an Anglican baptism that never took place. Yet others might persuade him merely to record the birth or to make reference to a baptism by another person. It is also undoubtedly the case that some Catholics resolutely avoided any involvement of the Anglican Church in the baptism of their children or the recording of their births.[72]

An example of how some Catholic gentry managed the situation concerns the children of William Stonor. In 1635 the vicar of Pyrton recorded the christenings of Mr Stonor's children in the parish register, even though none of them had been baptised in his church and he knew nothing whatsoever about the christenings. He did, however, record that the register entry was 'at the request of Mr Shepherd, Mr William Stonor's curate'. In other words, the Catholic chaplain based at Stonor Park, at the instigation of William Stonor, had persuaded the vicar to make the register entry. This indicates the influence recusant Catholic gentry could have over Anglican parish clergy.[73]

Until the 1880s a Catholic burial in consecrated ground in many places meant resort to the parish churchyard. Whereas in general the Catholic clergy discouraged baptism and marriage in the Anglican Church, they had no objection in principle to burial in the formerly Catholic and now Anglican churchyard. But a Catholic service officiated over by a Catholic priest was illegal. Moreover, an unrepentant convicted recusant was in Anglican eyes excommunicate and therefore could not be buried in consecrated ground.[74] On the other hand, and somewhat confusingly, from 1606 onwards it was a legal requirement that recusants be buried in the parish church or churchyard if they had not been excommunicated.[75]

In practice, a blind eye might be turned by the Anglican authorities allowing clandestine nocturnal Catholic burials. An influential lord of the manor (who might himself be a recusant, a church papist or merely sympathetic) might overrule or ignore the objections of the Anglican incumbent. It was commonplace for a squire to hold the advowson (right of patronage) of the parish church (although a convicted recusant was not allowed to retain these rights to nominate Anglican clergy).[76]

The Toleration Act of 1689 permitted Catholic cemeteries, but they were few and far between.[77] Normal practice by this time was for Catholics to be interred in the

---

72   Bossy, *English Catholic Community*, p. 133.
73   Ibid. p. 134.
74   Ibid. p. 140.
75   3 & 4 Jac. I, cap. 5.
76   Bossy, *English Catholic Community*, p. 141.
77   1 Gul. & M., cap. 18; Williams, *Catholic Recusancy*, p. 88.

churchyard or church by agreement with the Anglican clergy: nocturnal interments were no longer necessary. The correspondence of George Woodward, parson of East Hendred (then in Berkshire, now Oxfordshire) in the mid-eighteenth century, records how he dealt with the funeral in 1753 of 81-year-old Mrs Eyston, mother of the recusant lord of the manor, whose family still retain a private chapel in the Anglican parish church and a medieval Catholic domestic chapel attached to their house. Parson Woodward cut short a trip to Salisbury 'because I thought it would not be so respectful to the family (though they be Catholics) to leave the interment of her to another person'. He added: 'as soon as she was dead, all the Catholics in the town were summoned together, and to chapel they went, to say Mass for her soul: the funeral was very private, she was carried by six of the tenants, followed by her eldest son and daughter, the servants and tenants'. Thus, a Catholic Requiem Mass was followed by an Anglican burial. Despite the parson's Protestantism, he and the Eystons had a cordial relationship, dining together from time to time. It is significant that he referred to 'Catholics' rather than 'Roman Catholics' or 'Papists'.[78]

At Dorchester, the Davey family were key supporters of Catholicism through the penal period and then post-Emancipation. As late as 1863, John Davey, founder and benefactor of the new Catholic church built in 1848, was buried in the parish churchyard by the Anglican vicar. This followed a Requiem Mass celebrated in the Catholic church by Bishop Ullathorne of Birmingham. The case was cited nationally in the 1880s in support of legislation that would finally allow the burial of non-Anglicans by their own clergy.[79]

The position of Catholics 1660–88

The Clarendon Code of the 1660s was intended primarily to crush Protestant dissent in the aftermath of the Civil War and to proscribe those Dissenters who had left the Church of England in 1662. Its provisions were directed primarily at Protestant dissenters but in most respects also applied to Catholics.[80] One of the four Acts in the Code was the Corporation Act,[81] a precursor of the later Test Acts that precluded legal election to the governing body of any city or corporation unless the candidate had recently taken communion according to the Anglican rite and the oaths of supremacy and allegiance, sworn belief in the doctrine of passive obedience,[82] and renounced the Scottish Covenant.[83]

---

78 D. Gibson (ed.), *A Parson in the Vale of White Horse: George Woodward's Letters from East Hendred, 1753–61* (Gloucester, 1982), pp. 48–50.
79 K. Tiller, 'Religion and Community: Dorchester to 1920', in K. Tiller (ed.), *Dorchester Abbey: Church and People 635–2005* (Stonesfield, 2005), pp. 75–6.
80 Bettenson, *Documents of the Christian Church*, pp. 293–7.
81 13 Car. II, stat. 2, cap. 1.
82 The doctrine of passive obedience is the belief that there is a moral duty to obey the law.
83 The Covenant was an anti-Anglican and anti-Catholic agreement between Scottish Presbyterians and leaders of the English Parliamentarians during the Civil War.

As the ecclesiastical courts at Canterbury and York were not revived after the Restoration, enforcement of the recusancy laws was localised and inconsistent. An indication of non-enforcement is that, for the first four years of Charles II's reign, his average annual income from recusancy fines was a minuscule £37 against a projection of £18,600 per annum. In 1672 he issued a Declaration of Indulgence which, among other things, suspended the recusancy laws and permitted the private celebration of Mass. The Declaration was withdrawn after a year, during which it faced strong Anglican opposition. There followed a concentrated campaign of anti-Catholicism which led to the King issuing a proclamation in 1673 banishing priests and commanding the enforcement of the recusancy laws. The following year, Catholics who were neither householders nor servants of the aristocracy were ordered to leave London and almost all priests were ordered to leave England.[84]

The first Test Act was introduced in 1673. It imposed on most holders of civil or military office the requirement to take the oaths of supremacy and allegiance, to make a declaration denying Catholic eucharistic doctrine and to receive Anglican communion. The Act also stipulated that a widow must conform within four months of her husband's death or forfeit her inheritance.[85] In the same year a proclamation banned Catholics from the royal court and renewed the call for enforcement of the recusancy laws.[86] In Oxfordshire both recusants and Protestant dissenters experienced periodic investigations, notably during the episcopate of the energetic John Fell.[87] In 1676 the Bishop of London, Henry Compton, instituted a census of 'conformists', 'papists' and 'nonconformists'.[88] The Oxfordshire data from the resulting Compton Census is shown in Map 1 in relation to centres of Catholicism in the county.

The Popish Plot of 1678–81 was a fiction created by Titus Oates; he was eventually convicted of perjury but not before he was elected a freeman of the City of Oxford. The supposed Catholic conspiracy led to the execution or death in prison of many innocent men and the issuing of various royal proclamations. These latter commanded, for example, the expulsion of most Catholics from London, restrictions on travel in other parts of the country, the disarming of recusants, and tendering of the oaths of allegiance and supremacy. The Popish Plot also resulted in a second Test Act, passed in 1678.[89] This disqualified Catholic MPs unless they

---

84 Williams, *Catholic Recusancy*, pp. 17–23.
85 25 Car. II, cap. 2.
86 Williams, *Catholic Recusancy*, p. 22.
87 See M. Clapinson (ed.), *Bishop Fell and Nonconformity* (ORS 52, 1980); Hodges, 'Roman Catholic recusants', in Tiller and Darkes, *Historical Atlas of Oxfordshire*, pp. 84–5, 172; M. Clapinson, 'Early Protestant nonconformity', in Tiller and Darkes, op. cit. pp. 86–7.
88 A. Whiteman (ed.), *The Compton Census of 1676: A Critical Edition* (British Academy Records of Social and Economic History, n.s. 10, 1986).
89 30 Car. II, cap. 2.

took the oath of supremacy and denied not only Catholic eucharistic doctrine but also the Mass and adoration of the saints and the Virgin Mary.

On Charles's death in 1685, his brother, already an enthusiastic Catholic convert, succeeded as James II. The new King ordered suspension of all legal cases against recusants, subject to their production of a certificate of loyalty, and the refund of recusancy fines.[90] A Declaration of Indulgence was issued in 1687 granting religious toleration to Catholics and Protestant dissenters.[91] James claimed the right to dispense with laws and promoted Catholics to positions of influence, to the great annoyance of Protestants. The changed situation led to a number of high-profile conversions to Catholicism, such as that of the Poet Laureate, John Dryden. Many recusants felt secure enough to refurbish Catholic chapels or open new masshouses.

Protestant opposition to the King's Catholicising policies led to the Revolution of 1688. James fled to France and was replaced by his daughter Mary and son-in-law (and nephew) William of Orange, who reigned as Protestant joint monarchs. After Mary's death in 1694, William continued on the throne until his death in 1702.

The legal position of Catholics 1688–1829

After the Revolution of 1688, new oaths of allegiance and supremacy were introduced. These could be tendered to anyone. Every holder of an official position had to take the new oaths and observe the Test Act requirement of being an Anglican communicant. Failure to do so could result in a fine or imprisonment. Moreover, the offender could be deemed a 'popish recusant convict', despite not having been convicted by a court of law.[92] This novel process of 'constructive recusancy' came to be used increasingly as an easy method of rooting out Catholics.[93] In London and the counties around the capital, the Test declaration was to be tendered to all suspected Catholics.[94] Catholics were to remain within five miles of their homes unless granted a travel licence.[95] Proclamations of this sort became frequent during the reigns of William and Mary and of Anne.

Catholics were banned from owning weapons. Justices of the Peace could authorise any person, accompanied by a constable, to search the house of a suspected Catholic for arms.[96] The Universities of Oxford and Cambridge were awarded the patronage of any rectory hitherto held by a Catholic and no recompense was to be made.[97] Catholics were not allowed to keep horses worth more than £5.[98]

---

90   Williams, *Catholic Recusancy*, p. 38.
91   Patent Roll, 3 James II, 3, 18.
92   1 Gul. & M., sess. 1, cap. 8.
93   Williams, *Catholic Recusancy*, p. 44.
94   1 Gul. & M., sess. 1, cap. 9 (as corrected by cap. 17).
95   Williams, *Catholic Recusancy*, p. 44.
96   1 Gul. & M., sess. 1, cap. 15.
97   1 Gul. & M., sess. 1, cap. 26.
98   1 Gul. & M., sess. 1, cap. 15.

The possession of landed property by the Catholic gentry and nobility was an important factor in the survival of Catholicism. The government therefore introduced several measures to penalise Catholic landowners and thus, encourage them to abandon their religion. When the Land Tax was introduced in 1693, Catholic landowners who refused the oaths of supremacy and allegiance had to pay double the normal rate. Catholics refusing the oaths and the Test declaration against transubstantiation could by a statute of 1700 be deprived of their inheritance by their Protestant next of kin. Under the same statute no Catholic, regardless of whether they took the oaths or made the Test declaration, could purchase real estate.[99] From 1696, those Catholics hitherto entitled to vote were deprived of their electoral franchise. Catholics were also forbidden to act as lawyers. Subsequently, many practised instead in the more junior role of 'conveyancers under the bar'[100] and became experts in trust law, whereby they attempted to mitigate government attempts to deprive Catholics of their real estate and the income from it. Another statute deprived Catholic gentry of control of their local militia although they were still required to pay for its provision.[101]

The 1698 Popery Act introduced bounties for informers against Catholic clergy, and life imprisonment for clergy celebrating Mass and Catholics running schools. Informers against parents sending children to Catholic schools abroad, or against Catholic priests, were to be paid £50 for each successful conviction. Apprehended clergy could be sent to high security gaols, such as Hurst Castle off the Hampshire coast, for life in solitary confinement.[102]

The reign of Queen Anne saw further anti-Catholic legislation. In 1706, making converts to Catholicism was deemed to be treason. A census of papists was ordered and judges were instructed to enforce the treason laws against conversions to Catholicism. Two years later, in reaction to the failed Jacobite invasion of Scotland, horses and weapons held by Catholics were briefly seized and Catholics were expelled from London and instructed to stay within five miles of their homes. As Williams points out, if the new legislation dealing with the purchase and inheritance of land had been rigorously enforced it would have 'eliminated the Catholic nobility and gentry and with them (since they were the principal supporters of priests and providers of mass-centres) almost all that remained of English Catholicism'.[103]

George I, the first Hanoverian King of England and Scotland, reigned from 1714 to 1727. Despite their Jacobite inclinations, many southern English Catholic gentry were prepared to swear allegiance to George, abjure the Stuart cause and reject papal authority in temporal matters, if suitable wording could be agreed. Even before the 1715 Jacobite rising, an oath was drafted but it was not endorsed by the Vicars

99   11 Gul. III, cap. 4.
100   7 & 8 Gul. III, cap. 27.
101   10 Gul. III, cap. 18.
102   11 Gul. III, cap. 4.
103   Williams, *Catholic Recusancy*, p. 51.

Apostolic. In the immediate aftermath of the rising a group of Catholics, led by the Duke of Norfolk and acting independently of the Vicars Apostolic, devised an oath that the government and the Vatican both appeared to find acceptable. But three of the four Vicars Apostolic argued with Rome against it; the Jacobite cause still had considerable support in the Vatican and among English secular clergy. Negotiations continued unsuccessfully for several years.[104]

A spur to the gentry's desire to take an oath of allegiance was the Act, passed in reaction to the 1715 rising, obliging Catholics to register their names and landed property. The gentry hoped that if they took such an oath, they might be spared registration. The Registration Act was supplemented by a statute three years later, under which convicted recusants were liable to confiscation of two thirds of their property.[105] Any property allocated to 'superstitious uses' (e.g. to help fund a Catholic mission) was forfeited to the Crown.[106]

In 1723 a special levy of £100,000 was imposed on Catholics after the failure of the Atterbury plot.[107] Twenty-one years later only two thirds of the target had been received, an indication of the difference between the aims of anti-Catholic legislation and the practicalities of enforcement.[108]

The reign of George II (1727–60) was noteworthy for a complete absence of new anti-Catholic legislation. Unsurprisingly, however, the last major Jacobite rebellion in 1745 caused existing legislation to be invoked. Early in 1744, when it became clear that a Jacobite invasion was being planned, Catholics were commanded to leave London and stay at home. Local officials were instructed to administer the oaths of supremacy and allegiance and the Test declaration. They were also required to search Catholic homes for arms and to seize horses worth more than £5.[109]

In 1753, the Hardwicke Marriage Act set out new requirements 'for the Better Preventing of Clandestine Marriages' at a time before civil registration. All marriages (except those of Jews and Quakers)[110] were required to be conducted by an Anglican minister in an Anglican church according to the Anglican rite. Any minister conducting a wedding in violation of these requirements could be transported for fourteen years. Any marriage not complying with the Act's requirements was invalid. These stipulations held until 1836.[111] The Act was

---

104 E. Duffy, 'Englishmen in vaine: Roman Catholic allegiance to George I', *Studies in Church History*, xviii (1982), pp. 345–65. A group of Catholics, headed by Sir Robert Throckmorton of Coughton and Buckland, had taken the standard Oath of Allegiance to William III but this met with widespread disapproval in Catholic circles.
105 1 Geo. II, st. 2, cap. 55; 3 Geo. I, cap. 18.
106 1 Geo. I, st. 2, cap. 50.
107 9 Geo. I, cap. 18.
108 Williams, *Catholic Recusancy*, p. 60.
109 Ibid. pp. 62–3.
110 Jews and Quakers were considered to have sufficiently rigorous and accessible record-keeping, and were exempted.
111 26 Geo. II, cap. 33.

not intended to be specifically anti-Catholic and the government accepted that Catholics could treat the Anglican marriage service merely as a civil requirement. It had, in any case, long been common for Catholic gentry to partake in two wedding services: a private Catholic ceremony for religious reasons and a Church of England service, with register entries evidencing a legal marriage and the legitimacy of offspring. From 1754, this practice of having two weddings became more common for Catholics of lower rank.[112] Many poorer Catholics, however, merely went through the Anglican marriage ceremony, thus meeting the legal requirement while saving the cost of two ceremonies. As far as Catholic sacramental compliance was concerned, according to Catholic theology the ministers of the sacrament of matrimony are the couple; the priest merely officiates. Jesuit missioners had stressed this point during the seventeenth century.[113] Thus, a wedding conducted by a Catholic priest was not strictly necessary for a marriage to be valid in the eyes of the Catholic Church.

An entry in the Waterperry registers records a Catholic ceremony following marriage in the Anglican Church. The Latin translates as:

> On Sunday evening, 10 February 1771, James Maloni and Elizabeth Pratt were joined in marriage. The marriage contract was previously witnessed by the Protestant pastor according to an anti-Catholic decree of the parliament of Great Britain, and the sacrament has now been conferred by the priest.

A strange effect of the Hardwicke Act was that a Catholic priest who officiated at a Catholic wedding would then be very keen to ensure that the couple hastened to the Anglican church as quickly as possible, lest he be exposed to the risk of transportation for having conducted an illegal clandestine marriage. There is no record of any such transportation happening, however; another example of the, often limited, enforcement of anti-Catholic legislation as the eighteenth century progressed.[114]

At any time during the eighteenth century, existing legislation could have wiped out Catholicism in England, if the authorities had so wished. The fact that they did not do so could easily be misconstrued as implying an increasing reluctance to enforce anti-Catholic measures as time passed, coupled with steadily increasing toleration of Catholicism in general. For example, in the 1760s a systematic campaign of informing against Catholic priests for financial gain led to a series of prosecutions. In 1767 a priest was condemned to life imprisonment on the evidence of one such informer but the punishment was widely regarded as disproportionate: it led to a ruling in 1769 by Lord Mansfield that, for such a prosecution to succeed, evidence of ordination must be produced. Thereafter no prosecution of this type

---

112 Williams, *Catholic Recusancy*, pp. 65–6.
113 Bossy, *English Catholic Community*, p. 137.
114 Ibid. p. 139.

succeeded.[115] But toleration did not increase, nor conflict decrease, in a synchronised and linear manner.

In this confusing context, Catholics were able discreetly to contravene or work around many aspects of the legislation with relative impunity for much of the time. They were nonetheless excluded from public life, and the double land tax was a significant problem for Catholic landowners. Moreover, the great weight of rarely invoked but draconian legislation always hung over them, and there was always the possibility of an outbreak of anti-Catholic violence.

In 1778 the First Catholic Relief Act was introduced to Parliament.[116] The Act's genesis and the violent reaction provoked by it are discussed above (p. 9). Its key features were an oath denouncing Stuart claims to the throne, denial of the civil jurisdiction of the Pope in England, and rejection of the power of Rome to release Catholics from their oaths. A Catholic taking the oath could now purchase and inherit real estate legally, without the risk of an Anglican heir taking over his estate: no longer was there the need to create complex trusts involving Protestant collaboration to minimise such risks. The oath also enabled Catholics to serve legally in the British armed forces. It ended formally the prosecution of Catholic clergy by bounty hunters and lifted the threat of life imprisonment for running a Catholic school.[117]

The Second Catholic Relief Act in 1791 legalised Catholic worship by giving legal existence to registered places of worship, provided that the officiating clergy took an oath of allegiance.[118] The newly legalised Catholic chapels were not allowed to have steeples or bells for fear of confusion with Anglican churches; and they were not to be 'locked, barred or bolted' during services. Catholic clerical dress was not to be worn in the street. The Act also reopened the professions to Catholics.[119] Three years later a separate measure abolished double land tax on Catholic landowners.[120]

The 1829 Catholic Emancipation Act (see p. 10) prescribed a new parliamentary oath for MPs and Lords. Catholic clergy were not to officiate except in Catholic places of worship. Catholics could now become members of corporations and most public offices became open to them.[121]

After 1829 some anti-Catholic laws remained on the Statute Book, with no general attempts to enforce them but with occasional controversies and changes, as in the case of burial rights.

---

115 Williams, *Catholic Recusancy*, p. 66.
116 18 Geo. III, cap. 60.
117 Norman, *Roman Catholicism in England*, p. 55.
118 31 Geo. III, Cap. 32.
119 Mathew, *Catholicism in England*, p. 156.
120 34 Geo. III, cap. 8.
121 10 Geo. 4, cap. 7.

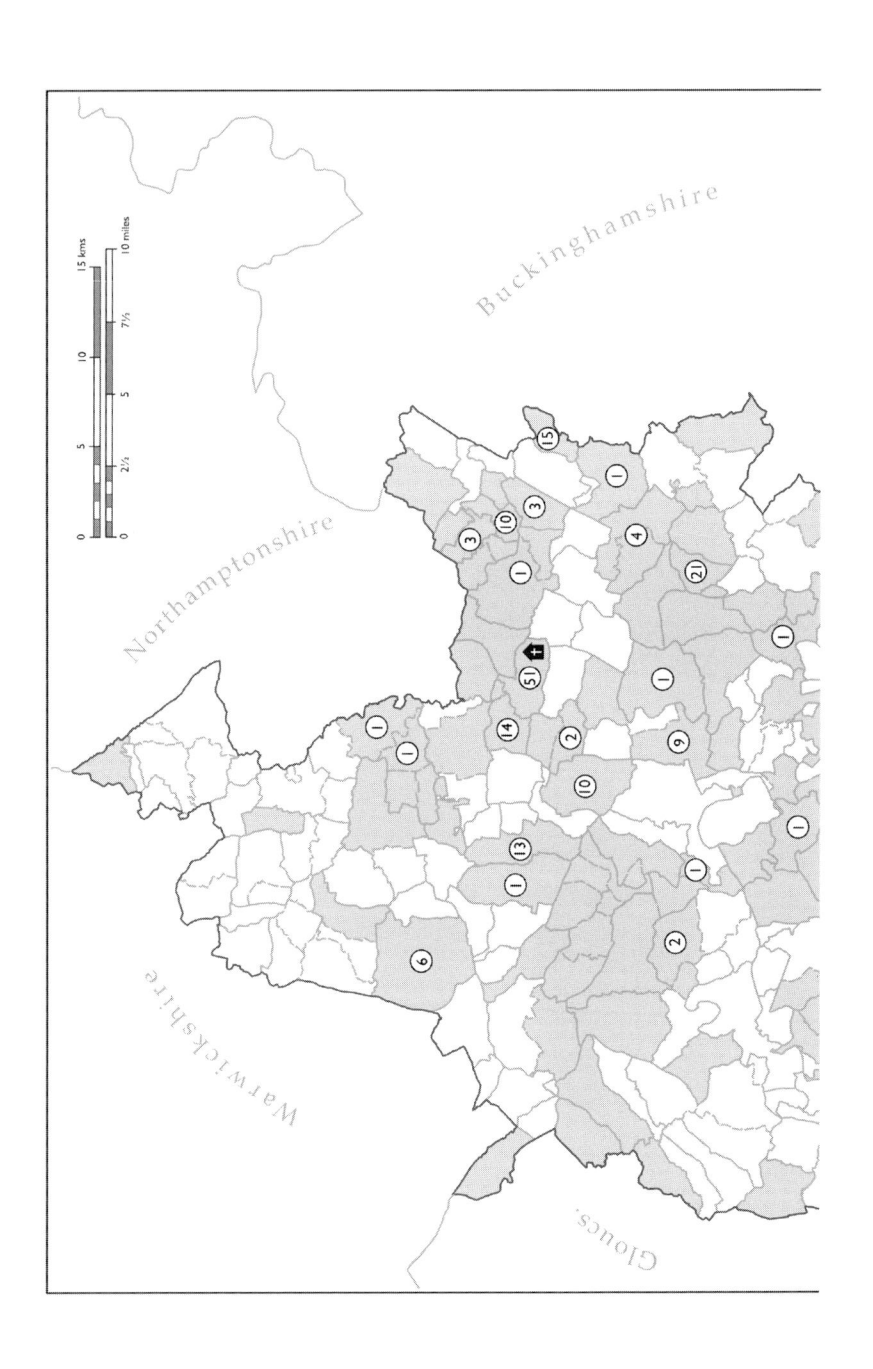

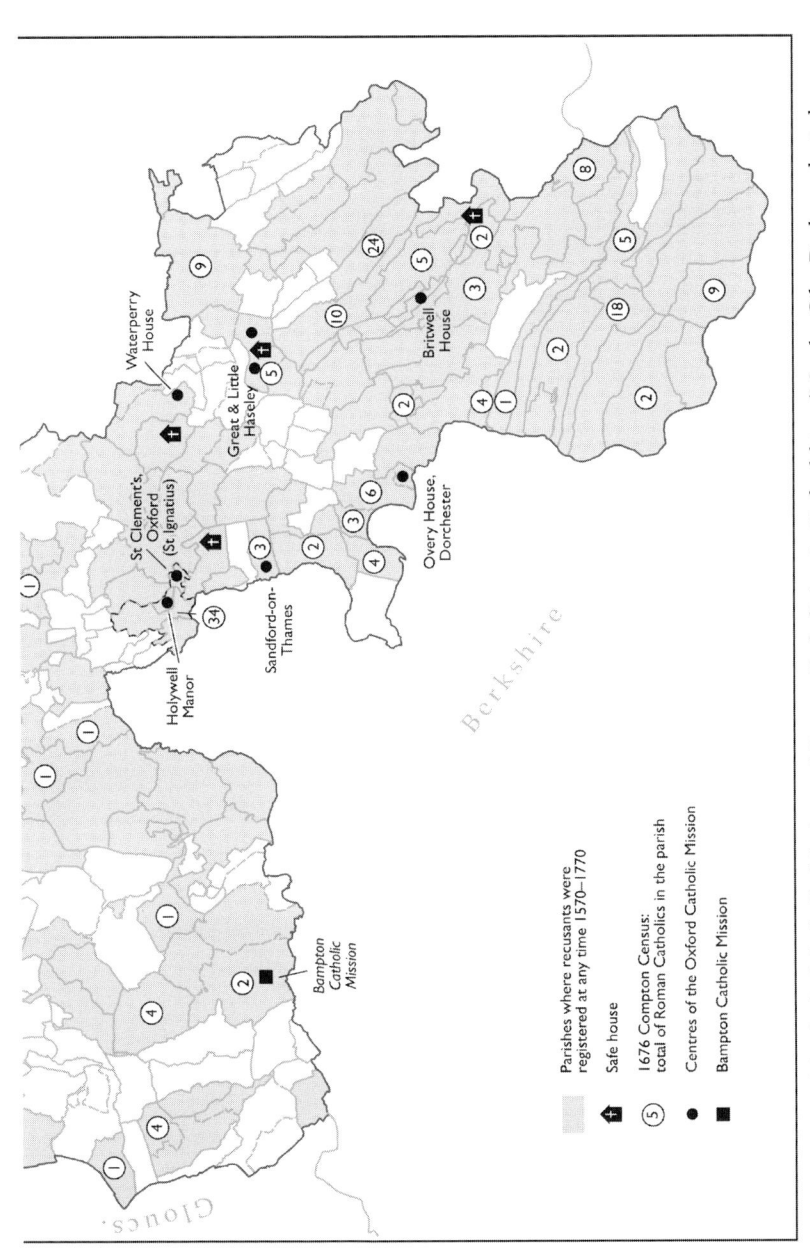

Map 1. The Oxford Catholic Mission and Roman Catholicism in Oxfordshire. (Map by Giles Darkes, adapted from K. Tiller and G. Darkes (eds), *An Historical Atlas of Oxfordshire* (ORS 67, 2010), p. 85)

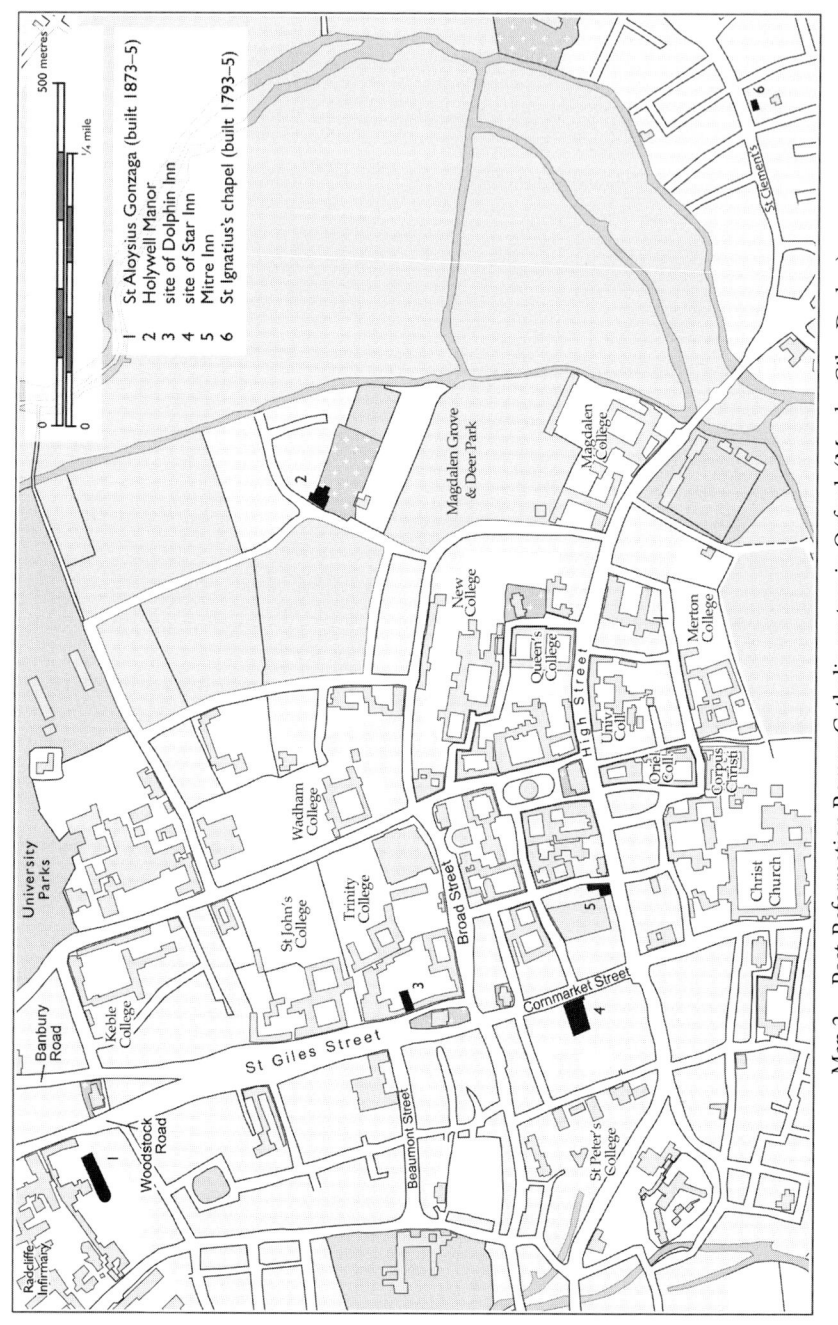

Map 2. Post-Reformation Roman Catholic centres in Oxford. (Map by Giles Darkes)

Locations of the Oxford Mission

The Oxford Catholic Mission during the period covered by the registers presented in this volume was first based principally at Waterperry and later at St Clement's, Oxford. It was also represented at various times at Britwell, the Haseleys, Holywell, Overy in Dorchester, and Sandford-on-Thames. This section outlines the Catholic presence in these places (see Map 1).

Oxford

As Alan Davidson has observed: 'Oxford was not a quiet country manor where Catholics might live undisturbed, nor a metropolis where they could submerge themselves in a teeming crowd. It was a small town with a fairly rigidly controlled academic population, and a town of which the authorities took especial care'.[122] In the two decades following the Restoration of the monarchy in 1660, the population of Oxford increased to more than 10,000. The principal trades were building, tailoring, gloving, shoemaking, brewing, innkeeping and dealing in textiles. The university expanded and many new college buildings were erected.[123]

A number of Oxford inns were regular meeting places for recusants and some were managed by Catholics (Map 2). In particular, the Mitre was a longstanding recusant venue where it seems that Mass was celebrated in a cellar at one stage in the seventeenth century.[124] The diarist Thomas Hearne noted a meeting that took place in about 1718: 'I had been six Years ago with this Mr Sexton [a lawyer acting for recusants] at the Mitre, with Mr Blount of Maple Durham, & Mr Blount's Lady, & some other truly virtuous, good people of the Roman Catholick perswasion'.[125] The Dolphin, at what became No. 1 St Giles, was also a recusant haunt in the seventeenth century,[126] as was the Star at 34 Cornmarket Street, which like the Mitre remained in Catholic hands into the 1700s. Mass was sometimes celebrated at the Mitre and the Star.[127] But the most enduring location close to the city centre to hear Mass in the seventeenth century was at Holywell Manor.

Holywell

Holywell, also known as St Cross, is a small parish of about 235 acres which lay just outside the Oxford city limits (Map 2). The name Holywell derives from a spring or

---

122 A. Davidson, 'Roman Catholicism in Oxfordshire from the late Elizabethan period to the Civil War' (unpubl. Bristol PhD thesis, 1970), p. 621.
123 A. Crossley, 'Oxford before 1800', in Tiller and Darkes (eds), *Historical Atlas of Oxfordshire*, p. 72.
124 J. Bertram, *St Aloysius' Parish, Oxford: The Third English Oratory* (Birmingham, 1993), p. 8.
125 D.W. Rannie (ed.), *Remarks and Collections of Thomas Hearne*, viii (Oxford Hist. Soc. 51, 1907), p. 268.
126 Stapleton, p. 215.
127 *VCH Oxon.* iv, pp. 412–13.

Fig. 1. Holywell Manor, just outside Oxford: home of the Catholic Napiers for much of the seventeenth century, and recognised as a place to which Oxford Catholics resorted to hear Mass.

well, dedicated to St Winifred and St Margaret. Most of the parish was agricultural until the mid-nineteenth century.[128]

The recusant Napier family of Holywell Manor were graziers of Scottish descent.[129] They leased the manor of Holywell from Merton College and lived at the manor house, which still exists though much altered (Fig. 1). In the reign of Elizabeth I, William and George Napier, whose mother was the sister of a cardinal,[130] received a Catholic education abroad. William ran the family livestock and butchery business. He married into the Catholic Powell family of Sandford-on-Thames and was described by Cardinal William Allen as 'a renowned and virtuous Catholic'. Allen was the head of the English Catholic Church in exile and the former principal and proctor of St Mary's Hall, Oxford.[131]

Being a grazier, William Napier also had pasture and a farmhouse at Temple Cowley. His land included a remote property called Hockley in the Hole. The diarist Anthony Wood noted that William Napier leased it to a recusant mason called Badger, who came from the Oxford parish of St Peter in the East, near Holywell. Late in the reign of Elizabeth I, Badger built a safe house on the plot, complete with a secret hiding place. This refuge later became an ale house. About 1678, it

---

128 Ibid. pp. 271–4.
129 The Napiers were also referred to as the Nappiers or Nappers.
130 William Peto, an English Franciscan friar.
131 Stapleton, pp. 211–12.

was sold and demolished.[132] One of the users of this safe house may have been William Napier's younger brother George, a Catholic priest. After training and ordination on the Continent, George Napier returned to England in 1603 and spent seven years on the English mission. In 1610 he was captured at Kirtlington, Oxfordshire, and hanged, drawn and quartered at Oxford. His head was exhibited on the steeple of Christ Church and each of his quarters was displayed on one of the city's four gates. At least one of his quarters was retrieved by his brother-in-law, Mr Powell of Sandford-on-Thames, and buried in the former Templars' chapel at Powell's home.[133]

Most of the Napiers were buried at Holywell, in the chancel of St Cross parish church, notwithstanding the official ban on the interment of recusants. Holywell Manor and the farm at Temple Cowley remained in the Napier family into the 1670s. In 1671 Holywell passed to a Napier daughter who had married into the Neville family of Holt and moved away. The Nevilles continued to hold the property, leasing it to the Catholic Harding family. The Hardings occupied the Manor until 1684 when they were succeeded by another Catholic family, the Kimbers, who were stewards to the absentee Nevilles.[134]

Holywell Manor was an unusual example of country house Catholicism in a suburb, a short walk from Oxford city centre. Thus, it was able to serve both as a family chapel and as an urban masshouse where, in the reign of James II, one of the king's chaplains celebrated Mass and where, as Anthony Wood recorded, 'all papists there retired to do their devotions'.[135] That this was possible for so long is indicative of the unofficial tolerance extended to Catholicism in Oxford before the Revolution of 1688. But the fate of George Napier also illustrates the potential severity of the anti-Catholic laws when they were invoked.

After the accession of William and Mary, which had been preceded by anti-Catholic rioting in Oxford,[136] and following the subsequent crackdown on Catholicism, recusancy in Oxford declined significantly, leading to the transfer of the mission's main focus to Waterperry. In 1706 only fourteen recusants were known to the authorities in Oxford, half of them apparently members of the Kimber family of Holywell.[137] Thomas Kimber senior died in 1716 and his son, also Thomas, in 1725. Hearne described the younger Thomas Kimber as his friend and 'a man of excellent sense and versed in history & antiquities'.[138]

---

132 A. Clark (ed.), *The Life and Times of Anthony Wood*, iii (Oxford Hist. Soc. 1894), p. 122.
133 Bishop Richard Challoner, *Memoirs of Missionary Priests and other Catholics of Both Sexes that have Suffered Death in England on Religious Accounts*, ii (Philadelphia, 1839), p. 35; Stapleton, p. 215.
134 Stapleton, pp. 216–17.
135 Ibid. p. 217.
136 Clark (ed.), *Life and Times of Anthony Wood*, iii, p. 286.
137 *VCH Oxon.* iv, p. 413.
138 Stapleton, p. 220.

The following priests have been identified as serving the mission at some time during the seventeenth century while its primary base was at Holywell:

> George Napier (executed 1610, beatified by the Catholic Church 1929)
> Adam Greene
> ? Truckines, SJ
> Richard Blount, SJ
> Thomas Kimber
> William Lacey
> John Nicholas Day, OSF
> F. Fairfax, SJ
> Henry Pelham (alias Warren, 1690)

Thereafter, at Holywell until the mid-eighteenth century, Mass continued to be celebrated as and when possible by any available priest but with no permanent missioner in residence.

Waterperry

Waterperry is a very small village about seven miles due east of Oxford and on the borders of Oxfordshire with Buckinghamshire (Map 1). Its one street has a mix of houses ranging from seventeenth-century timber-framed cottages to twentieth-century social housing. At the south-east end of the road, in close proximity, are Waterperry House and the parish church. The parish of Waterperry comprises 2,500 acres and is bounded at its southern end by the River Thame. The terrain is generally flat, mostly exceptionally good meadowland and pasture. In the north-west corner of the parish is the surviving remnant of the once-extensive Bernwood Forest. During the period of the registers Waterperry was 'a small and humble labouring community with few substantial yeomen'. In the early eighteenth century there were fifteen tenant farmers. Later in the century the population exceeded 100 but only eight people were rich enough to contribute to the poor rate. By 1801 the population was 195: in 2001 it was 170.[139]

By the time of the Reformation the Curson family, originally from Derbyshire, was living in the manor house. The family concentrated on sheep-farming, converting almost all the land in the parish to enclosed pasture, with little regard for the rights of their tenants, the parson or the commoners. Sir Francis Curson inherited Waterperry manor from his father in 1580. He was related to a number of recusant families, including the Belsons, Dormers, Stonors and Vachells, and between 1592 and 1612 his wife Ann (née Southcote) was listed several times as a recusant, though her husband seems to have been a church papist. The couple's daughters Elizabeth and Anna were Benedictine nuns at Brussels. Mary Curson of Rotherfield Peppard was listed as a recusant and was probably a third daughter.

---

139 *VCH Oxon.* v, pp. 295–6, 302–3.

The sons, Sir John and Richard, were recorded in 1612 as failing to take Anglican communion, and Sir John married a recusant, Magdalen Dormer.[140] In accordance with the Harleyford strategy of basing Catholic priests in the homes of Catholic gentry, the Jesuit priest John Gerard visited Waterperry about 1600 and stationed the Jesuit priest Edward Walpole at the house. When it was rebuilt in 1713, several coffins were discovered under the foundations. One was covered with black velvet and contained a silver candlestick and crucifix. The coffins are likely to have dated from the early days of the first Jesuit mission at Waterperry.[141]

Some time later, the Cursons of Waterperry conformed to Anglicanism. In the Compton Census of 1676 no Catholics were recorded in the parish.[142] The first Protestant Curson of the main line was probably Sir John's son and heir, Sir Thomas, first Baronet Curson of Waterperry. He married Elizabeth Burrough and the couple were noted as model Protestants. But Sir Thomas's sister Elizabeth married into the family of a local Catholic martyr, Thomas Belson,[143] and this connection probably maintained some Catholic influence within the family. Sir Thomas died in 1682 and soon afterwards his son Sir John married Penelope Child, a Catholic from Worcester. The re-founding of the Catholic mission at Waterperry stems from this marriage: Sir John 'himself soon after turn'd papist', as Anthony Wood noted.[144] The marriage produced two daughters and six sons, one of whom, Sir Peter, became a Jesuit priest. When Lady Penelope died, some time before 1695, Sir John married another Catholic, the widow Anne Powell (née Dormer) of Sandford-on-Thames.

For many years the Powells of Sandford Manor maintained a Catholic domestic chapel. However, the family's male line failed, leaving two daughters as heiresses. One of them, Winefred, married Sir John Curson's son and heir, Sir Francis. After his death in 1760 she sold Sandford Manor, which ceased to be a Catholic mission base.[145] Sir John Curson maintained a Catholic chapel in Waterperry House, although its precise location is not recorded. The only surviving remnant of the late seventeenth-century house is a two-storey service wing. The rest was rebuilt from 1713 and further remodelled after 1815 (Fig. 2).[146]

The priest who previously served Oxford probably lived at Waterperry after the Revolution of 1688. In 1695 Sir John and his second wife Lady Anne were listed as recusants. Five years later, about the time the Waterperry registers begin, Sir John was the subject of an enquiry by a commission investigating the landed property of

---

140   Ibid. pp. 298–9; Davidson, 'Roman Catholicism in Oxfordshire', p. 214; A.G. Petti (ed.), *Recusant Documents from the Ellesmere Manuscripts* (CRS Records Series 60, 1968), pp. 215, 237–9.
141   Stapleton, p. 204; Hodgetts, *Secret Hiding-places*, p. 143.
142   *VCH Oxon.* v, p. 308.
143   Executed with three other Catholics at Oxford in 1589 and beatified in 1987.
144   Clark (ed.), *Life and Times of Anthony Wood*, iii, p. 2.
145   Stapleton, pp. 198–202.
146   A. Brooks and J. Sherwood, *The Buildings of England: Oxfordshire North and West* (New Haven and London, 2017), pp. 530–1.

Fig. 2. Waterperry House in 1787, when it was owned by the Catholic Curson family and was the main focus of the Oxford Catholic Mission.

recusants.[147] From the returns of papists compiled by the Diocese of Oxford in 1706, we know that the Catholic household at Waterperry comprised Sir John and Lady Curson and ten 'servants' (presumably including resident estate workers), listed as 'Dan Padwick, Jon Lucas, Rich Arnold, Geo Howard, Hen Price, Mrs Eliz Ryder, Eliz Wilmore, Mary Margaret Woodward, Ann & Mary Padwick wife'.[148] From a dozen in 1706, the Catholic population of Waterperry grew to thirty-two by 1767, but dropped to fifteen by 1780 and in 1790 was just six.[149]

In the eighteenth century the Cursons continued to hold the advowson of Waterperry, enabling them to nominate the vicar, despite the Presentation of Benefices Act which was expressly intended to confiscate advowsons from Catholics. Robert Twycross was the vicar at Waterperry for fifty years from 1739–89. In the 1770s he was in dispute with the Cursons about the poverty of the living. He complained that no tithes had been paid 'since time immemorial' and that the Cursons had enclosed waste land without licence and without making an allotment to the poor or the vicar for their loss of common rights. This may be why in 1777 John Curson demolished the decrepit old vicarage and built a new one at his own expense, but this did not stop the vicar's complaints. There are no known

147   *VCH Oxon.* v, pp. 308–9.
148   W.O. Hassall, 'Papists in early eighteenth-century Oxfordshire', *Oxoniensia*, xiii (1948), p. 80.
149   *VCH Oxon.* v, p. 308.

enclosure records for Waterperry where the Cursons appear to have enclosed land unilaterally.[150]

Although the eighteenth-century Catholic presence at Waterperry was a typical example of country house Catholicism, the Cursons planned ahead for a transition to Oxford. In his will made in 1749, Sir Francis Curson provided for his chaplain to celebrate Mass at Oxford on alternate Sundays.[151] In 1790 Charles Leslie, the last chaplain, was given notice to quit Waterperry and immediately moved to St Clement's in Oxford.

The last mention of the surname Curson in the mission registers is dated 1804. The Waterperry estate had been inherited by Henry Francis Roper, who adopted the surname Curson as required by the will of Sir Francis Curson but who was not a blood relative. He lived much of the time in London and formally repudiated Catholicism. This enabled him to stand for Parliament in 1812. The following year he changed his name by Royal Licence to Henry Francis Roper-Curzon. The family left Waterperry in 1814, and sold the estate in 1830. Despite rejecting Catholicism himself, Roper-Curzon campaigned for Catholic Emancipation, but ended up disliked by both sides.[152]

Country house Catholicism at Waterperry provides a good example of the success of the strategy devised at Harleyford in 1588, keeping alight an ember of Catholicism until a time when the faith could be practised openly, but it also highlights how tenuous that survival was. In the seventeenth century the Catholic mission temporarily ceased to exist when the main Curson line conformed to Anglicanism. Sir Francis Curson, 3rd Baronet, was the mission's saviour, marrying into a recusant family and becoming a Catholic, maintaining a devout household with a chaplain, producing a son who became a priest, and leaving a will that encouraged and partly funded the transfer of the mission to suburban Oxford. Fortunately, the timing was such that urban Catholicism was growing.

The ultimate disappearance of Catholicism from Waterperry is characteristic of many of the old Catholic missions. In such cases there could be various contributory factors: financial and social decline resulting in sons and daughters opting for a celibate religious life; the consequent lack of a Catholic heir; sons moving into business and abandoning Catholicism; family members conforming to Anglicanism, through genuine conversion or to improve social and financial standing (or for mixed motives); or simply an indifference to religion in general. A surprising number of families that had remained Catholic for two hundred years or more, like the Roper-Curzons, abandoned the faith during the very period when it became easier to be a Catholic.

For a list of priests known to have served Waterperry after 1700, see Appendix A.

---

150   Ibid. pp. 302–6.
151   Stapleton, pp. 209, 227.
152   *VCH Oxon.* v, p. 299; A. Fraser, *The King and the Catholics: The Fight for Rights, 1829* (London, 2018), pp. 219–20.

Sandford-on-Thames

Sandford is a parish of about 1,000 acres, three miles from Oxford city centre (Map 1). It lies on the east bank of the River Thames, the boundary between Oxfordshire and Berkshire. The Thames and the main road through Sandford were major communication routes towards Reading and London.[153]

In 1542 a Welshman, Edmund Powell, bought the manor of Sandford, the former Knights Templar estate in the north-west of the parish known for many years as Manor Farm and later as Temple Farm. The Powells settled in Sandford and became recusants. Edmund Powell's eldest granddaughter married William Napier of Holywell, making her a sister-in-law of the martyred priest George Napier. John Powell, the last of his line to own the Sandford estate, had two daughters: Winefred, who married Sir Francis Curson of Waterperry, and Catherine, who married Henry Roper, tenth Lord Teynham. John Powell was a friend of the antiquary Thomas Hearne and an acquaintance of the diarist Anthony Wood. He died in 1730, the estate passing to his daughter, Lady Curson, who sold it in 1760.[154] The Sandford mission then merged with Waterperry, six miles away. As the Waterperry registers show, there were still a few Catholics at Sandford until at least 1768.

Mrs Stapleton suggested that Franciscans may have served the mission. There is no hard evidence for this but the Powells were well disposed towards the Franciscans: in the first half of the seventeenth century, two Powell daughters became Franciscan nuns and a son of the second Edmund Powell of Sandford left an annuity to the Franciscans.[155]

There appears to be no record of the names of priests who served Sandford Manor in the seventeenth century. It was a Jesuit mission by the start of the eighteenth century[156] and the first recorded Jesuit chaplain was Charles Collingwood from Northumberland, who arrived about 1701. Five years earlier he had been Prefect of the Jesuit College at St Omer, Pas-de-Calais. He appears to have stayed at Sandford until his death in 1719. His brother George, also a Jesuit, was executed at Liverpool for taking part in the 1715 Jacobite rising.[157] In 1724 Peter Inghilby was listed as being at 'Sandon, Oxfordshire', which has been interpreted as meaning Sandford. His death in 1741 is mentioned in the Waterperry registers.[158]

Britwell Prior (Newington)

The Catholic mission at Britwell was based at Britwell House (originally Britwell Prior House), in the parish of Newington thirteen miles from Oxford (Map 1).

---

153 *VCH Oxon.* v, p. 267.
154 Stapleton, pp. 200, 212.
155 Ibid. p. 202; Davidson, 'Roman Catholicism in Oxfordshire', p. 214.
156 H. Foley, *Records of the English Province of the Society of Jesus* (London, 1875–80), xi, p. 569.
157 Stapleton, p. 201.
158 Ibid. p. 343; Oxford Oratory Archives, 'Priests of St Aloysius' (undated list).

INTRODUCTION

In contrast to the low-lying riverside parishes of Holywell, Overy, St Clement's, Sandford and Waterperry, much of the historic parish of Newington was mixed arable and pasture in south Oxfordshire, lying 400 to 500 feet above sea level and including foothills rising to woodland at 735 feet on the Chiltern ridge.[159]

Recusancy at Britwell Prior can be traced back to 1577, when John Oglethorpe was a recusant. However, it was the Simeon family who did most to support the Britwell mission, albeit intermittently. John Simeon, who died in 1615, had two sons, both of whom were knighted. One studied at the English College in Rome, the other had a son who became a Jesuit, Edward Simeon. But the Simeons also had an estate in Staffordshire and they moved there in the late seventeenth century, leading to a collapse of recusancy at Britwell.[160]

Sir Edward Simeon, a bachelor and last of his line, rebuilt Britwell Prior House as his principal residence, a project which he completed in 1728. Much later, he built onto the house an external oval chapel, which was completed at a cost of £1,000 in 1769 shortly after his death.[161] It is noteworthy that this chapel was built twenty-two years before the second Catholic Relief Act legalised registered Catholic chapels.

Sir Edward's nephew, Edward Weld of Lulworth in Dorset, inherited Britwell Prior House and took the name Simeon, but died soon afterwards. His nephew, Thomas Weld, moved to the house on his marriage and three children were born there. But in 1775 he succeeded to five estates, including Lulworth, and moved back to Dorset.[162] The house was then let to the Catholic Joseph Blount of Mapledurham. After Revd George Bruning's departure in 1788, the Britwell mission apparently ceased to have a resident chaplain, although Revd James Charles Hunter, SJ (alias Weldon) was living there in 1792.[163]

In 1799 a community of English nuns, the Poor Clares of Aire in Artois, were allowed to leave house arrest in France and travel to the relative safety of England. Thomas Weld's sister Mary was one of the nuns and he allowed the community to stay at Britwell Prior House. He died in 1810 and the nuns left Britwell in 1813, moving to Coxside near Plymouth. (For a list of their chaplains, all Franciscans, see Appendix A.)

James Weld, a son of the owner of Britwell Prior House, came to live there when he married. In 1832 the Welds sold the house, at which point there ceased to be a Catholic presence at Britwell. The oval chapel became a billiard room and then a dining room, which still exists.[164]

---

159 *VCH Oxon.* xviii, pp. 303–6.
160 Stapleton, pp. 278–9.
161 Ibid. p. 279.
162 F.J. Turner, 'Weld, Thomas', *ODNB*.
163 Stapleton, pp. 279–80; J.S. Hansom, 'Catholic registers of the domestic chapel at Waterperry manor house, Oxon, and St Clement's church, Oxford, 1701?–1834', in CRS Records Series 7, *Miscellanea VI* (1909), p. 389.
164 *VCH Oxon.* xviii, pp. 313–15, 336–7.

A small Catholic register (c.29 × 22 cm.) for the Britwell mission survives and is dated 1769.[165] It was compiled by the chaplain, George Bruning.[166] In the register he records that he was preceded at Britwell by William Brown, who arrived in 1729, and John Richardson, a Jesuit, from 1751. He also provides a list of the villages served by the Britwell mission: Burcot, Chinnor, Ewelme, Ipsden, Overy, Shirburn, Wallingford and Watlington. The register includes a description of the new oval chapel and a list of conversions, baptisms, confirmation and marriages. Sixty-four people are listed as forming the congregation in 1769. This was shortly after the Haseley Court mission was merged into Britwell. The last entry is for the baptism in 1788 of John Davey at Overy, where his family had maintained their own Catholic chaplain, five miles from Britwell.

Great and Little Haseley

Great Haseley is a village eight miles from Oxford and three miles from Waterperry (Map 1). Next to the manor house stands its unusually large medieval parish church with a tithe barn. The ancient parish of Great Haseley was comparatively large, comprising some 3,250 acres of rolling farmland and incorporating Great Haseley, Little Haseley, Latchford and Rycote. Its economy was predominantly agricultural, with mixed arable and pasture. In 1801 the population of the parish was 608.[167]

The Jesuits listed Great Haseley and Haseley Court in Little Haseley as places that they served in 1620.[168] Catholicism persisted for some time among the Lenthalls of Latchford and for longer with the Huddlestons of Haseley Court, both gentry families. Yeoman recusants included the Horsemans of Great Haseley.[169] Haseley Court had a private Catholic chapel, served by its own chaplain during the Huddlestons' time. However, the family was financially ruined by their support for Charles I during the Civil War and moved away. The new occupiers were not Catholic and the chapel was converted into a stable.[170]

In 1737 John Wolfe married into the Boulter family and acquired Haseley Court. Wolfe was a Catholic and for a while Haseley again had a Catholic presence. He and his wife had three sons, all of whom died unmarried. The last died at Brussels in 1768 and the Haseley mission then merged into Britwell. When Britwell ceased to have its own chaplain, in the interval between the departure of the Blounts and the

---

165 Printed in J. Edge (ed.), 'The Catholic registers of Britwell Prior or Brightwell, Oxfordshire, 1765–88', in CRS Records Series 13, *Miscellanea VIII* (1913), pp. 292–8; the original register is in the Oxford Oratory Archive.
166 Revd George Bruning died in 1802 and was interred in the Eyston family's private chapel within the Anglican parish church at East Hendred.
167 *VCH Oxon.* xviii, pp. 235–8.
168 Foley, *Records of the English Province of the Society of Jesus*, vii, p. 569.
169 *VCH Oxon.* xviii, pp. 267–8.
170 Stapleton, p. 258.

arrival of the Poor Clares, Charles Leslie of Waterperry ministered to the Catholics of Haseley 'out of charity'.[171]

Overy (Dorchester)

Overy is a hamlet within the parish of Dorchester-on-Thames, eight miles from Oxford (Map 1). The main Oxford to London road passes close to Overy. The River Thame joins the Thames at Dorchester, and forms most of Overy's western and northern boundary, separating the hamlet from Dorchester itself. The landscape of Overy is flat and low lying. Overy Farm, some 345 acres, was held by the recusant Davey family. Overy House, the Daveys' family home, bears the initials HWD (for Helen and William Davey) and the date 1712.[172]

The survival of Catholicism along the three-mile stretch of the Thames from Clifton Hampden through Burcot to Dorchester was unusual in that it was fostered not by the gentry but by a group of farming families. The Catholic yeomen and tenants of the Dorchester district were predominantly members of the Davey, Day and Prince families. The Daveys of Overy became the most prominent and enduring recusants of the area. They grew in status in the late eighteenth and early nineteenth century. The famous agriculturalist, Arthur Young, in 1809 considered 'Mr Davey one of the most intelligent farmers in the county'. The family were leaders of the community in Dorchester and, in 1808, purchased land making them tithe holders with responsibility for repairing the chancel of the local parish church (formerly Dorchester Abbey).[173] William Davey was married to Sarah Haskey, whose family were stewards to the Stonors.

Before 1712, the Daveys lived in a substantial house and farmstead 150 yards south-west of their new Overy House.[174] A family memoir describes a room in the old house that served as a Catholic chapel, fully equipped with altar furniture and used for Mass seven times a year.[175] The Waterperry registers mention confirmands being sent to Waterperry by Gilbert Wells, the Jesuit chaplain at Overy. A few relics of this chapel still exist: some ancient vestments, an oil painting and an old mission chalice, which is small and takes apart for easy concealment.[176]

Later on, the Daveys and other Catholics from the Dorchester area attended Mass at Britwell. After the Britwell mission closed, one of the French exiled clergy, Monsignor Michel Desvalpons, Archdeacon and Vicar General of Dol in Normandy, was a house guest of William Davey at Overy. The University of

---

171   Ibid. pp. 258–60.
172   *VCH Oxon.* vii, pp. 39, 42; E.C. Davey, *Memoirs of an Oxfordshire Old Catholic Family* (London, 1897).
173   Tiller, 'Religion and community: Dorchester to 1920', p. 62.
174   Overy House is sometimes referred to as Overy Manor or Overy Manor House, although it was not actually a manor house.
175   Davey, *Memoirs*, p. 23.
176   Hadland, *Thames Valley Papists*, p. 144.

Oxford's Vice-Chancellor was a founding member of the relief committee established to support the émigré clergy, and some of the exiled French priests, including Desvalpons, were patronised by university dignitaries. When the monsignor died at Overy House in 1798, he was buried with honour in Dorchester Abbey, at the expense of the Warden of New College.[177] From 1796 to 1802 Overy was served by other exiled French priests,[178] probably from the hostel at Thame. Otherwise, the Daveys travelled to St Clement's for Mass. A Jesuit, William Ibbotson, served the mission for a short time prior to 1823. Thereafter Robert Newsham, the priest from St Clement's, served Overy on alternate Sundays until 1849.[179]

Newsham then became first priest of the new Catholic church of St Birinus at Dorchester, built at the expense of John Davey (1787–1863) and designed in Gothic Decorated style by William Wardell. (Wardell went on to design Catholic cathedrals in Sydney and Melbourne.) Robert Newsham contributed £1,000 to the endowment of the new church[180] and brought with him to Dorchester a small school for 'boys of the upper classes' that he had started at St Clement's seventeen years earlier. He lived in a large and handsome Georgian house (still the presbytery) next to St Birinus church. His household in 1851 included his niece, two scholars and a female servant. After a decade at Dorchester, Robert Newsham died in 1859.

As we have seen (p. 19), John Davey's funeral in 1863 was an occasion of controversy over Catholic burial rights. The relationship between High Church Anglicanism, Protestantism and Catholicism was to remain a constant theme in Dorchester life through the nineteenth and into the twentieth century, sometimes tense, sometimes stable, sometimes cordial.[181] St Birinus remains a centre for Catholicism in Dorchester and its hinterland today.

Oxford, St Clement's to Woodstock Road

It has been suggested that the siting of the Oxford Mission in St. Clement's, rather than in the city itself, was probably determined 'by motives of discretion and economy; yet the parish had some sort of Roman Catholic tradition associated, perhaps, with the occasional residence of foreign craftsmen'.[182] This tradition was to continue in the nineteenth century.

The road to Oxford from London ran through St Clement's parish and was greatly improved under the Mileways Act of 1771 when Magdalen Bridge and its approaches were reconstructed (Map 2). The population of St Clement's grew by

---

177 D.A. Bellenger, *The French Exiled Clergy* (Bath, 1986), p. 31; Davey, *Memoirs*, p. 46.
178 M. Gandy, *Catholic Missions and Registers 1700–1880*, ii (Whetstone, 1993), p. 34.
179 Stapleton, p. 248.
180 Davey, *Memoirs*, p. 49.
181 K. Tiller, 'Priests and people: Changing relationships in south Oxfordshire, 1780–1920', in Berkshire Local History Association, *People, Places and Context: Essays in Local History in honour of Joan Dils* (Purley, 2016), pp. 27–42.
182 *VCH Oxon.* iv, pp. 258–66.

more than five times in the first half of the nineteenth century, from just over 400 to more than 2,100, partly due to families moving from the city centre.[183] In the second half of the century the population of St Clement's expanded by a further two and a half times to 5,200.[184] The parish formally became part of the city of Oxford in 1835.

In 1791 Charles Leslie, a former Jesuit of the Scottish province, bought a 700-year lease on a house in St Clement's Street.[185] Leslie was the last chaplain at Waterperry and the second son of Patrick Leslie Duguid, 21st Baron of Balquhain, 10th Baron of Auchinhove and Count of the Holy Roman Empire.[186] Sir Francis Curson's will made in 1749 left £800 'for the maintenance of a priest of the Society of Jesus … for ever amongst the Catholics of Waterperry … whether the said Priest live in the Family of Waterperry at the Mansion House, or do not live in the said Family'. His widow, Lady Winefred, added a further £200 to the trust fund.[187] The Waterperry chaplain was expected to serve Oxford and Waterperry on alternate Sundays. For many years this had been impracticable, as after Holywell Manor ceased to have Catholic tenants, there was no safe place for the regular celebration of Mass at Oxford.[188]

The collateral relatives who succeeded Sir Francis and Lady Winefred Curson were less enthusiastic about having a resident chaplain. In 1790 they gave Charles Leslie formal warning to leave Waterperry immediately. The intention had always been that the Waterperry mission should also serve Oxford. Having secured the lease on the house at St Clement's, Leslie celebrated Mass on alternate Sundays there and at Waterperry. At the same time, he succeeded in recovering £1,400 that had belonged to the Oxford district of the Jesuits before their suppression.[189] At the Quarter Sessions in January 1792, following the legalisation of registered Catholic places of worship by the Second Catholic Relief Act, Leslie registered a room in his house as a chapel.[190]

The attitude of the University authorities towards Catholicism had meanwhile mellowed somewhat: they had made two large donations for the relief of French clergy exiled after the French Revolution; they had employed three exiled French priests to teach modern languages; they had bestowed honorary law degrees on several Catholic gentry; and Oxford University Press, printer to the Church of England, had produced a Vulgate edition of the New Testament for these Catholic

---

183   J. Nash, 'Population change 1801–1851', in Tiller and Darkes (eds), *Historical Atlas of Oxfordshire*, p. 136; *VCH Oxon.* iv, pp. 258–66.
184   J. Nash, 'Population change 1851–1901', in Tiller and Darkes (eds), *Historical Atlas of Oxfordshire*, p. 138.
185   The foundation date of the Catholic mission at St Clement's as given in *Kelly's Directory of Oxfordshire* (1895) was 1785. It is possible that Leslie had a short-term tenancy before the 700-year lease of 1791. The address was then known as 79 High Street (now 81 St Clement's Street).
186   C. Leslie, *Pedigree of the Family of Leslie of Balquhain* (Bakewell, 1861), p. 19.
187   Bertram, *St Aloysius' Parish*, p. 3.
188   Hansom, 'Catholic registers of Waterperry and St Clement's', pp. 391–2.
189   Bertram, *St Aloysius' Parish*, p. 3.
190   Stapleton, pp. 226–7.

Fig. 3. The chapel of St Ignatius at St Clement's, Oxford, built in 1793–5 in the garden of the former Jesuit Charles Leslie, Waterperry's last chaplain.

priests, free of charge. In the light of this greater tolerance of Catholicism, Charles Leslie proposed building a chapel in the grounds of his house at St Clement's. He sought the approval of the Vicar Apostolic, an Oxfordshire man born at Heythrop where Leslie had recently licensed a Catholic chapel. The bishop was enthusiastic about the Oxford proposal, making a large donation and persuading other rich Catholics to do likewise. However, so many exiled French clergy and nuns were arriving in England that fundraising for the new chapel was postponed for some years, their need being considered greater.

Leslie meanwhile started the construction of the chapel in the garden of his house, using borrowed money. The chapel, which had its own burial ground, was set back from the road as required by the law and as a precaution against anti-Catholic vandalism. By 1793 Mass could be celebrated in the shell and two years later the building was substantially complete. It was constructed of stone, the plain façade facing the road surmounted by a pedimented gable and featuring a roundel window above the arched doorway (Figs. 3–5).[191] Leslie wrote, 'I completed this solemn and handsome edifice as soon as possible, and I decorated it in a style of Elegant Simplicity, which has hitherto met with universal approbation'. The first burial at the chapel of St Ignatius took place in 1798. Shortly afterwards Charles Leslie was joined at St Clement's by fellow ex-Jesuit William Hothersall, who had been chaplain

---

191 The former chapel, now 81 St Clement's Street, was awarded a Blue Plaque in 2018.

Fig. 4. The nave of St Ignatius's chapel in 1906, looking east to the sanctuary.

Fig. 5. The sanctuary of St Ignatius's chapel in 1906.

to the Earl of Abingdon at Thame Park and, before that, the last Jesuit rector of the English College in Rome.[192]

In 1796 a trust fund administered by the 'Gentlemen of Stonyhurst' (former Jesuits) was established to administer the Oxford Mission.[193] When Charles Leslie started a major fundraising campaign, the Catholic community responded generously, more than forty individuals donating a total of just over £534. The donors included clergy, nobility, gentry, yeomen and even servants. Vestments and altar furnishings were also donated. Charles Leslie's mother, Countess Leslie, left the considerable sum of £1,000 to the mission.[194]

Charles Leslie died suddenly in 1806 and was succeeded by his elder brother James, also a former Jesuit.[195] James Leslie moved to Yorkshire after six years at St Ignatius and was succeeded as resident priest by John William Conolly, an Irish Jesuit (d. 1818) and then by Robert Newsham, SJ, who served the mission for three decades. In 1828 about 110 people received Easter Communion at St Ignatius. Shortly afterwards the presbytery (known as Leslie House after its first occupier) was completely rebuilt, and a few years later Robert Newsham established a small private school there for about eight pupils, including boarders.[196]

J.H. Newman converted from Anglicanism to Catholicism in 1845. It was at St Ignatius that he attended his first public Mass, having walked with friends from Littlemore. A few years later, following an argument with his Jesuit superiors, Robert Newsham resigned from the Society of Jesus and moved to Dorchester, taking the school with him. Henry Brigham, SJ, a Yorkshireman, became the new resident priest at St Ignatius.[197] When the national religious census was taken in 1851 Brigham declined to provide information unless compelled. The local registrar discovered from 'a friend of that religion' that the chapel had 70-80 sittings, about half free, and an average congregation of fifty.[198] In 1854 the Burial Act closed inner city graveyards, including that at St Ignatius.

With the restoration of the Catholic episcopal hierarchy in 1850, Oxfordshire became part of the new Diocese of Birmingham, and the mission of St Ignatius was handed by the Jesuits to the new diocese in 1859. James Nary, previously chaplain at Stonor and famous as a musician, took over in 1868 and established an excellent choir at St Ignatius. About the same time a new school began with eighteen pupils at the presbytery, possibly succeeding an earlier dame school as the 1861 census shows a resident school mistress. The Diocese of Birmingham handed the mission of St Ignatius back to the Jesuits in 1871.[199]

192 Stapleton, pp. 226–30.
193 Bertram, *St Aloysius' Parish*, p. 5.
194 Stapleton, p. 231.
195 Bertram, *St Aloysius' Parish*, p. 6.
196 Stapleton, pp. 232, 237.
197 Ibid. pp. 238, 240.
198 K. Tiller (ed.), *Church and Chapel in Oxfordshire 1851* (ORS 55, 1987), p. 76.
199 Stapleton, p. 239.

Fig. 6. The interior of the church of St Aloysius Gonzaga on Woodstock Road, Oxford, in 1906. The church was built in 1873–5 by J.A. Hansom & Son.

Nary's successor in 1871, James Corry, found that his predecessor's financial management skills had not matched his musical talents. In a letter written on the last day of 1871 he detailed the income and outgoings, conveying a fairly bleak picture. He had received little more than half the endowment of £33 and in the nine months he had been there had paid out £9 more than he had received. The school was costing £70 a year but its subscriptions were bringing in less than £40. The weekly offertory from the congregation of 'about 45 seat holders' (who presumably paid a pew rent) was not much more than fifteen shillings, reflecting the relatively low income and status of most of the congregation.[200]

The Jesuits realised that the chapel of St Ignatius was now too small, and poorly located to serve the potential Catholic community of Oxford. A site at 25 Woodstock Road was given by the Marquess of Bute, a Catholic convert, and the foundation stone of the much larger church of St Aloysius Gonzaga was laid in May 1873 by the Bishop of Birmingham. In November 1875, in the presence of the Archbishop of Westminster, the Bishop formally opened the new church (Figs. 6–7).[201] St Ignatius became a chapel of ease for Sunday Mass until 1911; Catholic primary education continued on the site until 1968.

For a full list of priests known to have served St Ignatius, see Appendix A.

200 Ibid.
201 K.D. Reynolds, 'Crichton-Stuart, John Patrick, 3rd marquess of Bute', *ODNB*; https://taking-stock.org.uk/building/oxford-st-aloysius/.

Fig. 7. The west front of St Aloysius's church. The presbytery (at right) was added in 1878, designed by William Wilkinson.

Local timeline

- 1680   The revived Catholic mission at Waterperry House began about this time when Sir John Curson converted to Catholicism having married Penelope Child, a recusant.
- 1688   Oxfordshire became part of the newly formed Midland District of the Catholic Church under Bonaventure Giffard, Vicar Apostolic.
- 1688   Invading Dutch troops desecrated the Catholic chapel at East Hendred. At Oxford they burned an effigy of a Catholic priest dressed in vestments stolen from the chapel.
- 1700   Earliest entry in registers of the Waterperry Catholic mission. Sir John Curson was accused of mortgaging his estates to help fund the Jesuits.
- 1703   George Witham became Vicar Apostolic of the Midland District.
- 1704   The recusant Austin Belson of Aston Rowant was arrested on suspicion of being a subversive.
- 1705   Catholic residences in the south Chilterns (Shirburn Castle, Stonor and Watlington Park) were searched for arms but none were discovered.
- 1715   The recusant Thomas Gage conformed to Anglicanism and disposed of Shirburn Castle near Watlington.
- 1716   John Talbot Stonor became Vicar Apostolic of the Midland District, often staying in Oxfordshire at Heythrop, Stonor or Watlington Park.
- 1722   Richard Hudson ran a small Catholic school at Kidlington with books supplied by the antiquary and diarist Thomas Hearne.
- 1723   Oxfordshire Catholics alarmed by the new levy on their estates.
- 1727   Sir John Curson of Waterperry died and was succeeded by his son Sir Francis.
- 1729   The first Catholic chaplain arrived at the new house built at Britwell Prior (Newington parish) by Sir Edward Simeon.
- 1750   Sir Francis Curson of Waterperry died childless. The Curson baronetcy passed to his brother Peter, a Jesuit priest. Sir Francis's widow retained the estate.
- 1753   The Vicar Apostolic administered confirmation at Waterperry.
- 1756   John Joseph Hornyold, the first Catholic bishop to be consecrated in England since the Reformation, became Vicar Apostolic.
- 1758   The Vicar Apostolic administered confirmation at Waterperry.
- 1763   The Vicar Apostolic again administered confirmation at Waterperry.
- 1764   Lady Winefred Curson (née Powell) of Waterperry, widow of Sir Francis Curson, died. The estate subsequently went through various changes of ownership but the Catholic mission was maintained. New owners adopted the surname Curson.
- 1765   Sir Peter Curson, SJ, died and the Curson baronetcy became extinct.

1767	A government census of Catholics showed Britwell Salome with 8, Dorchester 19, Haseley 11, Newington (including Britwell Prior) 15, Oxford 23 and Waterperry 32.
1768	Following the death of the recusant John Wolfe, the Catholic mission at Haseley Court lost its resident chaplain and was thereafter served from Britwell. Sir Edward Simeon of Britwell also died and was succeeded by his nephew Thomas Weld of the Dorset recusant family.
1769	The new Catholic chapel at Britwell House was completed at a cost of at least £1,000. It attracted a congregation of sixty-four from within a six-mile radius.
1778	Thomas Joseph Talbot became Vicar Apostolic.
1788	The Britwell mission, including Haseley, was absorbed into Waterperry.
1790	Charles Leslie, a former Jesuit and the last Catholic chaplain at Waterperry, was given formal notice to leave Waterperry immediately.
1791	Charles Leslie purchased a 700-year lease on a house at St Clement's, Oxford.
1792	Charles Leslie registered a room in the house at St Clement's as a Catholic chapel. He celebrated Mass on alternate Sundays at Waterperry and Oxford.
1793	Charles Leslie had the chapel of St Ignatius built in the grounds of his house.
1795	The chapel of St Ignatius at St Clement's was completed. Only a handful of Catholics remained at Waterperry but the Oxford congregation numbered about 60 and was growing. Charles Berington became Vicar Apostolic.
1796	A hostel was established at Thame House for about 100 Breton refugee priests.
1798	The exiled Catholic Vicar General of Dol in Normandy died at Overy and was buried with honour in Dorchester Abbey.
1798	First burial at the chapel of St Ignatius.
1799	Charles Leslie was joined at St Clement's by fellow ex-Jesuit William Hothersall, formerly chaplain to the Wenmans at Thame Park. English nuns of the Poor Clares order, exiled from Aire in Picardy, took refuge at Britwell House.
1800	Gregory Stapleton became Vicar Apostolic of the Midland District.
1800	Start of a new volume of sacramental registers for the combined mission of Oxford and Waterperry.
1803	John Milner became Vicar Apostolic of the Midland District.
1804	Last mention of the surname Curson in the Waterperry/Oxford registers. The Waterperry estate had been inherited by Henry Francis Roper, who adopted the surname Curson but was not a blood relative.
1806	Death of Charles Leslie.
1807	James Leslie, a former Jesuit and elder brother of Charles Leslie, succeeded the latter as priest at St Ignatius.

INTRODUCTION

1812   John William Conolly, an Irish Jesuit, became priest at St Ignatius. The Poor Clares left Britwell House.

1812   Henry Francis Curson, fourteenth Baron Teynham, formally repudiated Catholicism and stood for Parliament.

1813   Henry Francis Curson changed his name by Royal Licence to Roper-Curzon.

1814   The Roper-Curzon family left Waterperry.

1818   Death of John William Conolly, succeeded by Robert Newsham, SJ.

1823   The University of Oxford, the Anglican Diocese of Oxford, the City of Oxford and various Oxford residents opposed the Earl of Fingall's Catholic Relief Bill.

1826   Thomas Walsh became Vicar Apostolic of the Midland District. John Henry Newman was curate at St Clement's Anglican parish church, where he organised fundraising for its new church building, completed in 1828.

1829   Presbytery at St Ignatius completely rebuilt and called Leslie House.

1832   Small private school established for about eight pupils (including boarders) in the presbytery. The Weld family sold Britwell House and it passed out of Catholic ownership.

1840   Midland District renamed Central District. Nicholas Wiseman became its Vicar Apostolic.

1845   Newman converted from Anglicanism to Roman Catholicism. The following Sunday, he attended Mass at St Ignatius, close to the Anglican Church of St Clement's where he had once been curate.

1848   William Bernard Ullathorne became Vicar Apostolic of the Central District.

1849   Following an argument with his Jesuit superiors about the school he ran at St Ignatius, Robert Newsham resigned from the Society of Jesus and moved to Dorchester, taking the school with him. Henry Brigham, SJ, became the new resident priest at St Ignatius.

1850   Oxfordshire became part of the new Diocese (later Archdiocese) of Birmingham. William Bernard Ullathorne became Bishop of Birmingham.

1851   According to the religious census, approximately fifty people regularly attended Sunday morning Mass at St Ignatius.

1854   Francis Chadwick, SJ became resident priest at St Ignatius. The Burial Act closed inner city graveyards, including that at St Ignatius.

1857   Following the death of Francis Chadwick, Charles Blackett, SJ became resident priest, rapidly succeeded by Francis Jarrett, SJ.

1859   The mission of St Ignatius was handed by the Jesuits to the Diocese of Birmingham.

1860   Alexander Comberbach, a secular priest of the Diocese of Birmingham, became resident priest at St Ignatius.

1869   James Nary became resident priest at St Ignatius.

1869   St Ignatius school began with eighteen pupils in a room at the presbytery.

1871 The Diocese of Birmingham handed the mission of St Ignatius back to the Jesuits. James Corry, SJ became resident priest. Over the next four years, other Jesuit priests serving the chapel included John Morris, Francis Goldie, William Johnson and Thomas Parkinson.
1873 The foundation stone of the church of St Aloysius Gonzaga was laid by Bishop Ullathorne.
1875 Formal opening of the Church of St Aloysius. St Ignatius became a chapel of ease for Sunday Mass. During the week, the school used the chapel, a curtain screening off the altar.
1875 Nazareth House was founded by the Sisters of Nazareth on the corner of Pembroke Street (now Rectory Road) and Cowley Road as a Catholic alternative to the workhouse.

The registers: editorial method and description of their contents

The editor has transcribed, translated into English from the Latin, and tabulated all the entries of baptisms, confirmations, marriages, deaths and burials, and conversions.

First volume: 1700–1800

The registers in this earliest volume are almost entirely in English. They are in a small notebook approximately 15.5cm × 10cm, which was later bound together with the second volume. The entries up to 1756 were transcribed, probably by the Jesuit priest Francis Pole, from one or more lost sources. These sources were probably easily concealed pocketbooks, or notes made by missioners, at a time when possession of such material was incriminating.

In 1909 the Catholic Record Society published a transcript of the Catholic registers of the domestic chapel of the Curson family at Waterperry House and of its successor, the chapel of St Ignatius at St Clement's, Oxford, up to 1834.[202] The CRS transcript was the work of the architect Joseph Stanislaus Hansom (1845–1931), and the historian the Hon. Mrs Bryan Stapleton provided historical notes placing the transcript in context. Hansom did not translate Latin entries into English. The present editor made his own transcript from the original handwritten text and compared it with Hansom's version; he found very few disparities and none of any consequence.

Hansom was a founder member of the Catholic Record Society and was described by the Benedictine intellectual Cardinal Gasquet as its 'prime mover and energy'. J.S. Hansom was the son of Joseph Aloysius Hansom (1803–82), architect of the

---

202 J.S. Hansom, 'Catholic registers of the domestic chapel at Waterperry manor house, Oxon, and St Clement's church, Oxford, 1701?–1834', in CRS Records Series 7, *Miscellanea VI* (1909), pp. 388–422. (A scanned electronic copy of the volume, fully text searchable, is available at https://archive.org/details/publicationsofca06cath.)

church of St Aloysius, Oxford. He was also the nephew of Charles Francis Hansom, designer of the Catholic church at Buckland in the Vale of White Horse, who ran a separate architectural practice with his son Edward Joseph Hansom.

Second volume: 1800–54

The second volume is 20cm × 16.8cm, bound in boards, originally with a leather back. After partial transcription by the Catholic Record Society in 1909, the backs of the two volumes were broken and they were bound together. This volume is largely in Latin. The title page describes it as the second volume of the baptismal register of the combined Catholic mission of Oxford and Waterperry, beginning 4 November 1800.

Forenames are almost always recorded in their Latin forms. In translating them back into English, the present editor generally opted for the most usual versions of the time. The reader should be aware, however, that many Latin names can be translated in more than one form. Thus, to take an extreme case, the Latin form Joanna will usually mean Jane; but it could translate as Joanna, Joanne, Joan, Jean, Jeanette, or, bearing in mind the cosmopolitan congregation of the chapel, a non-English variant such as Jeanne, Giannetta, Ionna, Hanna, Sinead or Siobhan. The Latin form Anna will usually stand for Ann, occasionally for Anne (a rarer spelling at the time) but could also represent Anna or Nan. Similarly, Maria will usually mean Mary but could be Maria, Marie, Moira or Máire. It is quite possible that someone might have started life in Ireland with the Gaelic name Máire, be known in England as Mary and be registered by the Church as Maria. It is noteworthy that the English forms of some forenames may have more than one spelling. Winefride, a name spelled variously in these registers, is an extreme case, with at least ten variants.

In contrast to forenames, the surnames in the register are not Latinised. However, the spelling often varies considerably. As with other old church records, there were issues of pronunciation and lack of literacy on the part of the laity, and of lack of familiarity on the part of the clergy. Thus, a consistently used spelling may suddenly change, as in the case of Holyolk suddenly becoming Holyoak in 1821.

Combined volume: Baptisms (1854–65), confirmations (1854–73), marriages (1854–76), burials (1854–77)

From 1854 pre-printed registers were used in a standard format approved by the newly restored English Catholic hierarchy. Whereas the emphasis for the previous half century had been on recording baptisms, now registers were maintained also for confirmations, marriages and burials.

On the inside of the front cover of this combined volume is a note dated 29 March 1863 signed by Alexander Comberbach, the first diocesan priest at the mission. It lists obligatory masses to be said monthly or annually by the pastor of the congregation. A footnote, referring to an annual Requiem Mass for Arthur Beale, was added later and initialled by Comberbach: the reason for this is unclear.

This priest's use of the term 'pastor', which he applies to himself, is interesting, especially when viewed in the context of the English Catholic Church's transition from mission towards a normal diocesan and parochial situation. Dioceses had been re-established in 1850 but England was still officially missionary territory under Vatican control until 1908; not until 1918 did individual missions become parishes in the formal sense. Comberbach's register entries were originally signed as 'Pastor' but almost all, from 1859 to 1867, were later laboriously changed to 'Apostolic Missionary', reflecting Rome's view that England was still a mission.[203]

Baptisms (1865–78)

This standard format volume records the final decade of baptisms at the chapel of St Ignatius. It also contains records of later baptisms at St Aloysius, which are beyond the scope of the present volume.

Register of converts (1872–1909)

Whereas it was standard practice for Catholic missions to maintain registers of baptisms, confirmations, marriages and burials, there was no general requirement to keep a register of converts. However, in 1869 the fourth synod of the Diocese of Birmingham issued a decree that 'in each mission a register should be kept of those baptised conditionally and of converts to the faith', notwithstanding the fact that conditional baptisms should in any case be recorded in the normal baptismal registers.

As the requirement for registers of converts was not widespread, the book used at St Aloysius was not a pre-printed standard format volume but merely a sturdy exercise book with card covers and stitched binding. The register of converts covers thirty-seven years but the present volume is concerned only with those entries up to the end of 1875 when the church of St Aloysius Gonzaga replaced the chapel of St Ignatius as the main Catholic place of worship for the Oxford area.

Register of baptisms at the chapel of St Mary the Virgin, Bampton (1856–60)

This is a pre-printed register book in the format approved by the Catholic hierarchy. There was no significant historical link between the Bampton and the Oxford Catholic Mission (see Appendix B). The Bampton register passed to the Oxford Oratory as a convenient archival repository.

Commentary on entries in the registers

Where page numbers are quoted in this section, they refer to the original documents, the numbering starting with the first page of register entries.

Entries for events in the tabulated transcripts can be located by their date.

---

203 Norman, *Roman Catholicism in England*, p. 108.

First volume: 1700–1800

Days for Benediction

The register proper is preceded by a list of thirty days each year on which Benediction of the Blessed Sacrament was to be celebrated at Waterperry. Benediction is a service of hymns, litanies and adoration of the Blessed Sacrament.[204] Services and devotions other than Benediction are also listed under this heading, such as certain Masses, sermons, readings and prayers.

Supplement

Next is a supplement which provides further details of services and liturgical practice.

Names of members of the Congregation of Bona Morte at Waterperry

After five blank pages, we find a list of members of the Congregation of Bona Morte. Thirteen people are named in the undated first part of the list, headed by Sir Francis and Lady Curson. The first name is Miss Catharine Brinkhurst, Sir Francis's niece: the Brinkhursts were a Buckinghamshire family into which Sir John Curson's daughter Mary married. Five more names, all women (two married and three apparently unmarried), were added between 1751 and 1758.

Confirmations (1753–63)

After five blank pages there are three lists of confirmations at Waterperry in the decade commencing 1753. The first recorded confirmations at Waterperry took place on the fourth Sunday after Easter in 1753 (Fig. 8). They were administered by Bishop Hornyold, who confirmed fifteen people: six males and nine females. At the head of the list is Mary Padwick, who was no doubt related to the Padwicks listed as servants at Waterperry in 1706. Also named was Lucy Harding, presumably a member of the Harding family previously of Holywell.

The second list of confirmations dates from the ninth Sunday after Pentecost, 1758. Bishop Hornyold again presided. The list is headed by Lady Maria Bertie and Lady Sophia Bertie, the youngest daughters of Willoughby Bertie, Third Earl of Abingdon, and his wife Anna Maria (née Collins), Countess of Abingdon, who married in Florence in 1727. Seven of the confirmands came from the Catholic mission at Britwell, sent by its Jesuit chaplain John Richardson. Also confirmed was a female sent from Overy by Gilbert Wells.

A third list of confirmations is dated Pentecost (Whit Sunday) 1763, an appropriate occasion for confirmation. Bishop Hornyold again presided but this time there were only three confirmands, all female, two of whom were sent by the missioner at Britwell, Revd Brown.

---

204 The host, a consecrated communion wafer.

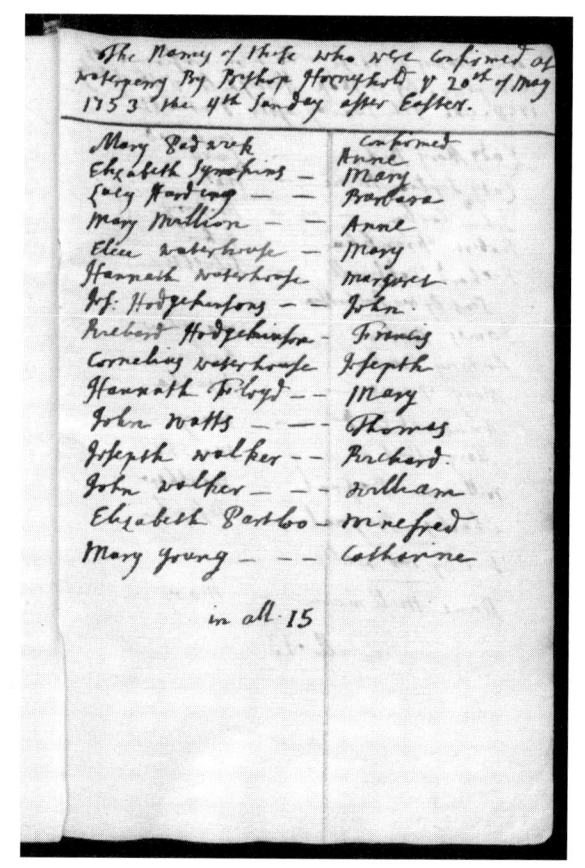

Fig. 8. List of those confirmed at Waterperry by 'Bishop Hornyhold'
(John Hornyold, Vicar Apostolic of the Midland District),
20 May 1753; from the 1700–1800 Waterperry register.

Anniversaries kept at Waterperry

Following the confirmation lists, an isolated marriage record dated 1770 and a blank page, there is a list of six anniversaries of deaths commemorated at Waterperry (Fig. 9). The people commemorated were Cursons or close relatives. The first anniversary is of Sir Francis Curson, who died in 1750; it highlights England's adoption of the Gregorian calendar in 1752. That year began not as hitherto on Lady Day (25 March) but on 1 January. So, for example, the anniversary of Sir Francis is given as 29 May Old Style and 9 June New Style.

Catalogue of the Dead (1700–79 and 1798–1807)

After three blank pages there follows what is described as a catalogue of the dead. This contains the earliest of the Waterperry register entries, which are two deaths

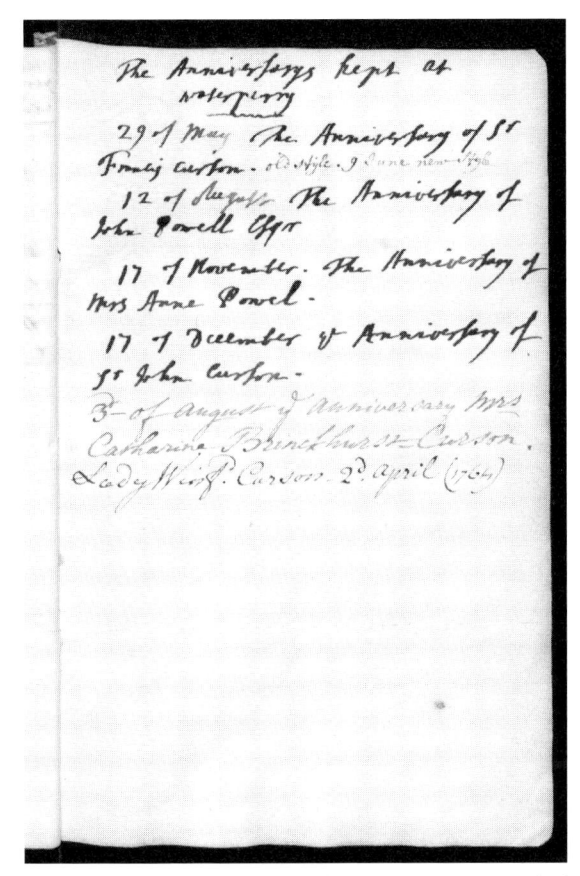

Fig. 9. List of death anniversaries kept at Waterperry in the late 18th century, naming members of the Curson family and their Powell relatives; from the 1700–1800 Waterperry register.

in 1700. More than a hundred deaths are listed in chronological order, the last being in 1807.

Most of the entries in the catalogue simply give a name and date of death, although the circumstances and ritual surrounding the deaths of the Cursons is described in detail. Sometimes a family relationship is highlighted. For example, the deaths of the sisters Mrs Mary Powell and Mrs Winefred White are mentioned as happening three days apart in 1703. Occasionally the place of death is recorded and from 1755 onwards, the location is mentioned more often. Usually, it is some village not far from Waterperry but occasionally locations much further away are cited, such as London, Essex or even Brussels, where Charles Wolfe of Haseley Court died in 1768.[205]

205 Stapleton, p. 259.

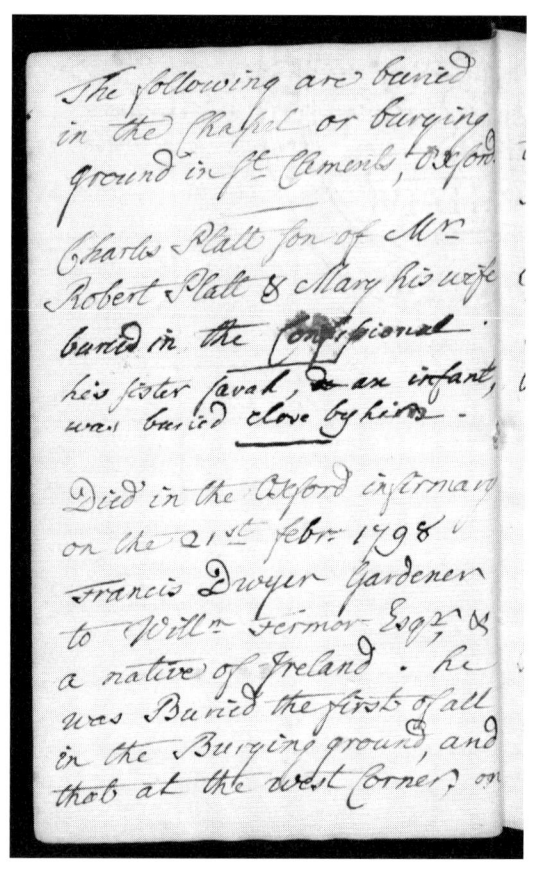

Fig. 10. First page of the burials list for St Ignatius's chapel in the 1700–1800 Waterperry register, noting two undated burials 'in the confessional', and the first burial in the 'burying ground' ('at the west corner') on 21 February 1798.

Thomas Phillips, listed as dying in 1742, was from Ickford, just over the Buckinghamshire border from Waterperry. His children included the abbess of the English Benedictine convent at Ghent and a Jesuit chaplain to Lord Shrewsbury.[206]

From 1771 Latin is used occasionally in the registers which are hitherto entirely in English. After an unexplained gap the list continues in 1798, stating that the burials listed were now in the new chapel or its burial ground in Oxford (Fig. 10). The brief list of burials at St Clement's concludes with two in 1807.

---

206 Ibid. 262.

Births and christenings (1701–1800)

After five blank pages there is a long list of christenings in chronological order, beginning in 1701. Until 1747 these entries are very brief, giving only the name of the person baptised and the date of the christening. Thereafter most additionally provide the date of birth, the location if not at Waterperry, and the names of the godparents, otherwise described as sponsors.

In the Waterperry christenings at this time we see the preoccupation with baptism following birth as quickly as possible. Often the christening took place within a day or two of birth, sometimes on the same day. Although not part of official Catholic theology, there was a widely held fear that if an unbaptised child died it would not go to Heaven, but instead be consigned to Limbo.[207] The christening of twins James and Winny Waterhouse illustrates the point. They were born on 25 July 1748 and baptised the same day *ob periculum* (Latin for 'because at risk'). The formal ceremonies were conducted six days later.

As with the other early entries in this volume, the baptismal records up to 1755 were evidently copied by Revd Pole from one or more other sources, now lost. Following his transcript of old records, he continued with a further eleven entries, apparently made when the christenings took place, at various dates between 1756 and 1764. The sole baptismal register entry for 1773 begins the practice of stating who officiated at the baptism. One baptism took place in 1780. The next christening was five years later. Another four years passed before the next baptism at Waterperry. There are eight more entries spanning 1792–6: three are explicitly stated as being at Oxford, the rest presumably at Waterperry. Two are of children of Henry Curson and his wife, Bridget.

After two stray marriage entries (Fig. 11), the births and christening register continues. The next two entries record baptisms at Little Haseley. Between the two is a note pointing out that, after the death of Mr Wolfe of Haseley Court, the Haseley Catholic community formed part of the Britwell congregation, but as that community was 'now without assistance', Charles Leslie served them 'out of Charity'.

An interesting development in the 1790s is the first use in this register of the term 'lawful'. Here it refers to Joseph Johnson's wife. Two entries later, we see mention of James Hart, lawful son of Joseph and Mary Hart. Some years later we find Joseph Johnson's wife Hannah again described as lawful. It seems likely that the Johnsons and the Harts were keen to have the fact recorded that they were legally married, in accordance with the Hardwicke Marriage Act, and that their children were deemed legitimate according to civil law. (In the early-nineteenth-century register entries, the term 'legitimate' is often used in the same way.)

An unusual entry entirely in Latin records the christening on 24 April 1797 of Marie Julie Anne, a daughter of the Count and Countess of Kerampuilh. They were French aristocrats from Brittany who had taken refuge in England from the

---

207   A supposed state of oblivion that is neither Heaven nor Hell.

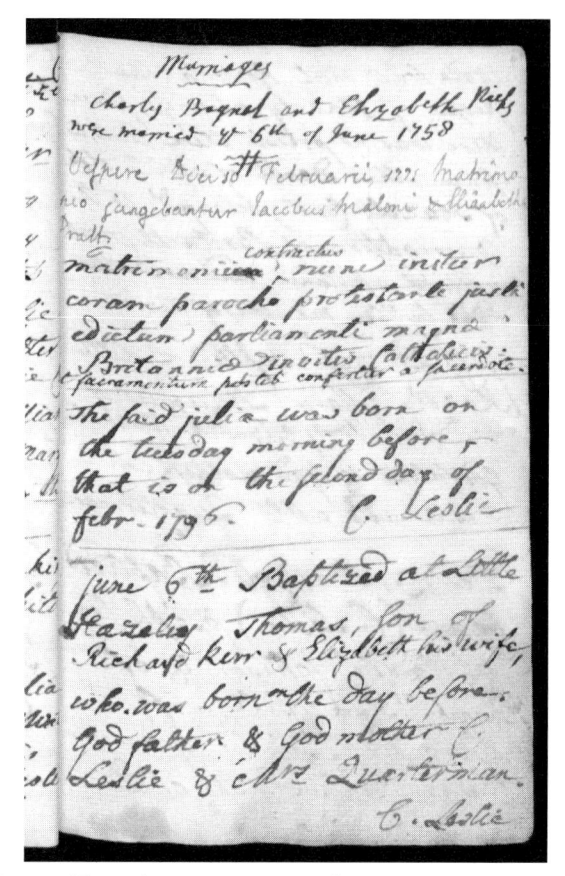

Fig. 11. The earliest register entries for marriages at Waterperry (6 June 1758 and 10 February 1771), followed by further baptisms including one at Little Haseley; from the 1700–1800 Waterperry register.

Revolution. Their surname was Saisy, rendered Saisi by Charles Leslie, presumably because classical Latin does not use the letter 'y'.

On the next page is the baptism of the daughter of an Irish soldier. There is also an entry recording the birth and christening of twins Vincent and Joseph Davey of Overy; the entry is singularly uninformative, lacking the names of the parents and the godparents, and may well have been an emergency baptism. The scantest entry of all is for the undated christening at Wheatley of John Shepherd, about whom nothing more is stated. It is clear however that it happened between mid-May 1799 and late February 1800.

Many of the entries on the last few pages of the register do not state who the baptiser was; we can safely assume that, unless otherwise stated, it was Charles Leslie, especially where he is named as godfather. On 31 January 1799, however,

INTRODUCTION

William Hothersall is noted as coming over to Waterperry from Thame to christen Bridget Kelly. Unusually, she was twenty weeks old, and it may be that her parents had only recently arrived in the area. Perhaps they were an army family returning from service abroad or itinerants. The first register volume of the Waterperry mission and its successor at St Clement's ends on 30 June 1800 with the christening of Sarah White of Warpsgrove near Haseley.

Second volume: 1800–54

Baptisms (1800–54)

Entries in this volume generally give the date of the christening, the date of birth (and sometimes the place), the parents' names (and normally the statement that they are married), the names of the godparents or sponsors, and the name of the baptiser. The first is for Peter Stephen Platt, which states that the godfather was represented by the French priest Mr Bertin. This was probably Georges Bertin, born 1733, of the Diocese of Rennes.[208] The second entry is for another child of Henry Curson of Waterperry. The third on 5 January 1801 is for Joseph Davey, born at Dorchester, who is described as the legitimate son of William Davey and his unnamed wife (Sarah, formerly Haskey).[209] This was an emergency baptism carried out by Mr Triquet, another French priest, probably Julien François René Triquet of the Diocese of Le Mans.[210]

An entry for 26 April 1801 involves two French priests, one the baptiser, the other a sponsor. The child was the three-year-old son of a dragoon guard and his wife, and had previously been baptised in a Protestant church. Consequently, he was conditionally baptised, the baptiser being Mr A. Rouxel, French priest and rector of the Diocese of Saint-Brieuc in Brittany, who presumably had come from Thame. The Catholic Church recognises baptism by anybody, provided they have the right intention and pour water on the child's head while saying 'I baptise thee in the name of the Father, and of the Son, and of the Holy Ghost'. Not all Protestant clergy followed this form, which is why the baptism was deemed conditional.

Also in 1801 is the baptism of Martha, the child of an apparently single mother, Mary Timbs. The register records the christening on 8 October 1804 of Charlotte, daughter of John Talbot, youngest brother of the fifteenth Earl of Shrewsbury. The mother's name is not given but she was Susan Harriet Anne (née Bedingfeld).

---

208 Bellenger, *French Exiled Clergy*, p. 149. Georges Bertin was one of the 5,621 exiled French Catholic priests, refugees from the French Revolution, who were in England receiving state aid in 1800. Most were from dioceses north of the Loire and on the western seaboard of France. In 1796 the King's Arms inn on Castle Hill, Reading, was requisitioned by the government as a hostel for more than 340 Norman priests. At Thame, the Mansion House in the High Street was similarly requisitioned for 100 Breton priests.
209 Davey, *Memoirs*, p. 46. William Davey married Sarah Haskey at the Catholic chapel at Stonor in 1784.
210 Bellenger, *French Exiled Clergy*, p. 251.

On page 8 Charles Leslie writes that he 'regularised the baptismal ceremonies, following an earlier baptism by a non-Catholic minister at Evesham'. In another entry on the same page, he records christening a child 'who had been baptised without a drop of water being present by a Protestant minister, or at least, that is what the mother of the child told me, who was present at the time of the ceremonies in the parish church of St Mary Magdalen, Oxford'.

With some entries, Charles Leslie clearly hoped to add missing details later: spaces are left, especially for unknown Christian names. In the entry for the christening of George Beek, 13 January 1806 it is clear that the priest failed to record an emergency baptism; but he recalled having baptised the child and was now supplying 'the missing ceremonies'.

For couples who had no Catholic friends or relatives nearby to be godparents, the priest of the chapel of St Ignatius often took the role of godfather, while a reliable female member of the congregation took that of the godmother. One such woman was Susanna Savage, whose name often appears as godmother from 1801 onwards.

On page 11, interspersed among the baptisms, is a stray wedding: that of Thomas Copus and Jane Bradl[e]y.

Two members of the Collingridge family appear on 2 August 1812: a family described as 'for many generations the mainstay of the several Catholic congregations supported by the Fermor family' in north Oxfordshire.[211]

In May 1813 we see the arrival of a new priest, replacing James Leslie who, the previous autumn, had become chaplain to the Middletons of Stockhold Park, Yorkshire. The new man was an Irish Jesuit, John William Conolly. From here on Irish surnames occur frequently in the registers.

An interesting development in the register entries during William Conolly's time at the chapel is the recording of the mother's previous surname, which may be a maiden name or, if she was widowed, the surname from her previous marriage. This is first seen in an entry for 5 September 1817 where it is stated that Lucy Davey, wife of William Davey, was formerly a Morgan.

After little more than six years at St Ignatius, William Conolly died. His successor was Robert Newsham, SJ, who was the resident priest for the next thirty-one years. It is clear that he was an effective evangelist: after his arrival there is an immediate increase in the baptisms (often conditional) of adults and sometimes of their Protestant-baptised children. There are six conditional baptisms of adults in the nine months to August 1819.

A stray burial is recorded in 1819, of Sir Richard Reade who died on 22 October 1819 'fortified by all the sacraments of the Catholic Church'. These would have comprised penance (also known as confession or reconciliation), holy communion and extreme unction (the anointing of the sick). This burial is discussed in greater detail in the Deaths and Burials section below.[212]

211 Stapleton, p. 89.
212 See below, p. 67.

In 1820 the register records more conditional baptisms of adults and children. The entry for John Smith, son of John and Elizabeth Smith is interesting, as Robert Newsham originally recorded the child as being legitimate then struck that word out. The high rate of baptisms continued and, in less than four years, filled seventeen pages of the register.

In 1829 the Catholic Emancipation Act was passed. It also saw the official lifting of the Vatican's suppression of the English Jesuits, after the Vicars Apostolic sent a memorandum to the Pope. That memorandum was presented by the agent for Oxfordshire-born Bishop Peter Collingridge. It was therefore appropriate that the first baptism at the chapel of St Ignatius following emancipation was that of Ignatius Collingridge on 24 May 1829.[213]

There is a somewhat mysterious and exotic entry for the baptism on 26 March 1833 of Adaline Domville Douglas, daughter of Sholto Douglas and his wife Julie Isabelle Gianetta (formerly de Montmorenci). The godparents were Compton Charles Domville and Victoire Schoelard. Seven years later, on 15 June 1840, she was baptised according to the Anglican rite at St Marylebone, London; in the Anglican register her first name is spelled Adeline rather than Adaline and her mother's names are anglicised to Isabella Jane. Adeline married Henry Drummond Charles Wolff at Livorno, some time between 1849 and 1854. She was the mother of the Victorian author 'Lucas Cleeve', whose real name was Adeline Georgiana Isabella Kingscote (née Wolff).

Another mysterious entry records the christening of James, son of Adam Heueritsi and his wife Totia (formerly Summala) on 21 September 1833. These surnames have not been traced anywhere else.

The Petres of Essex were one of the most famous recusant families. An entry dated 3 April 1834 records the conditional baptism of George Glynn Petre (1822–1905) who was then eleven years old. He had previously been christened at the Anglican parish church in Twickenham and later became Sir George Petre of Dunkenhalgh, Lancaster. He had a Catholic education at Stonyhurst College and Prior Park College and became an eminent diplomat in Argentina, Belgium, Denmark, France, Germany, Italy and Portugal.[214]

During 1834 the baptismal register format changes to a tabular layout, with the entries mostly in English rather than Latin. This is also the end point of the Catholic Record Society's untranslated transcription, published in 1909.

The entries in the new format continue to comprise mostly English and Irish surnames but with some other nationalities represented. For example, from 1834 to 1842 there is a Rentz, an Angleri sponsored by a Guanziroli and an Orletto, a Bianco sponsored by a Henrico and a Hoyos, a de Mascarène, a De Cardi, a Banclari and an Ortelli.

---

213 B. Bassett, *The English Jesuits: From Campion to Martindale* (London, 1967), p. 381.
214 T.H. Sanderson, rev. H.C.G. Matthew, 'Petre, Sir George Glynn', *ODNB*.

The new priest at St Ignatius from 1849 was Henry Brigham, SJ, a Yorkshireman, who changed the format of the baptismal register again, abandoning the tabular format used latterly by his predecessor. His first entry is dated 11 March 1849. Henry Brigham left the Oxford mission in 1854 and was succeeded by Francis Chadwick, SJ, who reverted to a tabular format for the baptismal registers in English but with Latin abbreviations. After completing just over one page, he transferred the entries to a new volume.

A note dated 27 September 1805 is signed by Charles Leslie. It records a donation from Thomas Day of Fritwell, lately of the nearby village of Hardwick, of £20 for the foundation of the mission. In return for this, various Masses were to be celebrated annually for the repose of the souls of all Catholics buried at Hardwick and for certain named members of the Day family, including Thomas and his wife Mary.

Another note dated 31 May 1822 and signed by Robert Newsham records a donation from Mary Cruse of £20 to the Catholic chapel at St Clement's. In return for this, various Masses were to be celebrated annually for certain named members of the Cruse and Davey families, including herself.

Combined volume

Baptisms (1854–65)

The standard format baptismal register was now required by the Catholic hierarchy to be in Latin. It commences with copies of the entries originally recorded by Francis Chadwick in the previous volume, spanning April 1854 to December 1855 (Fig. 12). Newer entries then follow, with most surnames being English or Irish. The last baptism by Francis Chadwick took place in January 1857. He died on 5 March 1857 and was quietly buried at night behind the chapel of St Ignatius. The interment was illegal because an Order in Council, obtained by the City of Oxford, had forced the closure of the burial ground for public health reasons. This legislation did not single out the Catholic cemetery: it also closed to new burials all ancient parish churchyards in the city (except existing vaults and walled graves), the Baptist, Wesleyan and Congregational burial grounds, and those of the workhouse, castle gaol and Radcliffe Infirmary.[215]

In 1859 the mission was passed by the Jesuits to the Diocese of Birmingham. Diocesan secular clergy then served the chapel from late 1859 until 1871. The first of the secular priests at the mission was Alexander Comberbach.

The baptism on 12 August 1855 of Elizabeth Devlin is notable in that the parents (James Devlin and Mary Donovan) clearly were not married. Such entries were very rare but this couple had three children baptised while not married: their second child, Daniel, was baptised on 6 September 1857, and their third child, Margaret, on 6 November 1859. In each case no condemnatory language is used in the register

---

215 Stapleton, p. 238; *Jackson's Oxford Journal* (12 May 1855), p. 5.

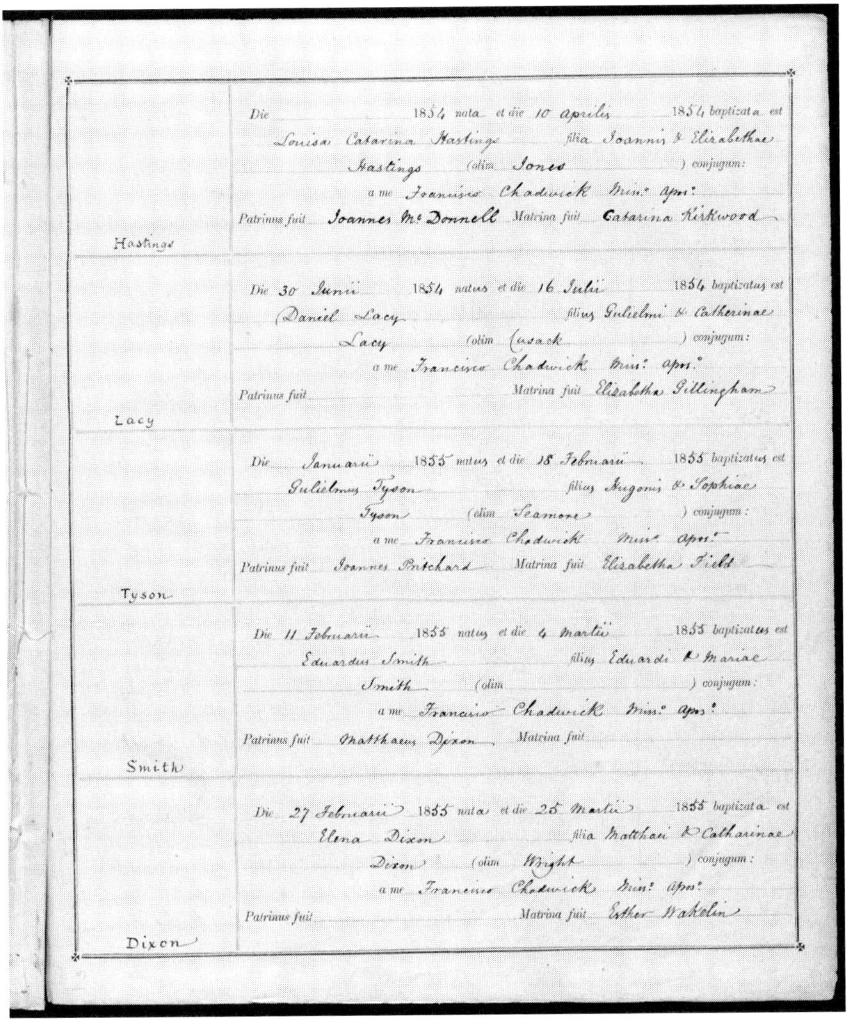

Die 1854 nata et die 10 aprilis 1854 baptizata est
Louisa Catarina Hastings filia Joannis & Elizabethae
Hastings (olim Jones) conjugum:
a me Francisco Chadwick Miss.° Ap.°
Patrinus fuit Joannes Mc Donnell Matrina fuit Catarina Kirkwood
Hastings

Die 30 Junii 1854 natus et die 16 Julii 1854 baptizatus est
Daniel Lacy filius Gulielmi & Catherinae
Lacy (olim Cusack) conjugum:
a me Francisco Chadwick Miss.° Ap.°
Patrinus fuit Matrina fuit Elizabetha Gillingham
Lacy

Die Januarii 1855 natus et die 18 Februarii 1855 baptizatus est
Gulielmus Tyson filius Hugonis & Sophiae
Tyson (olim Seamore) conjugum:
a me Francisco Chadwick Miss.° Ap.°
Patrinus fuit Joannes Pritchard Matrina fuit Elisabetha Field
Tyson

Die 11 Februarii 1855 natus et die 4 Martii 1855 baptizatus est
Eduardus Smith filius Eduardi & Mariae
Smith (olim) conjugum:
a me Francisco Chadwick Miss.° Ap.°
Patrinus fuit Matthaeus Dixon Matrina fuit
Smith

Die 27 Februarii 1855 nata et die 25 Martii 1855 baptizata est
Elena Dixon filia Matthaei & Catharinae
Dixon (olim Wright) conjugum:
a me Francisco Chadwick Miss.° Ap.°
Patrinus fuit Matrina fuit Esther Wakelin
Dixon

Fig. 12. First baptism entries in the new pre-printed register used at St Ignatius from 1854, and which also contains confirmations, marriages, and burials.

entry: the only differences are the parents' different surnames and the omission of the statement that the parents are a married couple.

Another rare type of entry is that recording the christening of Isabel Smith, daughter of single mother Mary Smith, on 10 October 1861. Entries of this type start becoming more common at this time. For example, there is the baptism of Charles Tarbuck, son of Catherine Tarbuck, on 18 November 1862.

The baptism of Vincent Albino on 16 February 1862 is interesting for several reasons. He was born the previous summer at Nottingham and his father, Blasio

Antonio Albino, appears to have been Italian. The godfather, Domenico Gargaro, also has an Italian name, as does the baptiser; he was Raphael Gorga, lector of theology for the Congregation of Passionist Priests, an order founded in Italy by the Italian mystic St Paul of the Cross in 1720. A sad little note, added to the entry later, notes Albino as a tramp but provides no further details.

There are also occasional conditional baptisms of adults, such as that of 21-year-old Mary Ann Tocque on 16 March 1863. On 14 March 1864, John Aloysius Louise, a young former Protestant minister, was conditionally baptised.

In the case of Florence Mary Collin, christened 30 November 1863, it seems probable that her mother was a Catholic but died during or soon after childbirth. We see the father being conditionally baptised immediately before his daughter, but there is no mention of the mother.

Compared with the eighteenth-century register entries, the length of time between birth and baptism has now lengthened considerably. Apart from cases where the baby was in danger of imminent death, no longer was it the norm for the christening to be within a few days of birth. Now, two to four weeks after the birth was normal, allowing travel arrangements to be made for relations and godparents to attend the ceremony. Occasionally the vital elements of the baptism were applied soon after birth, the formal completion of the ceremonial aspects taking place some time later. For example, Mary Monica Smith was christened on 9 January 1865 by Alexander Comberbach, apparently at the family home, ten days after her birth. Some six weeks later, the 'child was brought to the church' and the priest 'celebrated the holy ceremonies, said the prayers and conferred the names Mary Monica'.

By 1861 the three Hettich siblings from Baden in Germany were living at 19 High Street, St Clement's.[216] The two brothers were watch and clockmakers, and their sister was a milliner. They were all unmarried and in their twenties, and were able to employ a live-in teenage female servant. Karl Hettich married Josephine Fortwengler and the baptismal register records the christening of their daughter Mary Louise Josephine on 21 November 1864.

This baptismal register ends in June 1865 with four conditional baptisms. One was that of 17-year-old George William Phillips; the others were of Edward, Louisa and Elizabeth Young, whose ages are not given.

Confirmations (1854–73)

Confirmation at Waterperry was last given in 1763. Thereafter it took place at various Catholic missions in Oxfordshire at least seventeen times between 1770 and 1806 but never at Waterperry. The Vicar Apostolic of the Midland District, Dr John Milner, gave confirmation at the chapel of St Ignatius in 1805, 1807, 1811, 1819 and 1822 but no registers appear to exist for these events.[217] We know however that Bishop Milner also confirmed at Oxford on 15 July 1810 because the archives of

---

216 The Catholic presbytery was at 79 High Street. The road is now called St Clement's Street.
217 Stapleton, p. 231.

the Archdiocese of Birmingham hold a register for that occasion showing eighteen confirmands, all but five being women.[218] The next known set of confirmation registers comprises those in the combined volume under discussion here. The pages are from a pre-printed standard register in a format approved by the Catholic hierarchy. The first occasion covered was Sunday 6 November 1855, when William Bernard Ullathorne, Bishop of Birmingham, gave Confirmation at the chapel of St Ignatius. Eighteen people were confirmed, the sexes being equally represented.

The bishop returned on Sunday 3 June 1856. On that occasion, thirty-nine people were confirmed, of whom sixteen were male and twenty-three female. On a loose sheet of paper is a record of a much later visit by Bishop Ullathorne, on Sunday 23 February 1873. This time there were forty-seven confirmands, of whom twenty-three were male and twenty-four female.

Marriages (1854–76)

The requirement of the Marriage Act 1753 to marry in the Anglican Church was repealed in 1837. Plainly, it was unwise to record Catholic marriages conducted at Waterperry or Oxford during a period when such weddings were illegal. Nonetheless, three marriages were recorded in the first register volume but no record survives of any wedding before 1758, nor of any after 1771, until this new register, which commenced in 1854. The pages are from a standard printed register in a format approved by the Catholic hierarchy.

The first entry, dated 8 September 1854, records the marriage of William Last to Mary Ann Clarke of Bury St Edmunds. Nearly two years passed before the second entry for a marriage on 3 August 1856. One of the witnesses is Stanislaus Pfaff, who, like the Hettich brothers mentioned above, was a German clockmaker. Pfaff was born about 1826 and came from the Catholic village of Nussbach near Oberkirch in Baden-Württemberg. He lived at 17 High Street, St Clement's, and probably worked next door for the Hettich family.[219]

Most of the entries record marriages of English and Irish people, but with a sprinkling of French, German and Italian names. Sometimes the place of origin is mentioned, as in the case of Henry McHugo of Galway in 1861 and Philip Le Boutillier from Canada in 1864.

In 1869 Alexander Comberbach left St Clement's and became the chaplain at Stonor. He swapped roles with James Henry Nary, an accomplished musician who instigated the first choir at the chapel of St Ignatius. Its fine quality is said to have induced the Marquess of Bute to convert to Catholicism.[220] The last marriage entry

---

218 *The Bishops' Register of Confirmations in the Midland District of the Catholic Church in England, 1768–1811 and 1816* (Catholic Family History Society, 1999), p. 185. With the kind permission of the CFHS, and for the sake of completeness, the data from the 1810 register is included in this volume.
219 Birth year from the 1851 census.
220 Stapleton, p. 238.

by Alexander Comberbach was in October 1868; the first by James Nary almost two years later, in September 1870. During his brief time at St Clement's Nary officiated at five weddings, and another was conducted by J.P. O'Toole. These marriages cover a demographic spread of the mission's congregation, including those of a recusant yeoman, people who were apparently working-class or lower-middle-class locals, a German craftsman and a man who was probably an Irish immigrant.[221] The first wedding at which Nary officiated was that of Edward Davey of the recusant yeoman family to Teresa Turner on 25 October 1870. Davey was the author of *Memoirs of an Oxfordshire Old Catholic Family* (1897). The wedding on 26 November 1870 of Anthony Leonard Kirner and Crescentia Wangler highlights another two German families of clockmakers; Marcus and Lucas Wangler were working in Banbury by 1841 but Lucas and family were at 10 Castle Street, Oxford by 1852 and at 15 Market Street in 1861. The Kirners lived at 43 Queen Street.[222]

The first marriage conducted by James Corry was on 24 October 1871 when he married Henry Stevens and Bridget Ollington. He officiated at only two other weddings, the last being on 14 February 1872. Francis Goldie, SJ officiated at the next, which was on 15 May 1873. William Johnson, SJ conducted the next two weddings, and on 1 December 1875 Thomas B. Parkinson, SJ officiated at the last wedding recorded in this volume to be held at the chapel of St Ignatius, that of James Flynn and Mary O'Callaghan, both of Oxford. Of the fourteen surnames of the people married at St Ignatius from 1871 to 1875, eight were English and six Irish.

On 11 May 1876 the first wedding at the new church of St Aloysius was conducted by Thomas Parkinson. The couple were Joseph Ganter and Martha Hannah Facer. One of them, probably Martha, was not a Catholic, as the register entry states in Latin 'By dispensation of the Most Reverend Bishop of Birmingham, of the impediments of mixed religion'. Joseph Ganter was a German clockmaker.[223]

This register volume contains only one further wedding, that of Edwin Haynes and Helen Horseman, both of Marston, on 7 June 1876. Horseman is one of the few recusant surnames found in this marriage register, but whether Helen was actually of recusant descent is not known.

Death and burials (1854–77)

From 1807 until 1854 no register survives of deaths and burials, although more than a century ago Mrs Stapleton saw 'the first leaf of a Burial Register' from 1819.[224] On page 19 of the second volume of registers, among the baptisms, is a deleted but still legible death and burial entry. Mrs Stapleton's 'first leaf' has an entry that

---

221 The surname of the latter was Gara, probably an anglicisation of O Gadhra.
222 C.F.C. Beeson, *Clockmaking in Oxfordshire* (Oxford, 1989), p. 148.
223 B. Schaaf, *Schwarzwalduhren* (Karlsruhe, 2008), pp. 364–5. An earlier Joseph Ganter, together with Joseph Kammerer, is said to have brought the first Bohemian cuckoo clock to the Black Forest, c.1740.
224 Stapleton, pp. 233–4.

clearly refers to the same death and burial. However, she transcribed the name of the deceased as Richardus Eaves whereas in the deleted entry the surname is clearly Reade, followed by Eques, the Latin for a knight. The version cited by Mrs Stapleton states that he died 22 October 1819 and that he was a citizen of London, born in County Kilkenny, Ireland. There was certainly a gentry family of Reades at Rossenarra, County Kilkenny.[225]

The only other entry on the 'first leaf' seen by Mrs Stapleton records the death on Christmas Day 1819 of 'Reverendus Petrus Senechal', who was Pierre Michel François G. Senechal (1755–1819), an exiled French priest from the diocese of Amiens, who was a freelance teacher of French, Latin and Italian in Oxford for many years. Richard Reade and Revd Senechal were both buried by Robert Newsham in the graveyard at St Clement's parish church, on the 24 October 1819 and 3 January 1820 respectively.[226]

The fourth and last of the registers comprising this volume consists of pages from a pre-printed death register book. The format approved by the Catholic hierarchy provides for a statement that the deceased died 'in communion with Holy Mother Church' and 'fortified by the Sacraments'. In most cases the death and burial are both recorded, and also the age of the deceased (which may have been a guess or hearsay) and the domicile or supposed place of origin.

The register starts poignantly by recording the death on 17 May 1854 of a 22-year-old Irishman, John Bryan. He was buried by Francis Chadwick in the cemetery at Headington workhouse and was presumably an inmate there. Next is the death of a 29-year-old woman from Kidlington, buried in Jericho cemetery. Buried in the same place a fortnight later was a woman from Ireland. On the same page is another workhouse death, that of Ellen Dixon, a local woman, on 24 October 1854. She was buried in the Oxford workhouse cemetery. Two months later the death of Amand Mahieu is recorded, probably an immigrant from France, who was buried in Sandford cemetery.

Francis Chadwick completed the death and burial register entries from 1854 until his own death in 1857. He was buried by William Johnson, SJ and thereafter the diocesan priest Alexander Comberbach made all the entries until September 1868. James Corry, SJ maintained the register up to June 1872, when John Morris, SJ took over until September 1873. William Johnson then kept the register until July 1875. Thereafter the duties were divided between James Hoever, SJ and Thomas Parkinson, SJ.

Of the five deaths recorded on page 3, three give the ages of the deceased: they are one, twenty-one and twenty-two years. They include Fidel Pfaff (born about 1835)[227] from Freiburg, who was probably a younger brother or cousin of the Black Forest clockmaker Stanislaus Pfaff, mentioned in the marriage registers above. Both

---

225 C. Reade, *A Record of the Reades* (Hereford, 1899), p. 132.
226 Bellenger, *French Exiled Clergy*, pp. 246, 278.
227 Birth year from the death certificate of Fidel Pfaff.

lived in St Clement's High Street, near the chapel of St Ignatius, and Stanislaus was present when Fidel died of tuberculosis. On 29 January 1857, the death is recorded of Eliza Burel from Le Havre, France. On the same page is recorded the passing of Revd Francis Chadwick on 5 March 1857, at the age of 56, and his illicit burial four days later in the officially closed chapel cemetery.

There then appear to be four pages missing, as there are no entries for thirty-one months. They resume with the death on 19 November 1859 of John Curtis of Charlton-on-Otmoor, at the considerable age of eighty-two. In 1860 is recorded the passing of 55-year-old Frederick Oswald Joseph von Stockum from Düsseldorf and the death of William Morgan, aged 45, from the Isle of Man. In 1861 comes the death of 42-year-old Lucas Wangler, from Hinterzaten, near Freiburg, and the passing of his compatriot Joseph Pfaff, from Nussbach, near Oberkirch, both clockmakers from the Black Forest. Joseph Pfaff, born about 1821, was probably an older brother or cousin of the aforementioned Fidel and Stanislaus Pfaff.[228]

An entry records the death on 21 April 1863 of 44-year-old Daniel West. He came from the village of Woolhampton, in the Kennet valley between Newbury and Reading. By 1767 this had become the most Catholic parish in Berkshire, due to the presence of the recusant Wollascott family and their successors through marriage, the Plunketts.[229] Another Woolhampton man, John Paddey, died aged thirty-three in 1864.

The deaths of two women from East Hendred in the summer of 1866 are recorded. This village has long had a strong Catholic presence, due to the Eyston family who were unwavering recusants in penal times.

In July 1864 is recorded the death of William Jeffery, aged 50, from Old Wardour, Wiltshire. Unusually, he was taken back to Old Wardour for burial. Wardour Castle was the home of the recusant Arundell family; William Jeffery was their land agent, having succeeded his father John in that role.[230]

James Henry Corry notes the absence of entries from September 1868 until his first, which was in June 1871. This strongly suggests that another spread of four pages is missing. Here we see one of the few old recusant surnames that continue to appear in the registers: John Collingridge of Marston died 14 August 1871. Two entries in 1873 are particularly brief, recording little more than the names of the deceased; it is unclear whether the dates refer to the death or burial.

Karl Hettich, a Black Forest watchmaker and jeweller, died 30 April 1874 at the age of forty. The 1871 census shows him and his family living in Cowley Road, St Clement's, the name of his residence – Baden House – recalling his south German

---

[228] Birth year from the 1861 census.
[229] E.S. Worrall, *Returns of Papists 1767*, ii (CRS Occasional Publications 2, 1989), p. 166. Arthur Plunkett was the 8th Earl of Fingall, whose Catholic emancipation bill was rejected by Parliament in 1823.
[230] B. Williamson, *The Arundells of Wardour* (Salisbury, 2011), p. 146.

origins. Nonetheless, the census shows that he had become a naturalised British citizen. The Hettich family earlier lived in High Street, St Clement's.

Amyda Camponovo, a 69-year-old from Cowley Union (the workhouse) died on 17 November 1874. The only previous reference in the chapel's registers to someone with that Italian surname was eighteen years earlier, when Elizabeth Camponovo was confirmed. Littlemore asylum is also mentioned, in an entry recording the death of John Veal on 1 July 1875.

There is a particularly poignant entry for Christmas Eve 1874. This was the night of the Shipton-on-Cherwell rail disaster, in which thirty-four people died and sixty-nine were seriously injured. William Kavanagh (or Cavannah), a 55-year-old Irish bricklayer, was killed in the crash. Revd William Johnson visited Shipton; he buried Kavanagh and also Thomas Kennedy from Cowley, who had died the day before the crash.

The final entry in this volume records the death of James Charles Eagan from Cowley Barracks on the day he was born.

Baptisms (1865–78)

This volume records the final decade of baptisms at the chapel of St Ignatius. It also contains records of later baptisms at the church of St Aloysius but those are beyond the scope of the present volume.

Register of converts (1872–1909)

As noted above, the requirement for registers of converts was not national but decreed by the Diocese of Birmingham. The wording used for the entries varied but typically contained the following elements:

- Surname of convert
- Date of ceremonies
- Priest's statement 'I the undersigned baptised conditionally and received into the bosom of Holy Mother Church' (the second phrase sometimes being abbreviated to as little as 'received into the Church')
- Full name of convert
- Town or village where resident (optional)
- Parents' full names (sometimes including the mother's maiden name)
- Birth date of convert
- Signature of priest.

As with other registers during this period, the entries were in Latin. The register of converts covers thirty-seven years but only those entries up to the end of 1875 have been included in this volume.

Register of baptisms at the chapel of St Mary the Virgin, Bampton (1856–60)

There were five baptisms at this short-lived chapel: two by Franco Guaci Azzopardi and three by Daniel Donovan.

Themes found in the registers

The registers of the Oxford Catholic Mission from 1700 to the mid-1870s illustrate the transition from clandestine country house Catholicism to urban and suburban Catholicism. While the information provided is concerned primarily with the Catholic Church's desire to maintain a register of its administration of sacraments and rites of passage, it is also possible to use the register data to gain insights into the lives and demographics of the Catholic congregation.

A family history resource

For family historians the registers provide an excellent resource, although not widely known, sometimes ignored and relatively inaccessible. The fact that they are often in Latin is also a barrier, hence the translated, tabulated format used in this volume.

A major problem in family history research is that the possibility of having Catholic ancestors in the eighteenth or nineteenth century is rarely considered. This is often because no oral or written tradition of Catholicism survives in a family. But there are many families in which Catholicism existed (perhaps in only one branch) for a few decades or even several centuries before the descendants ceased to be Catholic for one reason or another. Such a change of denominational allegiance may have resulted in collective amnesia or possibly been deliberately omitted from a family history of resolute adherence to a particular denomination or because of an aversion to religion in general and Catholicism in particular.

Social class and immigration

The registers demonstrate an interesting contrast between the rural, gentry-dominated paternalistic community at Waterperry and the later much larger and demographically varied congregation at St Clement's. The early eighteenth-century congregation comprised the family of Sir John and Lady Curson and a small circle of their relatives, employees, friends and occasional gentry visitors. It is not clear whether any of the Cursons' tenants attended services at Waterperry House. The congregation was certainly a pious group, as highlighted by the descriptions in the registers of regularly celebrated services and devotions, and the list of members of the confraternity of Bona Morte. They led a rich but socially isolated devotional life, a far cry from the hurried clandestine celebration of Mass one might have imagined.

Families such as the Cursons employed Catholics as servants and labourers where possible. Though the Waterperry registers are short of detail, we may surmise that some families worked for the Cursons for a long time. For example, three of the ten Waterperry servants listed by the Anglican authorities in 1706 were Padwicks and that surname appears also in the registers in 1722, 1729 and 1753.

The social status of those who died at Waterperry was strongly reflected in the level of detail devoted to their passing in the register. The entry for James Kimberley, who died in 1756, is unusual inasmuch as it states that he was a stable boy: in most cases no occupation is mentioned and the facts recorded are minimal. This contrasts with the detailed entries for the Cursons, patrons of the mission. For example, we learn that Sir Francis Curson died just after nine in the evening on 29 May 1750, that the Dirge was sung by five priests on the night of 31 May, that the following day there were Masses and a sermon, that the funeral was on 7 June, and that the funerary hatchment was erected on 15 June.[231]

The influence that a Catholic squire could have on an Anglican vicar is demonstrated by the funeral in 1770 of the Catholic chaplain William Nelson. Like Sir Francis and Lady Curson, William Nelson was buried in the Anglican parish church of St Mary the Virgin, adjacent to Waterperry House.

The informal network of recusant families of which the Cursons formed part is highlighted by the surnames in the 'Catalogue of the Dead'. They include the names Belson, Brinkhurst, Chamberlain, Collingwood, Davey, Day, Dormer, Eyston, Grimsditch, Killby, Phillips, Powell, Stonor, Teynham and Wolfe. Some of these were yeomen families but most were gentry.

With the move to St Clement's at the end of the eighteenth century, the mission ceased to be dependent on a gentry family, though the first few resident priests had strong aristocratic connections. Charles Leslie, the last missioner at Waterperry who built the chapel of St Ignatius, was the son of a Scottish baron. He was succeeded by his elder brother and assisted by a former chaplain of the Earl of Abingdon.

Irish surnames are notably absent from the registers before the transfer of the mission to St Clement's, although the late William Nelson was actually an Irish O'Neil. However, the first interment at the new Catholic burial ground at St Clement's was that of an Irish gardener, a forerunner of the many Irish Catholics who came to the area during the nineteenth century. From 1813 the priest in charge was an Irish Jesuit, John William Conolly, whose first register entry recorded the christening of Henry Davis, whose parents came from Limerick in south-west Ireland. The names in the registers suggest that about a fifth of the congregation at St Clement's was of Irish origin.

From the early days at St Clement's, mainland European surnames appear in the registers, several being Italian. In the 1830s and 1840s there were about ten Italian surnames and a few from other nationalities. In the second half of the nineteenth century there were a French publican and his boat-builder son, a French Canadian and several families of watch and clockmakers from the Black Forest in southern Germany.

The St Clement's registers also contain entries for a few traditionally recusant yeoman families, in particular the Collingridges and the Daveys. After the building of the Catholic church at Dorchester in 1848 the Daveys are listed less frequently. The surnames of gentry and aristocratic recusant families only appear occasionally

---

231 A funerary hatchment is a lozenge-shaped full display of the heraldic arms, crest and supporters to which the deceased person was entitled. It is framed in black and would typically be erected in the family chapel or aisle of a parish church.

in the registers, principally because they lived elsewhere and only attended Mass at St Clement's when visiting Oxford.

Occupations are rarely recorded in the registers but soldiers are sometimes identified, as are vagrants. However, it is often possible to establish the occupations, ages, origins and addresses of the people named in the registers and of their family members from the national censuses.

In 1875 there were two baptisms of children of single mothers, hitherto a rarity. Both mothers were inmates of the newly opened Nazareth House. This was a Catholic home for orphans and old people run by the Sisters of Nazareth. It stood on the corner of Pembroke Street (now Rectory Road) and 99 Cowley Road and closed in 1994, after which the buildings were demolished.

The distinctive character of Catholic life at Waterperry

The Waterperry register provides a detailed description of the Catholic worship and liturgical life of the Cursons, their household and employees during the eighteenth century. A section on Benediction[232] is followed by a supplement describing other services, devotions and liturgical procedures. Benediction was to be celebrated on thirty different dates each year. Today the service is celebrated rarely and typically in early evening; however, the list for Waterperry includes many occasions when it was celebrated morning and night. The supplement includes other services and devotions, such as certain Masses, sermons, readings and prayers. The exhausting services to be held on Christmas Day commenced at midnight: they included the reading of the day from the Roman Martyrology,[233] the singing of the hymn *Te Deum*, three Masses, three periods of exposition of the Blessed Sacrament, three Benedictions and various prayers, sermons and readings.

On Sexagesima Sunday (the second Sunday before Ash Wednesday), candles were to be blessed as usual but not lit during Mass. The service of Tenebrae (shadows) was to be held at 7.00 p.m. on Wednesday, Thursday and Friday of Holy Week. Tenebrae, little known today, involves a gradual extinguishing of candles while psalms and readings are sung or recited. An Easter sepulchre is mentioned, into which the Blessed Sacrament was to be placed on Maundy Thursday and Good Friday. The host was 'buried' in the sepulchre on Good Friday, to be brought out at the first Mass of Easter, symbolically representing the Resurrection of Christ from his tomb.[234]

---

232 Benediction is a short service of hymns, litanies and adoration of the Blessed Sacrament. A consecrated communion wafer (the host) is displayed in a monstrance, an ornately decorated receptacle with a transparent holder for the wafer. The service culminates with a blessing by the priest, who makes the sign of the cross over the congregation while holding the monstrance. Although the precise form of the service has varied over time and place, mandatory elements have always included the singing of the hymn *Tantum Ergo*, the use of wax candles and the burning of incense.
233 A calendar commemorating the faith, deeds, lives and deaths of Christian martyrs.
234 Easter sepulchres were commonplace in English churches before the Reformation, and recusant Catholics continued to use them. The sepulchre was typically an arched structure on

Four plenary indulgences were granted annually by the Vicar Apostolic to the community at Waterperry. A note mentions that Mr Hornyold had altered these indulgences.[235] In Catholic theology, a plenary indulgence is the remission of all temporal punishment due to sin, the guilt of which has already been forgiven. Absolution following confession provides forgiveness of sins, whereas indulgences diminish (or, in the case of a plenary indulgence, eliminate) the punishment due to them. A plenary indulgence usually requires sacramental confession, the receiving of Holy Communion, prayer for the current Pope, freedom from attachment to sin, and the performance of one or more specific qualifying acts, such as defined acts of piety or charity.

The register includes a list of members of Waterperry's Congregation of Bona Morte. The original congregation was founded in 1648 at the mother church of the Jesuits in Rome. Its novel aim was a programme of devotions and spiritual exercises to assure its members of a good and happy death; previous death-oriented confraternities were usually more concerned with the charitable work of burying the dead.

The penal code

There is little direct reference to the penal laws in the registers, apart from a complaint in 1771 by the missioner at Waterperry about the Hardwicke Marriage Act: 'The marriage contract was previously witnessed by the Protestant pastor according to an anti-Catholic decree of the parliament of Great Britain, and the sacrament has now been conferred by the priest'.[236] The registers nonetheless reflect the penal code and its level of application in the following respects:

- The fact that in the eighteenth century the mission comprised a small and relatively secretive community based in a rural manor house.
- The sparse marriage records during the time when the Hardwicke Act was in force.
- The practice in register entries during that period to state that couples were 'lawful' or 'legitimate', thus highlighting that they had complied with the requirements of the Hardwicke Act.
- The rapidity with which the transfer to Oxford took place once it was legal to register a Catholic chapel.

---

the north wall of a church, sometimes cut into the masonry, otherwise of portable wooden construction.

235   R.J. Stonor, *Stonor: A Catholic Sanctuary in the Chilterns* (Newport, 1952), p. 290. In 1752, John Hornyold (1706–78) was consecrated bishop at Stonor House, Oxfordshire, by Bishop John Talbot Stonor, Vicar Apostolic of the Midland District. Hornyold was the first Catholic bishop consecrated on English soil since the reign of Mary I. The consecration was illegal but Stonor was of such high social status that he was able to act with impunity. Hornyold was initially Stonor's coadjutor and succeeded him as Vicar Apostolic.

236   The Act was not specifically anti-Catholic although it was often perceived as such by Catholics.

- The architecture of the new chapel in St Clement's, discreetly set back from the street, in compliance with the provisions of the Second Catholic Relief Act.

Numbers

The registers do not provide counts of the congregation but are nonetheless indicative of growth, decline, evangelistic activity and ageing. From other sources we know that the Catholic community at Waterperry comprised twelve people in 1706 and that it rose to thirty-two by 1767, dropping to fifteen by 1780 and just six in 1790, whereas in Oxford there were by then about sixty Catholics.[237] The registers suggest an average of about one baptism a year during the eighteenth century. Moreover, the rate was dropping fast towards the end of the century: there were only three baptisms in the 1780s. The death rate more or less matched the birth rate, at about one per annum up to 1807.

Numbers at St Ignatius were higher, probably about 110 in total, of whom about half attended Mass on any Sunday.[238] The larger congregation, coupled with a strong evangelistic push, saw baptisms rise to about twenty a year, a rate that was steadily maintained during 1865–75, the last decade before the opening of the church of St Aloysius. About a fifth were conditional baptisms of adults previously baptised into another Christian denomination. Most of the children and adults baptised had English surnames but about one in five had an Irish surname. A few had continental surnames, mostly German, with the occasional French or Italian example. There is little evidence of old recusant surnames among those baptised during this last decade.

Conversions

From 1833 onwards, the Oxford Movement made the case for an Anglican revival of aspects of Catholic theology, liturgy and devotional practice. This led to some Anglican laity and clergy converting to Roman Catholicism. Thus, in the baptismal register, we find an entry for 18 October 1844 recording the conditional baptism of William Goodenough Penny 'lately a Protestant Clergyman'.[239]

The register of converts starts in 1872: as the coverage of the present volume ends in 1875, only entries for the first three years are included here. It was clearly a trophy book, indicative of the competition between the resurgent Catholic Church and the Church of England.

---

237 *VCH Oxon.* v, p. 308; Worrall, *Returns of Papists 1767*, ii, p. 118.
238 Stapleton, pp. 232, 238.
239 He was a Bachelor of Arts who studied mathematics at Christ Church and then became perpetual curate at Dorton and Ashendon, Buckinghamshire.

Geographical reach

The geographical reach of the mission at St Clement's can be seen in its widest form in the burial registers. Some thirty cemeteries where Catholic burials had taken place are mentioned, including those at the Headington and Oxford workhouses, and the city parish churches of St Clement, St Giles, St Thomas, St Aldate and St Ebbes. Other burial grounds served included Abingdon, Abingdon Catholic, Banbury, Cowley, Dorchester Catholic, Freeland, Garsington, Headington, Hethe, Jericho, Kidlington, Littlemore, Marston, Osney, Radford, Sandford, Shipton, Summertown, Wheatley, Witney and Woodstock. Most of these places were within ten miles of St Clement's. Banbury, the most distant location, was twenty-two miles away, but was accessible by train from Oxford from 1850 onwards. In places with their own Catholic churches or chapels, such as Abingdon, Banbury, Dorchester, Hethe and Radford, the priest from St Ignatius was clearly helping out when the resident clergy were not available.

Mortality

It is noticeable that many of the deaths recorded were of very young people. The new burial register starts in 1854, a year when Oxford was affected by both cholera and smallpox. The cholera outbreak commenced at the beginning of August and lasted until the end of October, but there were plenty of other diseases around for much of the time. In some cases, the records show two or more members of the same family dying in quick succession, suggesting an outbreak of disease: for example, the deaths at Garsington in summer 1861 of a 14-year-old girl and her 7-year-old brother, just three days apart. The wide variation in life expectancy of this period is apparent: in the first six months of 1864 are recorded the deaths of a 70-year-old, a 50-year-old, a 22-year-old, a teenager of fifteen and a baby of four days.

The final entry in this volume is a sad reminder of the high rates of perinatal mortality. It records the death on 19 March 1877 of James Charles Eagan from Cowley Barracks on the same day that he was born. One can only hope that it was some consolation to the parents that their child died 'fortified by the Sacraments', which in his case would have been baptism and the anointing of the sick.

The Registers:
transcribed, translated, and tabulated

―◆―

Where no information is given, a dash is shown.
All dates are shown in New Style.
It may be assumed that where a priest is shown as a godfather/sponsor, he will also have been the celebrant.
+ after a name appears to signify the early death of a baptized infant.
Some of the mothers are given a former name: in most cases these are maiden names but they may be former married names.

Baptisms described as 'conditional': the Catholic Church recognizes baptism by anybody, provided they have the right intention and pour water on the child's head while saying 'I baptise thee in the name of the Father, and of the Son, and of the Holy Ghost'. If this form was not followed exactly the baptism was deemed conditional. Occasionally the vital elements of the baptism were applied soon after birth, with the formal and ceremonial aspects taking place some time later: hence 'completion later' or a second date with 'completion'.

WATERPERRY BAPTISMAL RECORDS

Date of baptism	Person baptised	Date of birth	Parents	Godparents or sponsors	Priest officiating
1701-06-12	Padwick, John	–	–	–	–
1701-10-23	Howard, Sarah	–	–	–	–
1708-03-05	Howard, Mary	–	–	–	–
1711-09-13	Howard, John	–	–	–	–
1712-06-08	Philips, Ed	–	–	–	–
1713-08-15	Howard, Anne	–	–	–	–
1713-09-06	Philips, Elizabeth	–	–	–	–
1715-01-12	Philips, Henry	–	–	–	–
1715-09-20	Howard, George	–	–	–	–
1716-03-09	Laurence, Jos.	–	–	–	–
1716-08-07	Philips, Samuel	–	–	–	–
1717-10-19	Howard, Martha	–	–	–	–
1718-05-11	Laurence, Frances	–	–	–	–
1723-05-01	Christmass, Anna	–	–	–	–
1719-03-02	Philips, James +	–	–	–	–
1720-08-15	Laurence, Mary	–	–	–	–
1722-01-29	Christmass, Simon	–	–	–	–
1722-04-04	Padwick, Mary +	–	–	–	–
1722-08-09	Howard, Catharine	–	–	–	–

Date of baptism	Person baptised	Date of birth	Parents	Godparents or sponsors	Priest officiating
1722-09-26	Lawrence, Richard junior	–	–	–	–
1723-03-03	Howes, Susan	–	–	–	–
1723-04-26	Padwick, Mary	–	–	–	–
1725-09-17	Christmass, William	–	–	–	–
1726-03-14	Padwick, Daniel	–	–	–	–
1726-03-14	Laurence, Jane	–	–	–	–
1728-08-27	Laurence, Margaret	–	–	–	–
1729-01-02	Padwick, John	–	–	–	–
1729-06-23	Bickerstaff, John	–	–	–	–
1731-03-06	Walker, Mary	–	–	–	–
1731-10-18	Clark, Sarah	–	–	–	–
1732-10-15	Winter, Susan	–	–	–	–
1733-06-17	Clark, Mary	–	–	–	–
1733-10-08	Walker, Anne	–	–	–	–
1734-11-15	Clark, Anne	–	–	–	–
1735-06-30	Waterhouse, Anne	–	–	–	–
1735-09-29	Stephens, Michael	–	–	–	–
1736-01-31	Clark, John	–	–	–	–
1736-08-01	Hodskinson, James	–	–	–	–
1737-05-08	Waterhouse, John	–	–	–	–
1737-09-04	Clarke, James	–	–	–	–

Date of baptism	Person baptised	Date of birth	Parents	Godparents or sponsors	Priest officiating
1738-10-29	Hodskinson, Joseph	–	–	–	–
1739-02-18	Waterhouse, Cornelius	–	–	–	–
1739-11-19	Clarke, George	–	–	–	–
1740-10-01	Waterhouse, Alice	–	–	–	–
1741-01-16	Hodskinson, Richard	–	–	–	–
1741-04-04	Clarke, Francis	–	–	–	–
1743-03-12	Waterhouse, Hannah	–	–	–	–
1743-04-09	Hodskinson, Anna +	–	–	–	–
1743-08-23	Christmass, Susan	–	–	–	–
1743-09-06	Clarke, William	–	–	–	–
1745-02-25	Waterhouse, Samuel	–	–	–	–
1745-06-07	Hodskinson, William	–	–	–	–
1745-09-19	Clarke, Sam	–	–	–	–
1747-06-19	Waterhouse, Francis	–	–	–	–
1747-08-09	Clarke, Catharine	1747-08-08	–	Lady Teynham, Mr Peter Curson	–
1747-08-10 Wheatley	Million, James	1747-08-09	–	William Hodskinson, Anne Yeates	–
1747-11-03	Hodskinson, Francis	1747-11-03	–	Thomas Jennings, Kitty Archer	–

THE REGISTERS   81

Date of baptism	Person baptised	Date of birth	Parents	Godparents or sponsors	Priest officiating
1748-07-25, completion 1748-07-31	Waterhouse, James	1748-07-25	–	A man and maid from Mr Wolfe's of Haseley Court	–
1748-07-25, completion 1748-07-31	Waterhouse, Winny	1748-07-25	–	Thomas Symkins, Amy Whorewood	–
1750-02-19	Clark, Charles	1750-02-18	–	Thomas Symkins, Anne Emerick	–
1750-07-02	Million, Mary	1750-06-28	–	Petrick Costigan, Anne Emerick	Thomas Brookes
1751-06-09	Waterhouse, Mary	1751-06-02	–	Francis Capè, Mary Hodskinson	–
1752-03-13	Hodskinson, Mary	1752-03-12	–	John Price, Catharine Hooper	–
1753-01-02 Milton	Symkins, James	1753-01-01	–	Mr Bagnal, Mrs Reynolds	–
1753-03-13	Million, John	1753-03-13	–	Thomas Skeps, Anne Yates	–
1754-02-18	Verni, Mary	1754-02-16	–	Richard Archer, Anne Weston	–
1754-11-24 completion later	Symkins, Thomas	1754-11-24	–	John Price, Anne Gatesfield	–

Date of baptism	Person baptised	Date of birth	Parents	Godparents or sponsors	Priest officiating
1755-03-12 completion 1755-03-16	Hodskinson, James +	1755-03-11	–	William Herbert, Elizabeth Nicks	–
1755-10-03	Waterhouse, James +	1755-10-01	–	Richard Archer, Elizabeth Styles	–
1756-10-21	Sympkins, Francis	1756-10-18	–	Mr Nandike, Lady Curson	–
1758-11-07	Sympkins, Catharine	1758-11-04	–	Mr Wells, Lady Teynham (proxy Lady Curson)	–
1759-03-26	Bagnal, Winifrid	1759-03-23	–	Mr Richardson, Lady Curson	–
1760-11-05	Hodgekinson, John +	1760-10-27 Wheatley	–	Jos Hodgekinson, Nelly Davis	–
1761-08-15	Bagnal, Appolonia	1761-08-13 Waterperry	–	Mr Bole, Mrs Lee	John Bernard Warmoll
1761-11-18	Hodgekinson, Anne	1761-11-15 Wheatley	–	Will Hodgeskinson senior, Elizabeth Symkins	–
1762-08-14	Symkins, Philip	1762-08-13	–	Mr Philip Roper, Miss Roper (proxy Lady Curson)	–
1763-08-30	Drothery, Mary	1763-08-23 St Clement's	–	Miss Macdonal, an Irishman	–
1763-10-09	Hodgekinson, John	1763-10-08 Waterperry	–	Mrs Bagnal junior, Jos. Hod[g]ekinson	–

THE REGISTERS

Date of baptism	Person baptised	Date of birth	Parents	Godparents or sponsors	Priest officiating
1763-09-10	Verni, Catharine	1763-09-09 Kingswood, Bucks	–	–	–
1764-06-24 completion 1764-07-01	Bagnal, Anne Ellen	1764-06-24	–	Miss Anne Brinkhurst (proxy Lady Teynham) Lord Teynham (proxy Mr Jackson)	–
1765-11-06	Hodgskinson, Joseph		–	Thomas Budd, Martha Bullock	Mr Woods
1771-08-03	Clark, Anne	1771-08-01	–	Richard Jackson, Anne Harris	
1773-03-01	Maloni, Joseph	1773-03-01	–	Grandmother and grandfather Maloni	John Jerome Butler
1775-01-06	Waterhouse, Francis	1775-01-06	–	Mr Jackson, Mary Waterhouse standing for their proxies	Francis Green
1775-04-09	Green, James	1775-04-09	–	Samuel Waterhouse, Elizabeth Symkins	James Lewis
1777-03-10	Waterhouse, Barbara Ann	1777-03-10	–	Thomas Thompson (proxy Richard Jackson), Mary Fisher (proxy Mary Green)	John Clossette
1777-06-22	Tilleman, Jane	1777-06-22 Oxford	–	Henry McGann, Mary McAllister	John Clossette

Date of baptism	Person baptised	Date of birth	Parents	Godparents or sponsors	Priest officiating
1777-09-29 (died about six weeks later)	Green, William	1777-09-29 Wheatley	–	Theodore Van Weddingen, Frances Clarckson	–
1778-10-18	Dougharty, Sarah	1778-09-03 Oxford	–	Mr Randolph McAllister, Catharine McAllister	John Clossette
1779-01-??	Waterhouse, Mary	1779-01-??	–	– (proxy Mr Richard Jackson), Mary Waterhouse (proxy Elizabeth Symkins)	John Clossette
1780-12-03	Clark, David	1780-12-03	John & Winifrid Clark	Thomas Simpkins, Martha –	Peter Jenkins
1785-12-28	Clark, William	1785-12-27	John & Winifrid Clark	P.P. Westby, Ann Jones	Peter Walker (alias Westby)
1789-12-19 Waterperry	Smith, Frances	1789-12-13	Mary & Henry Smith	William Haws, Winifrid Clark	James Taylor
1790-11-27	Curson, Thomas	1790-11-25	Henry & Bridget Curson	Thomas Hawkins of Nash Court, Lady Peter	Charles Leslie
1792-03-13	Platt, Charles	1792-03-13	Robert & Mary Platt	Charles Leslie, Sarah Kempster	Charles Leslie
1793-09-18	Platt, Alathea	1793-09-17	Robert & Mary Platt	Charles Leslie, Mrs Sparshatt	Charles Leslie
1793-09-16	Smith, Margaret	1793-09-15 Waterperry	Mary & Henry Smith	Thomas Sympkins	–

Date of baptism	Person baptised	Date of birth	Parents	Godparents or sponsors	Priest officiating
1794-04-09	Curson, Francis	1794-04-07	Henry & Bridget Curson	Charles Leslie (by proxy), Mrs Hawkins of Nash Court (by proxy)	–
1795-04-21	Kerr, Thomas	1795-04-19	Richard & Elizabeth Kerr	Charles Leslie, Mrs Quarterman of Haseley	–
1795-07-28	Platt, Robert	1795-07-27 St Aldate's, Oxford	Robert & Mary Platt	Charles Leslie, Sarah Kempster	Charles Leslie
1795-10-03 Waterperry	Smith, William	1795-09-29 Waterperry	Mary & Henry Smith	Charles Leslie, Mrs Simkins	–
1796-02-04	Curson, Julia	1796-02-02	Henry & Bridget Curson	Charles Leslie (by proxy), Mary Hawkins	Charles Leslie
1796-06-06 Lt. Haseley	Kerr, Thomas	1796-06-05	Richard & Elizabeth Kerr	Charles Leslie, Mrs Quarterman	Charles Leslie
1796-07-02 Lt. Haseley	Kerr, Mary	–	Richard & Elizabeth Kerr	Charles Leslie, Mrs Quarterman	–
1796-12-31	Johnson, Joseph	1796-12-29	Joseph & Hannah Johnson	Charles Leslie, Mary Timbs	Charles Leslie
1797-01-15	Curson, Caroline	–	Henry & Bridget Curson	Charles Leslie, Mrs Hawkins of Nash Court, Kent	Charles Leslie
1797-03-29	Hart, James	1797-03-28	Joseph & Mary Hart	Charles Leslie, Mary Timbs	–

Date of baptism	Person baptised	Date of birth	Parents	Godparents or sponsors	Priest officiating
1797-04-24	Saisy, Marie Julie Anne	1797-04-24	Lord Charles Marie François Saisy, Count of Kerampuilh & wife, Lady Marie Julie de la Boissière, Countess of Kerampuilh	Pierre Marie Saisy, Knight of Kerampuilh, Marcella Julie Françoise, Marchioness of Lanascol	Charles Leslie
1797-04-30	Platt, Robert	1797-04-28	Robert & Mary Platt	Charles Leslie, Mrs Sparshatt	Charles Leslie
1797-06-11	Kerr, William	1797-06-04	Richard & Elizabeth Kerr	Charles Leslie	
1797-09-24	Lee, Sarah	1797-08-20 Calne, Wilts	Morris Lee, Irish soldier, & wife Barbara	Charles Leslie, Mary Timbs	Charles Leslie
1798-09-27	Curson, George Henry	1798-09-26	Henry & Bridget Curson	Sir Thomas Webb, Bart (proxy Charles Leslie), Mrs Hawkins of Nash Court, Kent (grandmother)	–
1798-07-06	East, Charlotte	–	– East & wife – East	Charles Leslie, Mrs Quarterman	–
1798-10-29	Davey, Vincent	1798-10-29	– Davey of Overy & wife	–	–
1798-10-29	Davey, Joseph	1798-10-29	– Davey of Overy & wife	–	–
1798-12-06	Platt, Mary	1798-12-05	Robert & Mary Platt	Charles Leslie, Jane Philips	–
1799-01-31	Kelly, Bridget	1799-09-13 approx.	John & Jane Kelly	William Hothersall from Thame (priest)	–
1799-04-28	Kerr, William	1799-04-?? Gt Haseley	Richard & Elizabeth Kerr	Mr McHenry	–

THE REGISTERS 87

Date of baptism	Person baptised	Date of birth	Parents	Godparents or sponsors	Priest officiating
1799-05-13 Waterperry	Smith, Elizabeth	1799-05-10 approx.	Henry & Mary Smith	–	–
1799 Wheatley	Shepherd, John	–	–	–	–
1800-02-27	Johnson, Thomas	–	Joseph & Hannah Johnson	–	–
1800-05-01	Sheen, Mary	–	– Sheen & wife	John Hoy & his sister	–
1800-06-30	White, Sarah	–	– White & wife of Warpsgrove near Haseley	Charles Leslie, Mrs Quarterman of Haseley	–

ST IGNATIUS BAPTISMAL RECORDS, VOLUME 1

Date of baptism	Person baptised	Date of birth	Parents	Godparents or sponsors	Priest officiating
1800-11-04	Platt, Peter Stephen	–	Robert & Mary Platt	Mr Trant (proxy Mr Bertin), Mrs Trant (proxy Joanna Philips)	Charles Leslie
1800-12-05	Curson, Ellen	1800-12-03 Waterperry	Henry & Bridget Curson	Helen Hawkins	Charles Leslie
1801-01-05 d.o.d.	Davey, Joseph	1801-01-04 Dorchester	William Davey and his wife	–	Julien Triquet
1801-04-26 conditional	Short, Thomas	1798 approx.	John Short (a Dragoon Guard) & wife Eleanor	Jean Blot	A Rouxel, rector of the Diocese of Saint-Brieuc, Brittany
1801-10-08	Platt, Sarah	–	Robert & Mary Platt	Frances Leakey, Charles Leslie	Charles Leslie
1801-10-24	Johnson, William	–	Joseph & Ann Johnson	Charles Leslie	Charles Leslie
1801-11-29	Timbs, Martha	1801-11-27	Mary Timbs	Susanna Savage, Charles Leslie	Charles Leslie
1802-02-01	Salomone, Mary Ann	–	Mark & Martha Salomone	Fr William Hothersall, Mrs Sparshatt	Charles Leslie
1802	Salomone, Martha	–	Mark & Martha Salomone	Susanna Savage, Charles Leslie	Charles Leslie
1802-06-16	MacHenry, Ann	1802-06-16	John & Mary MacHenry	Mary Platt, Charles Leslie	Charles Leslie
1802-06-09	Mullen, John	1802-06-05	John & Susanna Mullen	Charles Leslie	Charles Leslie

Date of baptism	Person baptised	Date of birth	Parents	Godparents or sponsors	Priest officiating
1803-01-27	East, Elizabeth	1803-01-24 Gt Haseley	William & Elizabeth East	Charles Leslie	Charles Leslie
1803-03-20	Clancy, Bridget	–	Peter & Bridget Clancy from Co. Fermanagh, Ireland	Mr MacManus (the gardener), Susanna Savage	Charles Leslie
1803-08-13	Hopkins, George	–	William & Mary Hopkins	Joseph Hay, Mary Bridget Howell	Charles Leslie
1803-08-28	Hart, Henry	1803-08-27	Joseph & Mary Hart	Francis Copus, Susanna Savage	Charles Leslie
1804-10-08	Talbot, Charlotte	1804-09-08	Hon. John Talbot and his wife	Charles Browne (proxy Charles Leslie), Mrs Bridget Curson (proxy Sarah Clarkson)	Charles Leslie
1804-12-22	Hopkins, Mary Ann	1804-12-17	William & Mary Hopkins	Mr Goswell (proxy Charles Leslie), Mrs Goswell (proxy Sarah Clarkson)	Charles Leslie
1804-12-29	Platt, Ann Frances	1804-12-25	Robert & Mary Platt	Charles Leslie, Sarah Clarkson	Charles Leslie
1805-01-30 conditional	Quin, Peter	–	Peter & Bridget Quin	–	Charles Leslie
1805-02-06	Sheppard, Johanna	Wheatley	–	Charles Leslie, Susanna Sheppard	Charles Leslie
1805	Smith, –	–	Henry & Mary Smith	–	Charles Leslie

Date of baptism	Person baptised	Date of birth	Parents	Godparents or sponsors	Priest officiating
1805-09-27 conditional	–, Ann	–	–	–	Charles Leslie
1806-01-13 completion	Beek, George	–	Edward Beek & his wife	James Beek (brother of Edward), Mrs Hopkins (proxy for Mary, sister of Edward Beek)	Charles Leslie
1806-02-01	Cooney, Susanna	–	Dennis & Sarah Cooney from Nenagh, Co. Tipperary, Ireland	Charles Leslie, Susanna Savage	Charles Leslie
1806-02-24	Conway, Philip	–	Philip & Mary Conway from Ireland	Charles Leslie	Charles Leslie
1806-03-19	Brewerton, John	1806-03-16	William & Ann Brewerton	Charles Leslie, Susanna Savage	Charles Leslie
1806-05-03	Platt, John	–	Robert & Mary Platt	Charles Leslie, Mrs Sparshatt (absent)	Charles Leslie
1806-06-15	Cooney, John	–	John & Mary Cooney	Mr Fordham, Susanna Savage	Charles Leslie
1806-06-24	Downey, Rosamund	1806-06-17	Charles & Mary Downey from Dublin	Charles Leslie, Susanna Savage	Charles Leslie
1807-06-??	Cole, Mary	–	Mr Cole & his wife	Georges Bertin, Mary Hopkins	Georges Bertin
1807-07-28	Beek, James Charles	–	Edward & Mary Beek	William & Catherine Beek	James Leslie
1807-11-13	Conway, John	1807-11-12	Philip & Mary Conway	Mary Machery	James Leslie

Date of baptism	Person baptised	Date of birth	Parents	Godparents or sponsors	Priest officiating
1808-04-14	Goldby, Mary Elizabeth	–	Mr & Mrs Goldby	Joseph Bushel, Mary Hopkins	James Leslie
1808-05-01	Carr, Martha	–	Mr & Mrs Carr	James Leslie, Ann Davies	James Leslie
1809-01-15	Salomone, George	1809-01-04	Mark & Martha Salomone	Thomas Copus, Ann Davies	James Leslie
1809-12-21	Goldby, Martha	–	Mr & Elizabeth Goldby	James Leslie, Mary Hopkins	James Leslie
1810-03-13	Cole, Robert	–	John Cole & his wife	James Nash, M Hopkins	James Leslie
1810-09-09	Copus, Joanna Elizabeth	–	Thomas & Jane Copus	James Leslie, Martha Salomoni	James Leslie
1811-03-10	Backford, James	–	James & Phillida Backford	Francis & Rachel Copus	James Leslie
1811-07-07	Salomone, Thomas	–	Mark & Martha Salomone	James Leslie, Susanna Clarkson	James Leslie
1811-10-??	Copus, Maria Elizabeth	–	Thomas & Jane Copus	James Leslie, Ann Davies	James Leslie
1812-05-12	Foy, Margarita	–	William & Ann Foy	Mark & Martha Salomone	James Leslie
1812-08-02 Charlton-on-Otmoor	Courtis, Augustus John	–	John & Elizabeth Courtis	Felix & Sophia Collingridge	James Leslie
1812-08-16	Carr, Elizabeth	–	Richard & Elizabeth Carr	James Leslie, Ann Davies	James Leslie

Date of baptism	Person baptised	Date of birth	Parents	Godparents or sponsors	Priest officiating
1813-05-16	Davis, Henry	–	John & Mary Davis from Limerick, Ireland	J.W. Conolly, Mary Connelly	James Leslie
1813-06-11	Woodward, Sarah	–	William & Ann Woodward	J.W. Conolly, Frances Sparshatt	John William Conolly
1813-06-13	Hanlon, James	–	Charles & Sarah Hanlon from Witney	J.W. Conolly, Frances Sparshatt	John William Conolly
1813-10-27	Gaverick, Caroline	–	John & Margaret Gaverick	William Hopkins, Frances Sparshatt	John William Conolly
1813-11-07	Salomini, William	–	Mark & Martha Salomini	William & Mary Hopkins	John William Conolly
1813-12-04	Corry, John	–	John & Elizabeth Corry from Leeds	J.W. Conolly, Frances Sparshatt	John William Conolly
1814-02-04	Copus, John	–	Thomas & Jane Copus	J.W. Conolly, Frances Sparshatt	John William Conolly
1814-05-01	Foy, Elizabeth	–	William & Ann Foy	Michael Neil, Frances Sparshatt	John William Conolly
1815-03-04	Wells, Alicia	–	Henry Wells & wife Mary (formerly Fagan) both from Ireland	John & Bridget Allen	John William Conolly
1815-03-23	Charleton, William	–	John & Winifrid Charleton from Ireland	James McVeigh, Elizabeth Merry	John William Conolly
1815-05-21	Copus, William	1815-04-27	Thomas & Joanna Copus	Ambrose Smith, Frances Sparshatt	John William Conolly

Date of baptism	Person baptised	Date of birth	Parents	Godparents or sponsors	Priest officiating
1815-06-22 conditional	Ryan, Helen	–	Patrick Ryan & wife Joanna (formerly Bohan) both from Ireland	J.W. Conolly	John William Conolly
1815-10-15	Allison, William	–	James & Catharine Allison	J.W. Conolly, Elizabeth East	John William Conolly
1816-01-07	Foy, David	–	William & Ann Foy	Thomas Copus, Frances Sparshatt	John William Conolly
1816-11-10	Copus, John William	1816-10-27	Thomas & Joanna Copus	William Foy, Ann Murphy	John William Conolly
1817-09-05	Davey, William	1817-09-04	Robert Davey & wife Lucy (formerly Morgan)	William Davey, Lucy Morgan	John William Conolly
1817-10-06	Tool, Anna	1817-09-23	Arthur & Catharine Tool living in Ireland	J.W. Conolly, Frances Sparshatt	John William Conolly
1817-10-19	Salomini, Frances	1817-10-01	Mark & Martha Salomini	Angelo Campino, Frances Sparshatt	John William Conolly
1818-11-15	Copus, Peter	–	Thomas & Joanna Copus	William Foy, Mary Ann Morgan	Robert Newsham
1818-11-29	Foy, Elizabeth	1818-11-24	William & Ann Foy	Stephen Fox, Mary Ann Morgan	Robert Newsham
1818 conditional	Viner, William	adult	–	–	Robert Newsham
1819 conditional	Shorter, Ann	adult	–	–	Robert Newsham

Date of baptism	Person baptised	Date of birth	Parents	Godparents or sponsors	Priest officiating
1819 conditional	Brain, Mr	adult	–	–	Robert Newsham
1819 conditional	Brain, Mrs	adult	–	–	Robert Newsham
1819-07-20 conditional	Shaw, Michael	adult	Thomas & Rosanna Shaw	–	Robert Newsham
1819-08-24 conditional	Milburn, John	adult	–	–	Robert Newsham
1819-08-20 conditional	Whitaker, Ann	–	Samuel & Frances Whitaker, father deceased.	–	Robert Newsham
1819-10-01 conditional	Hanley, Ann	–	Charles & Sarah Hanley father deceased.	–	Robert Newsham
1819-10-01 conditional	Hanley, Daniel	–	Charles & Sarah Hanley father deceased.	–	Robert Newsham
1819-10-01 conditional	Hanley, Elizabeth	–	Charles & Sarah Hanley father deceased.	–	Robert Newsham
1819-12-30 conditional	Hanley, Sarah, widow of Charles	–	–	–	Robert Newsham
1820-01-04 conditional	Smith, John	–	John & Elizabeth Smith	–	Robert Newsham
1820-01-17 conditional	Holyolk, James	–	George & Sarah Holyolk	–	Robert Newsham
1820-01-22 conditional	Jackson, Peregrine	–	Paul & Ann Jackson	–	Robert Newsham

THE REGISTERS 95

Date of baptism	Person baptised	Date of birth	Parents	Godparents or sponsors	Priest officiating
1820-01-28	Davey, Robert	1820-01-28	Robert Davey & wife Lucy (formerly Morgan)	Richard Morgan, Sarah Davey	Robert Newsham
1820	Holyolk, Maria	–	John & Ann Holyolk	George & Ann Holyolk	Robert Newsham
1820-03-30 conditional	Holyolk, Ann, wife of George	–	–	–	Robert Newsham
1820-04-04 conditional	Holyolk, Sarah (mother)	–	–	–	Robert Newsham
1820-04-04 conditional	Holyolk, Sarah (dau.)	–	Sarah Holyolk	–	Robert Newsham
1820-04-23	Salmoni, Mark	1820-04-23	Mark & Martha Salmoni	Angelo Campano, Sophia Collingridge	Robert Newsham
1820-06-12 conditional	Holyolk, John	–	–	–	Robert Newsham
1820-06-12 conditional	Holyolk, Ann	–	John Holyolk	–	Robert Newsham
1820-07-25	Higgins, Sarah	1820-06-24	Thomas Higgins & wife Sarah (formerly Mahoney)	Robert Newsham, Caroline Leonard	Robert Newsham
1820-07-30 conditional	Marcum, Thomas	–	–	–	Robert Newsham
1820-08-10 conditional	Sparshatt, John	–	–	–	Robert Newsham
1820-10-06	Copus, Arabella	–	Thomas Bradley & wife Joanna (formerly Bradley)	Robert Newsham, Rose Dawkins	Robert Newsham

Date of baptism	Person baptised	Date of birth	Parents	Godparents or sponsors	Priest officiating
1821-01-10 conditional	Mcafie, Maria	—	William Mcafie & wife Elizabeth (formerly Rumble)	—	Robert Newsham
1820-10-09	Kelly, Henry	1820-09-13	Michael Kelly & wife Mary (formerly Green)	Robert Newsham, Rose Dawkins	Robert Newsham
1821-01-20	Markum, Thomas Joseph	1821-01-17	Thomas Markum & wife Catharine (formerly McCann)	Thomas Hickey, Michael Haghan, Sarah Hanley	Robert Newsham
1821-02-13	Holyoak, John	1821-02-11	John Holyoak & wife Ann (formerly Holyoak)	George & Ann Holyoak	Robert Newsham
1821-02-13	Holyoak, Mary	1821-02-09	George & Ann Holyoak	Ambrose & Mary Smith	Robert Newsham
1821-02-24	Geoghegan, Thomas	1821-01-28	James Geoghegan & wife Elizabeth (formerly Cormack)	Robert Newsham, Rose Dawkins	Robert Newsham
1821-03-03 conditional	Taylor, John	—	John & Esther Taylor	—	Robert Newsham
1821-03-23	Smith, Joseph	1821-03-22	John Smith & wife Margaret (formerly Long)	William & Mary Hopkins	Robert Newsham
1821-04-01	Poulton, Mary Ann	1821-03-03	William Poulton & wife Margaret (formerly Mansfield)	Robert Newsham, Catharine Markham	Robert Newsham
1821-04-25 conditional	Hitchman, James	—	—	—	Robert Newsham
1821-05-11	Tayler, Helen	1821-05-10	Charles Tayler & wife Sarah (formerly Davey)	Charles Tayler, Sarah Davey	Robert Newsham

THE REGISTERS

Date of baptism	Person baptised	Date of birth	Parents	Godparents or sponsors	Priest officiating
1821-05-29 conditional	Howell, Mary Ann	–	James Howell & wife Joanna (formerly Mellet)	–	Robert Newsham
1821-05-29 conditional	Howell, Samuel	–	James Howell & wife Joanna (formerly Mellet)	–	Robert Newsham
1821-05-29 conditional	Howell, Catharine	–	James Howell & wife Joanna (formerly Mellet)	–	Robert Newsham
1821-07-17	Wheeler, John	1821-07-04	William Wheeler & wife Mary (formerly Buckland)	James & Elizabeth Wheeler	Robert Newsham
1821-08-12	Green (alias Kelly), James	1818-12-29	James Keirsley & Mary Green	–	Robert Newsham
1821-08-16	Davey, George	1821-08-15	George Davey & wife Elizabeth (formerly Tayler)	William Davey, Mary Crusse	Robert Newsham
1821-08-17 conditional	Beechey, Martha	–	John Beechey & wife Mary (formerly Mason)	–	Robert Newsham
1821-08-17 conditional	Smith, Rebecca, wife of Mr Smith	–	–	–	Robert Newsham
1821-08-29 conditional	Goom, Elizabeth, wife of Mr Goom	–	–	–	Robert Newsham
1821-09-10 conditional	Kelly (formerly Green), Mary, wife of Michael Kelly	–	–	–	Robert Newsham
1821-09-20 conditional	Collyer, Phoebe	–	James & Mary Collyer	–	Robert Newsham
1821-09-21	Smith, Mary Ann	1821-09-04	Ambrose Smith & wife Mary (formerly Hickman)	George Holyoak, Ann Holyoak	Robert Newsham

Date of baptism	Person baptised	Date of birth	Parents	Godparents or sponsors	Priest officiating
1821-09-21	Auger, John	1781 approx.	Robert & Mary Auger	–	Robert Newsham
1821-10-01 conditional	Badcock, Mary, wife of William Badcock	–	Richard & Ann Warnham	–	Robert Newsham
1821-12-24 conditional	Baston, Ann	–	Stephen & Elizabeth Baston	–	Robert Newsham
1822-02-01 conditional	Pritchett, Thomas Henry	1796 approx.	–	–	Robert Newsham
1822-02-12	Holyoak, Ann	1822-02-05	George Holyoak & wife Ann (formerly Alcock)	Ambrose & Mary Smith	Robert Newsham
1822-05-09	Smith, Frances	1822-05-07	John & Margaret Smith	George Hopkins, Frances Whitaker	Robert Newsham
1822-09-02	Hickey, Michael	1822-08-29	Thomas Hickey & wife Sarah (formerly Hanley)	William Foy, Rose Dawkins	Robert Newsham
1822-10-12 conditional	Bloxham, Susanna	–	–	–	Robert Newsham
1822-10-14	Davey, Henry	1822-10-08	George Davey & wife Elizabeth (formerly Tayler)	William Davey, Sarah Taylor	Robert Newsham
1822-10-22	de Crusse, Bridget	1822-10-13	Joseph de Crusse & wife Mary (formerly Dunnaven)	Robert Newsham, Rose Dawkins	Robert Newsham
1822-11-03	Austin, Elizabeth (formerly Morgan)	1782 approx.	–	–	Robert Newsham
1822-11-24 conditional	Yates, Elizabeth	adult	–	–	Robert Newsham

Date of baptism	Person baptised	Date of birth	Parents	Godparents or sponsors	Priest officiating
1822-12-07	Mulhern, John Thomas	1822-12-05	Thomas Mulhern & wife Ann (formerly Baston)	George & Mary Hopkins	Robert Newsham
1822-12-23 conditional	Foy, Ann (formerly Douglas), wife of William Foy	–	–	–	Robert Newsham
1823-02-25	Davey, Joseph	1823-02-24	Robert Davey & wife Lucy (formerly Morgan)	William Davey, Mary Crusse	Robert Newsham
1823-04-12	Higgins, William	1822-07-26	Thomas Higgins & wife Sarah (formerly Mahoney)	–	Robert Newsham
1823-04-13	Foy, Ann	1823-04-08	William Foy & wife Ann (formerly Douglas)	Thomas & Sarah Hickey	Robert Newsham
1823-04-13 conditional	Baston, Lydia	–	–	–	Robert Newsham
1823-04-24 conditional	Yates, Ann	–	–	Abraham & Ann Yates	Robert Newsham
1823-04-28	Yates, Elizabeth	1823-04-27	Abraham & Ann Yates	George Hopkins, Mary Yates	Robert Newsham
1823-05-04	Smith, Ambrose Henry	1823-04-24	Ambrose Smith & wife Mary (formerly Hickman)	George Holyoak, Francis Lakey	Robert Newsham
1823-06-19	Tayler, Mary	1823-06-17	Charles Tayler & wife Sarah (formerly Davey)	William Davey, Mary Cruse	Robert Newsham
1823-??-22	Wheeler, Mary	–	William Wheeler & wife Mary (formerly Buckland)	John & Elizabeth Wheeler	P.P. Heffernon

Date of baptism	Person baptised	Date of birth	Parents	Godparents or sponsors	Priest officiating
1823-07-16	Markham, John	1823-07-03	Thomas Markham & Catherine (formerly McCarren)	Daniel Grant, Rose Dawkins	Robert Newsham
1823-10-26	Holyoak, James	1823-10-26	George Holyoak & wife Ann (formerly Allcock)	William & Mary Hopkins	Robert Newsham
1823-10-26	Holyoak, John	1823-10-26	George Holyoak & wife Ann (formerly Allcock)	William & Mary Hopkins	Robert Newsham
1823-12-14	Poulton, Nicholas	1823-11-23	William Poulton & wife Margaret (formerly Mansfield)	Robert Newsham, Ann Yates	Robert Newsham
1823-12-15 conditional	Teague, Alexander	–	–	–	Robert Newsham
1823-12-16 conditional	Teague, George Vivers	–	Alexander & Elizabeth Teague	–	Robert Newsham
1823-12-16 conditional	Teague, Diana Elizabeth	–	Alexander & Elizabeth Teague	–	Robert Newsham
1823-12-16 conditional	Teague, Joanna Tilly	–	Alexander & Elizabeth Teague	–	Robert Newsham
1823-12-16 conditional	Teague, Mary Syndercomb	–	Alexander & Elizabeth Teague	–	Robert Newsham
1823-12-28	Smith, Eliza	1823-12-26	John Smith & wife Margaret (formerly Long)	Robert Newsham, Mary Hopkins	Robert Newsham
1824-04-09 Conditional	Arrow, Henry	adult	–	–	Robert Newsham

Date of baptism	Person baptised	Date of birth	Parents	Godparents or sponsors	Priest officiating
1824-05-09	Mulhern, Mary Ann	1824-05-02	Thomas Mulhern & wife Ann (formerly Baston)	Henry Arrow, Lydia Baston	Robert Newsham
1824-05-08	Byrnes, Elizabeth Sara	1824-04-25	John Byrnes & wife May Ann (formerly Barrit)	Thomas & Sarah Hickey	Robert Newsham
1824-??-08	Yates, Frances	1824-??-06	Abraham Yates & wife Ann (formerly Haycraft)	Robert Newsham, Rose Dawkins	Robert Newsham
1824-12-20	Holyoak, Eliza Emilia	1824-12-17	George Holyoak & wife Ann (formerly Alcock)	Ambrose & Maria Smyth	Robert Newsham
1825-01-03	Davey, William	1825-01-01	George Davey & wife Elizabeth (formerly Taylor)	William & Sarah Taylor	Robert Newsham
1825-02-07	Taylor, Charles	1825-02-06	Charles Taylor & wife Sarah (formerly Davey)	John & Elizabeth Davey	Robert Newsham
1825-02-27	Smith, Elizabeth	1825-02-03	Thomas & Margaret Smith	Robert Newsham, Winifred McGuire	Robert Newsham
1825-07-04	Smith, Charles	1825-06-29	John Smith & wife Margaret (formerly Long)	Robert Newsham, Frances Whitaker	Robert Newsham
1825-07-10	Foy, Elizabeth	1825-07-03	Michael Foy & wife Mary (formerly Dale)	Lewis & Eliza Clifford	Robert Newsham
1825-07-22 conditional	Bloxham, – (f.)	adult	–	–	Robert Newsham
1825-08-07	Smith, Alfred	1825-07-20	Ambrose Smith & wife Mary (formerly Hickman)	John Smith, Frances Lakey	Robert Newsham
1825-10-02	Rodwell, Clementina	1825-09-29	James Rodwell & wife Joanna (formerly Smith)	James & Ann Collingridge	Robert Newsham

Date of baptism	Person baptised	Date of birth	Parents	Godparents or sponsors	Priest officiating
1826-01-15	Mulhern, Michael Stephen	1825-12-29	Thomas Mulhuan & wife Ann (formerly Baston)	–	–
1826-03-21	Davey, Mary Elizabeth	1826-03-16	George Davey & wife Elizabeth (formerly Tayler)	Charles Tayler, Sarah Davey	Robert Newsham
1826-04-15	Fitzgibbons, William	1826-03-20	Thomas Fitzgibbons & wife Ann (formerly Mahony)	Henry Cosgrave, Rose Dawkins	Robert Newsham
1826-04-25	Evans, Francis	1826-04-04	Francis Evans & wife Bridget (formerly Broderick)	Robert Newsham, Rose Dawkins	Robert Newsham
1826-08-17 conditional	Yates, John, husband of Amelia	adult	–	–	Robert Newsham
1826-08-17 conditional	Yates, Amelia, wife of John	adult	–	–	Robert Newsham
1826-08-29 conditional	Peake, Edwin	adult	–	–	Robert Newsham
1827-01-09	Smith, James	1827-01-04	John Smith & wife Margaret (formerly Long)	Mary Cecilia Rathbon, James Long	Robert Newsham
1827-02-19	Taylor, William	1827-02-18	Charles Taylor & wife Sarah (formerly Davey)	William & Mary Taylor	Robert Newsham
1827-02-19	Taylor, Mary	1827-02-18	Charles Taylor & wife Sarah (formerly Davey)	George & Elizabeth Davey	Robert Newsham
1827-03-18	Foy, William	1827-03-12	Michael Foy & wife Mary (formerly Dale)	William Foy, Ann Dale	Robert Newsham
1827-05-21	Yates, Thomas	1827-05-18	Abraham & Ann Yates	John & Emma Yates	Robert Newsham

Date of baptism	Person baptised	Date of birth	Parents	Godparents or sponsors	Priest officiating
1827-05-03	Welsh, John	1827-04-28	Martin Welsh & wife Ann (formerly Havert)	Kean & Bridget Havert	Robert Newsham
1827-??-14	Archibald, Sarah	1827-??-08	Joseph Archibald & wife Mary (formerly O'Brien)	William Foy, Ann Hanley	Robert Newsham
1827-07-31	Davey, John	1827-07-28	George Davey & wife Elizabeth (formerly Taylor)	John & Elizabeth Davey	Robert Newsham
1827-07-29	Mulhern, George	1827-07-17	Thomas Mulhern & wife Ann (formerly. Baston)	Abraham & Elizabeth Yates	Robert Newsham
1827-12-17	Smith, Mary Frances	1827-11-21	Ambrose Smith & wife Mary (formerly Hickman)	John & Margaret Smith	Robert Newsham
1827-11-01	Rodwell, Julia	1827-10-28	James Rodwell & wife Jane (formerly Smith)	John & Jane Smith	Robert Newsham
1827-09-10	Wheeler, Frances	1827-08-01	William Wheeler & wife Mary (formerly Buckland)	Abraham & Ann Yates	Robert Newsham
1827-12-13	Williamson, George Alexander	1824-??-14	George Williamson & wife Mary (formerly Egan)	Robert Newsham, Mary Ann Barnard	Robert Newsham
1827-12-13	Williamson, John	1827-10-19	George Williamson & wife Mary (formerly Egan)	Robert Newsham, Mary Ann Barnard	Robert Newsham
1828-03-15 conditional	Preston, Hannah	adult	John & Mary Preston	–	Robert Newsham
1828-07-16	Davey, John	1828-07-01	George Davey & wife Elizabeth (formerly Tayler)	John & Elizabeth Davey	Robert Newsham

Date of baptism	Person baptised	Date of birth	Parents	Godparents or sponsors	Priest officiating
1828-08-10	Markham, James	1828-07-14	Thomas Markham & wife Catherine (formerly McCann)	Daniel & Maria Phelan	Robert Newsham
1828-08-30	Smith, George Frederick	1828-08-01	John & Mary Smith	Ambrose & Mary Smith	Nicholas Sewall
1828-10-12	Hickey, Sarah	1828-10-07	Thomas Hickey & wife Sarah (formerly Rowels)	Owen O'Hare, Catherine Heffernan	Robert Newsham
1829-04-12	Brown, Louise	1829-03-11	William Brown & wife Sarah (formerly White)	Daniel Hanley, Charlotte Tyler	Robert Newsham
1829-04-12	Terry, Emma	1829-03-12	John Terry & wife Mary (formerly East)	Daniel Phelan, Elizabeth East	Robert Newsham
1829-05-24	Collingridge, Ignatius	1829-05-23	William Watts & wife Catherine (formerly Collingridge)	Joseph Richardson, Mary Ann Barnard	Robert Newsham
1829-10-04	Adams, Anne	1829-09-10	Thomas Adams & wife Sarah (formerly West)	Thomas Copus, Mary Richardson	Robert Newsham
1829-11-01	Yates, Abraham	1829-10-17	Abraham Yates & wife Ann (formerly Haycraft)	William Wheeler, Mary Ann Phelan	Robert Newsham
1829-12-03	Smith, James	1829-10-23	John Smith & wife Margaret (formerly Long)	Ambrose & Mary Smyth	Robert Newsham
1830-01-22	Adams, Thomas	adult	—	—	Robert Newsham
1830-01-25	Bernard, George	1829-12-29	Ambrose Smith & wife Mary (formerly Hickman)	John & Margaret Smith	Robert Newsham
1830-01-26	Fitzgibbon, Ann	1829-12-29	Thomas Fitzgibbon & wife Ann (formerly Mahony)	Bernard McCanvill, Sarah Johnston	Robert Newsham

THE REGISTERS

Date of baptism	Person baptised	Date of birth	Parents	Godparents or sponsors	Priest officiating
1830-02-02	Wheeler, William	1830-01-06	William Wheeler & wife Mary (formerly Buckland)	Daniel & Ann Hanley	Robert Newsham
1830-02-27	Sweeny, Thomas	1830-02-03	Thomas Sweaney & wife Ellen (formerly Corkery)	Patrick Sweaney, Mary King	Robert Newsham
1830-03-15	Phelan, John	1830-03-07	Daniel Phelan & wife Ann (formerly Powell)	John & Joanna Smith	Robert Newsham
1830-04-29	Davey, Robert	1830-04-27	George Davey & wife Elizabeth (formerly Taylor)	John Taylor, Ann Bisher	Robert Newsham
1830-05-13 conditional	Watts, William	adult	–	–	Robert Newsham
1830-05-16	Foy, Mary	1830-05-11	Michael Foy & wife Mary (formerly Dale)	Daniel Kinney, Mary Richardson	Robert Newsham
1830-08-19	Godfrey, Matilda May	1830-08-15	James Godfrey & wife Phoebe (formerly Yates)	Jane & Amelia Yates	Robert Newsham
1830-10-10	Brown, Elizabeth	1830-09-12	William Brown & wife Sarah (formerly White)	Joseph Richardson	Edward Scott
1831-01-07	Blake, Mary Anne	adult	–	–	Robert Newsham
1831-05-01	Terry, Elizabeth	1831-04-03	John Terry & wife Mary (formerly East)	Robert Newsham, Charlotte Tyler	Robert Newsham
1831-05-22	Johnston, Mary	1831-05-02	John Johnston & wife Sarah (formerly Norris)	Thomas & Anne Fitzgibbon	Robert Newsham
1831-06-04	Smith, Thomas	1831-05-10	John Smith & wife Margaret (formerly Long)	Ambrose & Mary Smith	Robert Newsham

Date of baptism	Person baptised	Date of birth	Parents	Godparents or sponsors	Priest officiating
1831-10-16	Fitzgibbon, John	1831-09-27	Thomas Fitzgibbon & wife Ann (formerly Mahony)	John Johnson, Sarah Hickey	Robert Newsham
1831-11-20	Bell, Benjamin	adult	–	–	Unsigned
1831-12-18	Yates, Mary Anne	1831-12-11	Abraham Yates & wife Ann (formerly Heycroft)	John Wilson, Elizabeth Yates	Robert Newsham
1832-01-13	Smith, Agnes Catherine	1831-12-18	Ambrose Smith & wife Mary (formerly Hickman)	John & Margaret Smith	Robert Newsham
1832-01-16	Davis, Frances Sophia	1831-11-15	James Davis & wife Mary (formerly McGedy)	Francis & Sophia McGedy	Robert Newsham
1832-02-02	Bell, Benjamin	adult	–	–	Robert Newsham
1832-03-17 conditional	Lamb, Sarah	adult	–	–	Robert Newsham
1832-03-26 conditional	Johnson, Sarah	adult	–	–	Robert Newsham
1832-06-03	Lamb, Elizabeth	1832-05-16	Patrick Lamb & wife Sarah (formerly Rider)	Michael Doran, Catherine Mayates	Robert Newsham
1832-07-15	Foy, Ann	1832-07-03	Michael Foy & wife Mary (formerly Dale)	Daniel Hanley, Ann Foy	Robert Newsham
1832-07-30 conditional	Collingridge, Jemima	adult	–	–	Robert Newsham
1832-08-12	Tyler, Emma	1832-07-10	William Tyler & wife Charlotte (formerly East)	Robert Newsham, Mary Terry	Robert Newsham
1832-09-25 conditional	Cecil, William	adult	–	–	Robert Newsham

Date of baptism	Person baptised	Date of birth	Parents	Godparents or sponsors	Priest officiating
1832-11-25	Monis, Ann Elizabeth	1832-11-04	Thomas Monis & wife Ann (formerly Hanley)	Daniel Hanley, Sarah Hickey	Robert Newsham
1832-12-06	Johnston, John	–	John Johnston & wife Sarah (formerly Norris)	Francis Campioni, Sarah Lamb	Robert Newsham
1832-12-23	Smith, Edward	1832-11-25	John Smith & wife Margaret (formerly Long)	Ambrose & Mary Smith	Robert Newsham
1832-12-30	Wheeler, Elizabeth	1832-12-06	William Wheeler & wife Mary (formerly Buckland)	Daniel Hanley, Ann Morice	Robert Newsham
1833-01-03 conditional	Whiting, – (f.)	adult	–	–	Robert Newsham
1833-01-15	Davey, Edward Charles	1822-01-09	George Davey & wife Elizabeth (formerly Tayler)	James & Catherine Tayler	Robert Newsham
1833-03-10	McCarthy, Jeremy	1833-02-27	Jeremy McCarthy & wife Mary (formerly Murrey)	John & Mary Shierman	Robert Newsham
1833-03-26	Douglas, Adaline Domville	1832-12-22	Sholto Douglas & wife Julie Isabelle Gianetta (de Montmorenci)	Compton Charles Domville, Victoire Schoelard	Robert Newsham
1833-03-31	Fitzgibbon, Helena	1833-03-10	Thomas Fitzgibbon & wife Ann (formerly Manning)	James Haley, Mary Ann Salmoni	Robert Newsham
1833-09-11	Davidson, Maria Louisa	1833-09-02	James Davidson & wife Mary (formerly McGedy)	Francis & Louisa McGedy	Robert Newsham
1833-09-21	Heueritsi, James	1833-09-18	Adam Heueritsi & wife Totia (formerly Summala)	James Tees, Ann Mary Delien	Robert Newsham

Date of baptism	Person baptised	Date of birth	Parents	Godparents or sponsors	Priest officiating
1833-10-20	Lamb, James	1833-09-21	Patrick Lamb & wife Sarah (formerly Rider)	William & Ann Foy	Robert Newsham
1833-12-20	Phelan, – (m.)	1833-11-11	Ann Phelan from Summertown	–	Robert Newsham
1834-04-03	Smith, Helen Theresa	1834-03-15	Ambrose Smith & wife Mary (formerly Hickman)	Joseph & Sarah Richardson	Robert Newsham
1834-04-03 conditional	Petre, George Glynn,	–	Henry Petre	–	Robert Newsham
1834-04-06	Fitzgibbon, John	1834-03-15	Thomas Fitzgibbon & wife Ann (formerly Mahony)	James Prendergast, Mary Ann Salmoni	Robert Newsham
1834-05-18	Daly, Mary Ann	1834-04-27	Michael Daly & wife Mary (formerly Sullivan)	Patrick Bresnahan, Catherine Dwyer	Robert Newsham
1834-06-22	Thick, Christina	1834-06-15	George Thick & wife Margaret (formerly Foy)	William & Ann Foy	Robert Newsham
1834-07-20	Croney, Cornelius	1834-03-11	Cornelius Croney & wife Anne (formerly O'Donnell)	Jeremy Murrey, Anne Murray	Robert Newsham
1834-08-16	Rany, Mary	1834-08-03	Garret Rany & wife Helen (formerly Dunaven)	Ann Gough, Bridget Rany	Robert Newsham
1834-08-31	Davey, Mary Theresa	1834-08-28	George Davey & wife Elizabeth (formerly Taylor)	William Davey, Mary Taylor	Robert Newsham
1834	Harris, Alfred	1834-08-29	John & Anna Harris	Ambrose & Mary Smith	
1834	Rentz, Henry	1834-09-18	Johnstein & Evastein Rentz	Carl Henrichi, Henrietta Smith	–
1834	Foy, Sarah	1834-11-23	Michael & Mary Foy	David & Ann Foy	–

Date of baptism	Person baptised	Date of birth	Parents	Godparents or sponsors	Priest officiating
1834	Morris, Ann	1834-09-01	Thomas & Ann Morris	Thomas Hickey, Frances Whitaker	–
1834	Brown, Emma	1834-11-20	William & Sarah Brown	Robert Newsham, Mary White	–
1834	Lamb, William Stephen	1834-12-26	Patrick & Sarah Lamb	James Lamb, M. Ann Salmoni	–
1835-04-06	Atkins, Edmund	1817 approx.	–	–	–
1835	Wood, Rose	1835-03-24	George & Margaret Wood	Robert Newsham	–
1835-05-08 conditional	Smith, Mary Louisa	–	–	–	–
1835-05-08 conditional	Maycock, Mary	–	–	–	–
1836-06-10	Phelan, Thomas	1836-03-11	Ann Phelan from Summertown	–	–
1836-06-16	Steen, Teddy	–	Michael & Mary Steen	Antony Saxton, Mary Carabine	–
1836-07-29	Halloway, Marcia	1836-06-17	William & Mary Halloway	William & Mary Halloway	–
1836-01-13	Thick, Ann	1836-01-03	George & Margaret Thick	William & Ann Foy	–
1836-03-21	Fitzgibbon, William	1836-03-08	Thomas & Ann Fitzgibbon	John Johnson, Mary Burns	–
1836-05-08	Brown, John	1835-05-01	Michael & Mary Brown	Patrick & Mary Cunningham	–
1836-05-09	Angleri, Antonio Giovanni Battista Alexandro Joseph	1836-05-01	Alexandro & Margherita Or. Maria Angleri	Giovanni Guanziroll, Maria Orletto	–

Date of baptism	Person baptised	Date of birth	Parents	Godparents or sponsors	Priest officiating
1836-05-10	Curl, Thomas	1836-04-08	Thomas & Anna Curl	–	–
1836-05-29	Morris, Sarah	1836-05-07	Thomas & Anna Morris	William McGowen, Sarah Hickey	–
1836-06-02	Davey, Frances Mary	1836-05-29	George & Elizabeth Davey	Felix & Sophia Collingridge	–
1836-06-?	Poulton, Jane	–	William & Margaret Poulton	–	–
1836-06-?	Poulton, Henry	–	William & Margaret Poulton	–	–
1836-06-10	Driscoll, Dennis	1836-06-10	Thomas & Nancy Driscoll	Dennis Driscoll, Margaret Curran	–
1836-08-07	Harris, Andrew	1836-07-18	John & Anna Harris	Ambrose & Mary Smith	–
1836-10-01 conditional	Tyson, Hugh	adult	–	–	–
1836-10-08	Driscoll, Mary	1836-09-12	John & Cremine Driscoll	Con Driscoll. Honora Riding	–
1836	Lamb, Jane	1836-10-22	Patrick & Sarah Lamb	Michael & Margaret Lamb	–
1836	Halloway, William	1836-10-12	William & Mary Halloway	George & Mary Halloway	–
1837	Smith, Frederic Augustus	1836-12-27	Ambrose & Mary Smith	Peter Hunt, Mary Ann Barnard	–
1837	January, Emery	1837-01-31	George & Phebe January	–	–
1837	Hanley, William Henry	1837-03-12	Daniel & Anna M. Hanley	Edmond Atkins Anna Morris	–

Date of baptism	Person baptised	Date of birth	Parents	Godparents or sponsors	Priest officiating
1837	Foy, John	1837-04-03	Michael & Mary Foy	John Johnston, Fanny Richardson	–
1837	Bianco, Angelina	1837-03-28	Peter & Anna Bianco	Francis Henrico, Agatha Hoyos	–
1837	Harris, Walter John	1837-10-12	John & Anna Harris	Ambrose & Mary Smith	–
1838	Morris, Charlotte	1838-03-10	Thomas Anna Morris	Daniel & Sarah Hickey	–
1838	Holloway, Thomas	1838-03-20	William & Mary Holloway	George & Mary Holloway	–
1838	Lamb, Mary Ann	1838-05-02	Patrick & Sarah Lamb	Thomas Fitzgibbon, Lucy Rouse	–
1838-10-23	Richardson, Ann	–	Mother of Joseph Richardson	–	–
1838-11-03	Fitzgibbon, Ellen	1838-10-01	Thomas & Ann Fitzgibbon	Patrick Lamb, Catherine Markham	–
1839	de Mascarène, Frederick Emanuel	1839-11-01	Paul & Matilda de Mascarène	Robert Newsham, Mary Ann Barnard	–
1838	Wood, Margaret	1838-10-15	George & Margaret Wood	Thomas & Ann Fitzgibbon	–
1839	Smith, Eliza Winefred	1838-12-23	Ambrose & Mary Smith	Job & Mary Turner	–
1839	January, Lucy Catharine	1838-12-14	George & Phebe January	–	–
1839	Thick, John	1839-02-11	George & Margaret Thick	William & Ann Foy	–
1839-04-04 conditional	Kear, Elizabeth	adult	–	–	–
1839-04-04 conditional	Kear, Eliza	–	Elizabeth Kear	–	–

Date of baptism	Person baptised	Date of birth	Parents	Godparents or sponsors	Priest officiating
1839	Delaney, John	1839-11-01	Hugh & Mary Delaney	John Moore, Mary Anne Barnard	–
1839	Terry, Frances	1839-04-10	John & Mary Terry	Robert Newsham, Charlot Tyler	–
1839-08-12 conditional	Prior, John	–	–	–	–
1839-08-23	Foy, David	–	Michael & Mary Foy	Thomas Hickey, Ann Goodman	–
1839-08-17	Hanley, Charles	–	Daniel & Hannah Maria Hanley	William & Ann Foy	–
1839-11-01	Hanley, Hannah H.	adult	–	–	–
1840-02-??	Chapman, Thomas	adult	–	–	–
1839-10-??	Prior, John	adult	–	–	–
1840	Johnston, Thomas Roberts Spokes	1839-10-18	Robert Spokes, Ann Johnston	Thomas Chapman, Eliza Barnard	–
1840-04-19	Lamb, Sarah	1840-03-25	Patrick & Sara Lamb	Thomas & Catharine Markham	–
1840-05-24	Johnston, George Spokes	1840-04-23	Robert Spokes & Ann Johnston	William Foy, Eliza Barnard	–
1840-06-12	McGowen, Mary	adults	–	–	–
1840-07-08	Morris, Thomas	1840-04-14	Thomas & Hannah Morris	Daniel Hanley, Sarah Hickey	–

Date of baptism	Person baptised	Date of birth	Parents	Godparents or sponsors	Priest officiating
1840-07-25	de Cardi, Gertrude	1829-08-10	John Baptist Zepherin de Cardi & wife Elizabeth de Cardi (formerly Weller)	Robert Newsham, Eliza Barnard	–
1840-07-25	de Cardi, Nicolette	1831-04-12	John Baptist Zepherin de Cardi & wife Elizabeth de Cardi (formerly Weller)	Robert Newsham, Eliza Barnard	–
1840-07-25	de Cardi, Mark Oliver	1833-10-12	John Baptist Zepherin de Cardi & wife Elizabeth de Cardi (formerly Weller)	Robert Newsham, Eliza Barnard	–
1840-07-25	de Cardi, Philip Antony	1835-09-19	John Baptist Zepherin de Cardi & wife Elizabeth de Cardi (formerly Weller)	Robert Newsham, Eliza Barnard	–
1840-07-25	de Cardi, Peter Louis	1837-05-01	John Baptist Zepherin de Cardi & wife Elizabeth de Cardi (formerly Weller)	Robert Newsham, Eliza Barnard	–
1840-08-30	McGowan, Frances	1840-08-08	William & Mary McGowen	William & Ann Foy	–
1840-12-25	Tison, Catharine	1840-10-05	Hugh & Catharine Tison	Thomas Molloy, Michael Breen, Ann Godman	–
1840-12-31 Adult	Sirett, Mary Ann	–	–	–	–
1841-01-14	Banclery, Vincent John Gilbert	1840-12-12	Vincent & Letitia Banclary	Robert Newsham, Sophia Chapman	–
1841	Tod, Robert Joseph Whitelock	1841-01-13	George & Eliza Tod	Revd Joseph Smith, Eliza Tate	–

Date of baptism	Person baptised	Date of birth	Parents	Godparents or sponsors	Priest officiating
1841	Turner, Teresa Mary	1841-03-08	Job & Mary Turner	Peter Hunt, Teresa Smallwood	–
1841-03-17	Brown, Mary Elizabeth	–	William & Sarah Brown	Robert Newsham, Sarah Tyler	–
1841	Holloway, James	1841-02-27	William & Mary Holloway	George & Mary Holloway	–
1841	Smith, Julia Lucy	1841-06-30	Ambrose & Mary Smith	John & Eleanor Smallwood	–
1841	Thick, Charles	1841-08-17	George & Margaret Thick	William & Ann Foy	–
1841 conditional	Brooks, Elizabeth	–	–	–	–
1841 conditional	Brooks, Mary Ann	–	–	–	–
1841 conditional	Brooks, Sarah	–	–	–	–
1841 conditional	Brooks, Jane	–	–	–	–
1841-09-06	Tobin, Edward	1841-05-30	James & Maria Tobin	John & Ann Roland	–
1841-09-06	Curril, Rachael	adult	–	–	–
1841-10-12	Holloway, George	1841-08-25	George & Charlot Holloway	William & Keziah Holloway	–
1841-11-19	Parker, John Robert Howell	1841-10-19	Robert & Mary Parker	Samuel & Catharine Howell	–
1841-11-14	Clark, William	1841-10-14	Giles & Catharine Clark	Robert Newsham	–
1841-11-24	Finmore, Maria Agnes	adult	–	–	–
1841-12-22 conditional	Gooch, John	adult	–	–	–

THE REGISTERS

Date of baptism	Person baptised	Date of birth	Parents	Godparents or sponsors	Priest officiating
1842-01-06 conditional	Gooch, Hanna	–	–	–	–
1842-01-06 conditional	Gooch, Samuel	–	–	–	–
1842-01-06 conditional	Gooch, Robert	–	–	–	–
1842-01-06 conditional	Gooch, John	–	–	–	–
1842-01-07 conditional	Gooch, Herbert	–	–	–	–
1842-01-07 conditional	Gooch, William	–	–	–	–
1842-01-07 conditional	Gooch, Alban	–	–	–	–
1842-01-07	Gooch, Hugh	–	–	–	–
1842-01-08	Lamb, John	1842-01-04	Patrick & Sarah Lamb	Hugh Tison, Mary Foy	–
1842-01-14	Thick, Charles	–	George & Margaret Thick	William & Ann Foy	–
1842-05-07	Chopping, Sarah Richardson	1841-10-18	Matthew & Amanda Chopping	Joseph & Sarah Richardson	–
1842-06-26	Tyson, Hugh	1842-04-19	Hugh & Catharine Tyson	Thomas & Catharine Markham	–
1842-07-03	Turner, Sarah Elizabeth	1842-06-13	Job & Mary Turner	Thomas & Mary Ann Smallwood	–

115

Date of baptism	Person baptised	Date of birth	Parents	Godparents or sponsors	Priest officiating
1842-08-21	Ortelli, Angela Lucy	1842-08-19	Defendente & Mary Ortelli	Antony & Angela Ortelli	–
1843-01-08	Hinton, Mercy	1842-06-06	William & Angelina Hinton	Robert Newsham, Eliza Barnard	–
1843-02-12 conditional	Hinton, Angelina	–	–	–	–
1843-02-12 conditional	Hinton, John	–	–	–	–
1843-02-26 conditional	Hinton, William (father)	–	–	–	–
1843-02-26 conditional	Hinton, William (son)	–	–	–	–
1843-02-12	McGowen, Maria	1842-12-24	William & Mary McGowen	Matthew Kear, Sarah Hickey	–
1843-04-05 conditional	Neville, Charles	–	–	–	–
1843-09-11	Holloway, John	1843-05-05	William & Mary Holloway	George & Mary Holloway	–
1843-09-12 conditional	Davies, William	adult	–	–	–
1843-08-12	Wood, Jane	1843-07-14	George Newman Wood & Margaret Wood	–	–
1843-09-14	Mellet, William Henry	1843-08-20	Robert & Mary Parker	Samuel & Catharine Howell	–
1843	Shevelin, Mary Ann	1843-09-09	Patrick & Catharine Shevelin	Edward & Ann Murray, Mary Ann Fahey	–

Date of baptism	Person baptised	Date of birth	Parents	Godparents or sponsors	Priest officiating
1843-10-10	Seager, Osmund	1843-07-30	Charles & Anna Seager	Revd John Moore & Elizabeth Moore	–
1843-10-23	Holloway, Mary	1843-09-??	George & Charlotte Holloway	William & Zechia Holloway	–
1843-11-19	Lamb, Charles	1843-10-21	Patrick & Sarah Lamb	John Prior (father), John Prior (son), Mary Foy, Catharine Ellis	–
1843-11-19	Lamb, Henry	1843-10-21	Patrick & Sarah Lamb	John Prior (father), John Prior (son), Mary Foy, Catharine Ellis	–
1843-11-20	Poulton, James P. Hans	1843-10-07	Dennis Sullivan, M. Ann Poulton	Michael Foy, Catharine Brodick	–
1843-10-10	Hussey, Sarah	adult	–	–	–
1843-12-22	Barnhill, –	adult	–	–	–
1843-12-24	Turner, Eliza Mary	1843-12-07	Job & Mary Turner	Frederic & Eliza Cerotti	–
1843-12-24	Marden, Thomas	1843-07-13	Thomas & Mary Anne Marden	Daniel Cochrane, Margaret Dormer	–
1844-02-04	Stanley, Mary Anne	1844-01-20	William & Anne Stanley	William Davis, Anne Wood	–
1844-02-20	Williamson, Eliza Lucy	1844-02-19	Charles & Eliza Lucy Williamson	John MacCann, C. Hickey	–
1844-03-30	Tyson, Agnes	1844-02-11	Hugh & Catharine Tyson	Thomas Markham, Eliza Barnard	–
1844-04-25	Green, Charles Samson	adult	–	–	–

Date of baptism	Person baptised	Date of birth	Parents	Godparents or sponsors	Priest officiating
1844-05-15 conditional	Green, Charles Samson	–	–	–	–
1844-05-15 conditional	Barnes, Elizabeth	–	–	–	–
1844-05-15 conditional	Barnes, Emma	–	–	–	–
1844-06-03 conditional	Grove, Mary	–	–	–	–
1844-08-10 conditional	Leader, Mary Anne	–	–	–	–
1844-09-08	McGowen, Frances	1844-09-08	William & Mary McGowen	Michael Breem, Sarah Hickey	–
1844-09-29	Dinnison, William	1844-09-11	William & Catharine Dinnison	Frederick Finnigan, Mary Sullivan	–
1844-10-06	Holloway, Mary Anne	1844-08-16	William & Mary Anne Holloway	George & Mary Holloway	–
1844-10-18 conditional	Penny, William Goodenough, former Protestant clergyman	–	–	–	–
1844-11-05 conditional	Smith, William	–	–	–	–
1844-11-24	McCarty, Donald	1844-11-17	Michael & Mary McCarty	Frederick Harvey, Mary Wilkins	–
1845-01-17	Gardiner, Harriet	1844-12-22	George & Ann Gardiner	Frederic & Betsy Gardiner	–

Date of baptism	Person baptised	Date of birth	Parents	Godparents or sponsors	Priest officiating
1845-02-19 conditional	Bultely, Elizabeth	adult	–	–	–
1845-03-23	Ortelli, Angelian Lucy Pasealina	1845-03-23	Defendente & Mary Ortelli	Fedeli Primavesi, Angelina Ortelli	–
1845-05-16	Twycross, Isaac	–	–	–	–
1845-05-23	Smith, Sarah	adult	–	–	–
1845-05-18	Kenrick, Mary Ann	1845-03-20	William & Ann Kenrick	Robert Newsham, Ann McGowen	–
1845-06-02	Jarvis, Edward	adult	–	–	–
1845	Richardson, Gertrude Agnes Annie	1845-06-17	Joseph & Rosabella Georgina Richardson	–	–
1845-06-22	Green, Mary Ann	1845-04-25	Charles & Harriett Green	Josef & Rosabella Richardson	–
1845-07-14	Morris, Charles	1845-04-25	Thomas & Anna Morris	Daniel Henley, Ann Foy	–
1845-07-16	Holloway, Mark	1845-06-10	George & Charlott Holloway	William & Zechia Holloway	–
1845-08-15	Lyden, Mary Ann Magdalen Mingay	adult	–	–	–
1845-10-02	Markam, Betsy	1845-08-26	Thomas & Betsy Markam	Thomas & Catharine Markam	–
1845-10-25 conditional	England, Mary Anna	–	–	–	–
1845-10-30 conditional	Bull, Elizabeth	–	–	–	–

Date of baptism	Person baptised	Date of birth	Parents	Godparents or sponsors	Priest officiating
1845-11-02	Shevlan, Catharine Elizabeth	1845-09-20	Patrick & Catharine Shevlan	Pat. Bennett, Elizabeth Gillingham, Elizabeth Ann Carn	–
1845-11-06	Parker, James Joseph Mills	–	Robert & Mary Parker	Samuel Simkin, Mary Howell	–
1845-12-10	Walton, Frederick Benjamin	1845-02-14	Frederick D'Arcey & Elizabeth Walton	John & Catharine Prior	–
1845-12-20	Lamb, Thomas	1845-12-06	Patrick & Sarah Lamb	Patrick & Catherine Shevlan	–
1845-12-30	Becket, Katharine Rachael	1845-12-15	Thomas & Ann Becket	William Carew, Rachael Becket	–
1846-01-26 conditional	Robinson, John	–	–	–	–
1846-01-29 conditional	Cripps, Mary Ann	–	–	–	–
1846-01-29 conditional	Cripps, Sarah	–	–	–	–
1846-02-04 conditional	Cripps, Temperance Ann	–	–	–	–
1846-02-10 conditional	Woodmason, Ann	–	–	–	–
1846-03-13 conditional	Wiblin, Ann	–	–	–	–
1846-02-19	Coleman, John	1846-02-16	Timothy & Ellen Coleman	Thomas Sullivan, Ann Hickey	–

THE REGISTERS

Date of baptism	Person baptised	Date of birth	Parents	Godparents or sponsors	Priest officiating
1846-04-20 conditional	Plumb, Emma	–	–	–	–
1846-05-20 conditional	Smith, Richard	–	–	–	–
1846-05-20	Holloway, Agnes	1846-03-31	William & Mary Ann Holloway	George & Mary Holloway	–
1846-06-09	Richardson, Augustin Joseph Mingaye	1846-05-27	Joseph & Rosabella Georgina Richardson	Robert Walker, Maria Finmore	–
1846-06-11	Hickey, Mary Jane	1846-05-16	Thomas & Sara Hickey	Daniel Hanley, Ann Hickey	–
1846-06-23	Castle, Charlott	adult	–	–	–
1846-07-19	Wiblin, Ann	adult	–	–	–
1846-07-24	Carter, Phebe	adult	–	–	–
1846-07-19	Howell, Jane	adult	–	–	–
1846-08-09	Ortelli, Maria Lucy Paulina	1846-08-08	Defendente & Maria Ortelli	Angelina Ortelli, Ildevaldo Primavesi	–
1846-08-06	Carter, Sibbia	adult	–	–	–
1846-09-01	Jones, Ann	adult	–	–	–
1846-09-28	Jones, Davey	adult	–	–	–
1846-10-03	Jones, Mary	adult	–	–	–
1846-10-19	King, Mahala	–	–	–	–
1846-10-19	King, Thirsa	–	–	–	–

Date of baptism	Person baptised	Date of birth	Parents	Godparents or sponsors	Priest officiating
1846-10-19	King, Ann	–	–	–	–
1846-10-19 conditional	Harwood, Richard Hall	–	–	–	–
1846-10-04 conditional	Carter, William	–	–	–	–
1846-10-05	Hope, Mary	adult	–	–	–
1846-10-05	Hope, Mary Jane	adult	–	–	–
1846-10-06	Wilkins, Elizabeth	adult	–	–	–
1847-02-01 conditional	East, William Justin	–	–	–	–
1847-02-03 conditional	Harwood, Elizabeth	–	–	–	–
1847-02-04	King, Sophia	–	–	–	–
1847-09-08 conditional	Miles, Elizabeth	–	Thomas & Mary Ann Miles	John & Elizabeth Prior	–
1847-02-11	Tarant, Sarah	adult	–	–	–
1847-02-14	Dennison, John	1847-01-03	William & Ann Dennison	Dan Coglan, Eliza Anderton	–
1847-02-17	McGowan, Margaret	1846-12-25	William & Mary McGowan	Matthew Kear, Eliza Quartermain	–
1847-02-24	Holloway, Ann	1847-01-08	George & Sarah Holloway	William & Zechia Holloway	–
1847	Green, Sarah Rose Hanna	1847-03-10	Charles & Harriet Green	Joseph & Mingaye Richardson	–

Date of baptism	Person baptised	Date of birth	Parents	Godparents or sponsors	Priest officiating
1847	Williamson, Ellen Elizabeth	1847-03-18	Charles & Eliza Lucy Williamson	Thomas J. Markam, Eliza Barnard	–
1847-09-01	Watson, Maria Elizabeth	1847-07-15	Frederic & Elizabeth Watson	Patrick Lamb, Eliza Williamson	–
1847-10-12 conditional	Brown, Robert	–	–	–	–
1847-10-14 conditional	Aldworth, William	–	–	–	–
1847-11-19	Lamb, Teresa	1847-10-04	Patrick & Sarah Lamb	Hugh Tison, Ann Foy	–
1847-11-20 conditional	McMullen, William	–	–	–	–
1847-11-26 conditional	Ellis, Charles	–	–	–	–
1847-12-15	Finnakin, William	1847-12-07	Frederici & Mary Finnakin	Robert Newsham, Margarite Matthews	–
1847	Ortelli, Paul John	1847-12-23	Defendente & Mary Ortelli	John Ortelli, Josephine Whitfield	–
1848-03-20 conditional	Snow, John	–	–	–	–
1848-03-20 conditional	Clare, Jacob	–	–	–	–
1848-03-20 conditional	Clare, Mary	–	–	–	–

Date of baptism	Person baptised	Date of birth	Parents	Godparents or sponsors	Priest officiating
1848-03-20 conditional	Clare, James	–	–	–	–
1848-03-20 conditional	Clare, Ann	–	–	–	–
1848-03-20 conditional	Clare, Emily	–	–	–	–
1848-03-20 conditional	Clare, David	–	–	–	–
1848-03-20 conditional	Clare, Mary Ann	–	–	–	–
1848-04-20	Parker, Kate Agnes Lester	1848-03-28	Robert & Mary Parker	Richard Simkins, Sarah Agnes Lester	–
1848-05-03 conditional	Davis, Lydia	–	–	–	–
1848-05-19 conditional	Woodley, Sarah	–	–	–	–
1848-07-23	Russell, James	1848-07-03	John & Ellen Russell	Thomas Fitzgibbon, Rose Green	–
1848-07-23	Read, Michael	1848-07-01	William & Mary Read	Hugh Tison, Julia Sullivan	–
1848-07-25	Richardson, Rosa Maria Mingaye		Joseph & Rosabella G.M. Richardson	Daniel Hanley, Anne P. Wainwright	–
1848-11-12	Dennison, Mary Ann	1848-10-27	William & Catharine Dennison	George French, Mary A. Forby	–

Date of baptism	Person baptised	Date of birth	Parents	Godparents or sponsors	Priest officiating
1848-12-06	Woodley, Gemima	adult	–	–	–
1848-12-13	Welland, Elizabeth	1848-11-18	William & Ester Welland	Robert Newsham, Eliza Barnard	–
1849-03-11	Halloway, Harriet	1849-02-05	George Halloway & wife Charlotte (formerly Smith)	William Halloway, Catherine Burnhill	Henry Brigham
1849-04-29	Murray, Thomas	1849-04-28	– Murray & wife Anne (formerly Donoghue)	Dennis Delay Catherine Cokeley	Henry Brigham
1849-06-28	Halloway, Anne	1849-06-02	– Halloway & wife Kezia Halloway	Hugh Tyson, Elizabeth Prior	Henry Brigham
1850-01-02	Develin, Mary Anne	1849-12-29	James Develin & wife Mary (formerly Donovan)	Hugh Tyson, Ellen Russell	Henry Brigham
1850-06-23	Hickey, John Thomas	–	– Hickey & wife Jane (formerly Collingridge)	Michael & Mary Foy	Henry Brigham
1851-03-09	Hanley, Maria Teresa	–	Daniel Hanley & wife Maria Frances (formerly Smith)	Ambrose & Ellen Smith, aunt & uncle of child	Henry Brigham
1851	Tyson, ?	–	Hugh Tyson & wife	John Keir, – Ellis	Henry Brigham
1851-04-06	Carter, Francis	–	Sarah Carter	William & Ann Carter	Henry Brigham
1851-06-15	Williamson, Charles	–	Charles Williamson & wife Eliza Lucy (formerly Markham)	Thomas Markham (grandfather of child), Mary Foy Snr	Henry Brigham
1851-06-22	Donovan, John	–	James & Mary Donovan	Eliza Lamb	Henry Brigham

Date of baptism	Person baptised	Date of birth	Parents	Godparents or sponsors	Priest officiating
1852-05-30	Hanley, Julia Frances	–	Daniel Hanley & wife Maria Frances (formerly Smith)	Ambrose & Mary Smith (grandparents of child)	Henry Brigham
1852-05-30	Smith, Mary Anne	–	Ambrose Henry Smith & wife Frances (formerly Kimber)	Daniel Hanley, Ellen Smith (aunt of child)	Henry Brigham
1852-12-12	Tyson, Francis	–	Hugh Tyson & wife Sophia (formerly Seymour)	– Ellis, Ann Carter	Henry Brigham
1852-12-14	Hickie, Katherine	–	Thomas Hickie & wife Jane (formerly Collingridge)	Stanislaus Pfaff, Maria Finmore	Henry Brigham
1853-09-04	Parker, Florence Mary Jermyns	–	Robert Parker & wife Mary (formerly Howel)	Ambrose Smith Snr, Catherine Adelaid Howel (aunt of child)	Henry Brigham
1853-12-11	Hanley, Charles Ambrose	–	Daniel Hanley & wife Maria (formerly Smith)	Charles Grafton, Helen Smith (aunt of child)	Henry Brigham
1854-01-08	Haynes, Thomas Murray	–	Thomas Haynes & wife Elizabeth (formerly Lamb)	Hugh Tyson, Ann Foy	Henry Brigham
1854-03-03	Smith, Ambrose Frederick	–	Ambrose Henry Smith & wife Frances (formerly Kimber)	Patrick Bennet, Maria Hanley	Henry Brigham
1854-04-10	Hastings, Louisa Catherine	1854-03-13	John Hastings & wife Elizabeth (formerly Jones)	John McDonnell, Catherine Kirkwood	Francis Chadwick
1854-07-16	Lacy, Daniel	1854-06-30	William Lacy & wife Catherine (formerly Cusack)	Elizabeth Gillingham	Francis Chadwick

Date of baptism	Person baptised	Date of birth	Parents	Godparents or sponsors	Priest officiating
1855-02-18	Tyson, William	1855-01-07	Hugh Tyson & wife Sophia (formerly Seamore)	John Pritchard, Mrs French	Francis Chadwick
1855-03-04	Smith, Edward	1855-02-11	Edward & Mary Smith	Matthew Dixon	Francis Chadwick
1855-03-25	Dixon, Ellen	1855-02-27	Matthew Dixon & wife Catherine (formerly Wright)	William & Esther Wakelin	Francis Chadwick
1855-06-18	Hanley, Mary Ann	1855-05-18	Daniel Hanley & wife Mary Francis (formerly Smith)	Charles Alban Buckler Winefride Smith	Francis Chadwick
1855-08-12	Devlin, Elizabeth	1855-06-29	James Devlin & wife Mary (formerly Donovan)	John Harrington, Catharine Ellis	Francis Chadwick
1855-09-30	Hemmins, Elizabeth Mary	1855-08-27	John Hemmins & wife Mary (formerly Foy)	Michael & Ann Foy	Francis Chadwick
1855-12-02	Williamson, Alfred John	1855-10-23	Charles Williamson & wife Eliza (formerly Markham)	Thomas Markham, Elizabeth French	Francis Chadwick

ST IGNATIUS BAPTISMAL RECORDS, VOLUME 2
(PART OF A VOLUME ALSO INCLUDING CONFIRMATIONS, MARRIAGES AND BURIALS)

The previous nine entries are repeated at the start of the volume but are not repeated here.

Date of baptism	Person baptised	Date of birth	Parents	Godparents or sponsors	Priest officiating
1855-12-12	Oger, Mary Gertrude	1855-11-15	Alexander Oger & wife Mary (formerly Reynolds)	Joseph Richardson, Ann Wainwright	Francis Chadwick
1856-01-28	Smith, Frances Georgia	1855-12-29	Ambrose Smith & wife Frances (formerly Kimber)	Frederick & Winefride Smith	Francis Chadwick
1856-02-17	Haynes, Joseph James	1855-11-02	Joseph Haynes & wife Elizabeth (formerly Lamb)	Matthew Kaer, Elizabeth Field	Francis Chadwick
1856-08-22 private, d.o.d.	Sullivan, Thomas	1855-11-02	John Sullivan & wife Sarah (formerly Jones)	–	Francis Chadwick
1856-09-25	Grafton, Charles Hardman	1856-09-02	Charles Grafton & wife Mary Ann (formerly Woollett)	Charlotte Mary Waring, John Hardman (proxy Joseph Richardson)	Francis Chadwick
1856-12-02	Hanley, Edmund Augustus	1856-11-19	Daniel Hanley & wife Mary Frances (formerly Smith)	Joseph Richardson, Winefride Smith	Francis Chadwick
1857-01-14	Hemmins, William John	1856-11-21	John Hemmins & wife Mary (formerly Foy)	John Donovan, Sarah Foy	Francis Chadwick
1857-01-18	Hill, Mary Helen	1856-12-28	John Hill & wife Hannah (formerly Brennan)	Ambrose Smith, Eliza Field or French	Francis Chadwick
1857-04-22	Savory, Mary Ann	1856-03-29	William Savory & wife Mary (formerly Egleston)	John Murphy, Eliza Field or French	George Harper

Date of baptism	Person baptised	Date of birth	Parents	Godparents or sponsors	Priest officiating
1857-04-27	Smith, Cecilia Frances	1857-04-04	Ambrose Smith & wife Frances (formerly Kimber)	Richard & Margaret Ann Pritchard	Charles Blackett
1857-06-19 conditional	Frankham, Harriet Mary	1840-03-26	Thomas Frankham & wife Sarah (formerly Daery)	–	Charles Blackett
1857-07-05	Harrington, John	1857-06-25	Daniel Harrington & wife Eliza (formerly Leech)	John Murphy, Catherine Ellis	Charles Blackett
1857-08-30	Dixon, Matthew	1857-08-10	Matthew Dixon & wife Catherine (formerly Wright)	James Wright	Charles Blackett
1857-09-06	Devlin, Daniel	1857-08-02	James Devlin & wife Mary (formerly Donovan)	Michael Donovan, Mary Foy	Charles Blackett
1857-09-20	O'Shea, Ann	1857-09-10	James O'Shea & wife Eliza (formerly Burke)	John & Bridget O'Shea	Charles Blackett
1857-11-28	Shea, Joseph	1857-11-25	John Shea & wife Bridget (formerly Burke)	Eliza Shea	Francis Jarrett
1858-03-28	Daly, Cornelius	1858-03-19	Michael Daley & wife Mary Ann (formerly Jeneway)	John Murphy, Hannah Hill	Francis Jarrett
1858-06-13	Wallace, William	1858-05-31	Patrick Wallace & wife Catherine (formerly Hopkins)	Michael Daly	Francis Jarrett
1858-06-29	Grafton, Mary Angela	1858-06-13	Charles Grafton & wife Mary Ann (formerly Woolbeth)	James Gibson, Ann Hardman	Francis Jarrett
1858-07-25	Hanley, George Daniel	1858-07-11	Daniel Hanley & wife Mary Frances (formerly Smith)	Frederick Augustus & Julianna Lucy Smith	Francis Jarrett

Date of baptism	Person baptised	Date of birth	Parents	Godparents or sponsors	Priest officiating
1858-09-05	Duffy, Elizabeth	1858-08-27	John Duffy & wife Elizabeth (formerly Matthews)	Alice Hall	Francis Jarrett
1858-11-14	Whelan, Mary Ann	1858-10-23	Edwin Whelan & wife Margaret (formerly Murphy)	John Shea	Francis Jarrett
1858-12-12	Bergin, John Charles	1858-12-02	Thomas Bergin & wife Mary Ann (formerly Compton)	Margaret O'Brian	Francis Jarrett
1859-01-06	Hill, John Patrick	1858-12-18	John Hill & wife Ann (formerly Brennan)	James & Eliza O'Shea	Francis Jarrett
1859-02-13	Hemmins, Teresa	1859-01-04	John Hemmins & wife Mary (formerly Foy)	Michael Foy, Mary Finmore	William Knight
1859-04-24	Daley, Sidney	1859-04-03	Michael & Mary Ann Daley	John Murphy, Mary Savorey	Francis Jarrett
1859-04-22	Smith, Ellen Elizabeth	1859-03-28	Ambrose Henry Smith & wife Frances Ann (formerly Kimber)	Job & Teresa Turner	Francis Jarrett
1859-05-09	Harrington, Mary	1859-04-30	Daniel Harington & wife Elizabeth (formerly Leach)	John O'Shea	Francis Jarrett
1859-06-27	Savin, Charles Joseph	1859-05-28	Isaac Savin & wife Sarah Elizabeth (formerly Turner)	Charles Turner	Francis Jarrett
1859-07-10	Brown, James	1859-06-23	William Brown & wife Mary (formerly Kough)	Margaret Keen	Francis Jarrett
1859-08-14	Carter, Andrew Edwin	1859-08-02	Edwin Carter & wife Ann (formerly Lane)	Sophia Tyson	Francis Jarrett

THE REGISTERS

Date of baptism	Person baptised	Date of birth	Parents	Godparents or sponsors	Priest officiating
1859-09-11	Killian, Rose Ann	1859-09-05	James Killian & wife Henrietta (formerly Hogg)	Michael O'Hagan	Francis Jarrett
1859-11-06	Devlin, Margaret	1859-09-06	James Devlin & wife Mary (formerly Donovan)	James Kylien	Alexander Comberbach
1859-11-22	O'Shea, Bridget	1859-11-20	John O'Shea & wife Eliza (formerly Burke)	John & Elizabeth O'Shea	Alexander Comberbach
1860-01-09 conditional	Ikky, Winefride	1859-12-20	—	Mary Cunningham	Alexander Comberbach
1860-01-20	Hanley, James Alexander	1860-01-16	Daniel Hanley & wife Mary (formerly Smith)	Alexander Comberbach, Winefride Smith	Alexander Comberbach
1860-01-30 conditional	Nutt, Maria Anna	1859-01-30	Joseph Nutt & wife Mary Ann (formerly Olington)	—	Alexander Comberbach
1860-02-12	Whelan, Thomas Edward	1860-02-04	Edwin Whelan & wife Margaret (formerly Murphy)	John Wrangler, Harriet O'Niel	Alexander Comberbach
1860-02-22	Grafton, Francis Henry	1860-02-13	Charles Grafton & wife Mary Ann (formerly Woollett)	Thomas Woollett (proxy Charles Buckler), Frances Kelley (proxy Mary Waring)	Alexander Comberbach
1860-05-09	Holloway, Anthony Joseph	1860-03-28	George Holloway & wife Charlotte (fomerly Smith)	Mark Holloway, Antonia Holloway	Alexander Comberbach
1860-05-25	Ikky, Thomas	1860-05-17	John Ikky & wife Mary (formerly Abatt)	Bridget Ikky	F. Engelbert, a Franciscan Capuchin
1860-05-26	Daly, Mary	1860-05-11	Michael Daly & wife Mary Ann (formerly Janaway)	Mary Cunningham	F. Engelbert, a Franciscan Capuchin

Date of baptism	Person baptised	Date of birth	Parents	Godparents or sponsors	Priest officiating
1860-06-24	Dixon, Catherine	1860-01-02	Matthew Dixon & wife Catherine (formerly Wright)	William & Esther Weeklein	Alexander Comberbach
1860-06-29	Berry, William	1860-06-25	Henry Berry & wife Mary (formerly MacHenny)	J. Richardson	Alexander Comberbach
1860-06-29	Smith, Mary Clotilda	1860-06-19	Ambrose Smith & wife Frances (formerly Kimber)	Daniel Henry, Julia Smith	Alexander Comberbach
1860-08-05	Nolen, John Francis	1860-07-02	John Francis Nolan & wife Helen (formerly Macdonell)	Margaret Macdonell	Alexander Comberbach
1860-09-30	Connell, Thomas	1860-09-20	Thomas Connell & wife Mary (formerly Wilcokx)	Thomas & Mary Thase	Alexander Comberbach
1860-12-02	Murphy, Catherine Mary	1860-11-27	John Murphy & wife Catherine Mary (formerly Hannah)	Michael McGough, Harriet O'Neil	Alexander Comberbach
1860-12-31	Taylor, Henry	1860-05-23	Thomas Taylor & wife Catherine (formerly Northcot)	Elizabeth Murphy	Alexander Comberbach
1861-01-25	Hill, Thomas	1861-01-09	John Hill & wife Ann (formerly Brennen)	Elizabeth O'Shea	Alexander Comberbach
1861-01-31	Savin, Mary Elizabeth	1861-01-02	Isaac Savin & wife Sarah (formerly Turner)	Louisa Turner	Alexander Comberbach
1861-05-05	Harrington, Edward	1861-04-29	Daniel Harrington & wife Eliza (formerly Leech)	Edwin & Margaret Whelan	Alexander Comberbach

Date of baptism	Person baptised	Date of birth	Parents	Godparents or sponsors	Priest officiating
1861-06-20	Taylor, Joseph	1861-06-20	William Taylor & wife Elizabeth (formerly Dockworth)	Mary Williams	Alexander Comberbach
1861-07-28	Grafton, Henry Albert	1861-07-23	Charles Grafton & wife Mary Ann (formerly Woollett)	Thomas Woollett, Mary Newsham	Alexander Comberbach
1861-10-10	Smith, Isabel	1861-01-05	Mary Smith	Mary Cunningham	Alexander Comberbach
1861-11-11	Dennis, William	1861-11-07	William Barnes & wife Ann (formerly Newsham)	Helen Barnes	Alexander Comberbach
1861-12-19	Smith, John Alfred	1861-11-25	Ambrose Smith & wife Frances Ann (formerly Kimber)	William Hanley, Elizabeth Reave	Alexander Comberbach
1862-01-06	O'Shea, John Baptist	1861-12-27	John O'Shea & wife Bridget (formerly Burke)	William Hanley, Jane Hill	Alexander Comberbach
1862-01-09 conditional	Wheeler, Clara	1842-06-21	William & Mary Ann Wheeler	–	Alexander Comberbach
1862-02-16	Albino, Vincent, became a tramp	1861-07-14 Nottingham	Blasio Antonio Albino & wife Emma (formerly Glass)	Domenico Gargaro, Elizabeth Bray	Raphael Gorga, a Passionist priest
1862-03-23	Cox, Mary Ann	1860-02-09	William Cox & wife Mary Ann (formerly Dawson)	Martin Fitz Mauris	Alexander Comberbach
1862-03-23	Cox, William Patrick	1861-09-15	William Cox & wife Mary Ann (formerly Dawson)	Martin Fitz Mauris	Alexander Comberbach
1862-03-31	Mannion, Ann	1860	Michael Mannion & wife Fanny (formerly Green)	Michael Kelly, Mary Burk	Alexander Comberbach

Date of baptism	Person baptised	Date of birth	Parents	Godparents or sponsors	Priest officiating
1862-04-01	Mannion, William	1861	Michael Mannion & wife Fanny (formerly Green)	Michael Kelly, Sarah Kelly	Alexander Comberbach
1862-04-18	Cambell, Jane	1862-04-06	George Cambell & wife Mary (formerly Healy)	– McDurmond (f.)	Alexander Comberbach
1862-05-12	Riley, Henry	1862-04-04	James Riley & wife Ann (formerly Doweek)	Michael & Ellen Ralf	Alexander Comberbach
1862-06-22	Conley, Christopher	1862-05-16	Christopher Conley & wife Sarah (formerly Smith)	Fitz Morris [Fitzmaurice], Mary Stanley	Alexander Comberbach
1862-07-21	Biovois, Victor Celestin	1862-07-03	Victor Celestin Biovois & wife Ann (formerly Prew)	Harman Hettich, Mary Crips	Alexander Comberbach
1862-09-07	Owen, John Thomas	1859-12-21	John Owen & wife Ruth (formerly Harris)	Lavinia Harris	Alexander Comberbach
1862-10-19	Adams, Frances	1862-10-03	John Adams & wife Margaret (formerly Brenhem)	Mary Cunningham	Alexander Comberbach
1862-10-27	Seillier, Alexander Miles	1862-07-21	Alexander & Cecily Seillier	Mary Cunningham	Alexander Comberbach
1862-11-01	Taylor, Martha	1862-10-02	William & Elizabeth Taylor	Lucy Taylor	Alexander Comberbach
1862-11-10	Markham, Frederick William John	1862-08-04	Thomas Markham & wife Jane (formerly Soundy)	Eliza Williamson	Alexander Comberbach
1862-11-18	Tarbuck, Charles	1862-10-26 Exmouth	Catherine Tarbuck	Mary Cunningham	Alexander Comberbach
1862-12-14	Finnighan, Mary Ann	1862-11-23	John Finnighan & wife Elizabeth (formerly Nolan)	Jane Cunningham	Alexander Comberbach

Date of baptism	Person baptised	Date of birth	Parents	Godparents or sponsors	Priest officiating
1862-12-28	Dixon, James	1862-11-23	Matthew Dixon & wife Catherine (formerly Wright)	Christopher Wright, Jemima Hume	Alexander Comberbach
1863-01-26	Grogan, Thomas	1862-12-04	Thomas Grogan & wife Susannah (formerly Holden)	Josephine Savoury	Alexander Comberbach
1863-01-26	Berry, Mary Ann	1863-01-15	Henry Berry & wife Mary (formerly McHenrey)	Mary Ann Lens	Alexander Comberbach
1863-03-16 conditional	Tocque, Mary Ann	1842	–	–	Alexander Comberbach
1863-03-16	Hill, Marion Josephine	1863-03-19	John Hill & wife Ann (formerly Brennen)	Mary Barrett	Alexander Comberbach
1863-04-11	Fisher, Sarah Esther	1863-04-10	John Fisher & wife Elizabeth (formerly Symon)	Elizabeth Cooper	Alexander Comberbach
1863-05-01	Savin, Teresa Mary	1863-03-17	Isaac Savin & wife Sarah (formerly Turner)	William Turner, Mary Gilston	Alexander Comberbach
1863-05-21	Harrington, Daniel	1863-05-12	Daniel Harrington & wife Elizabeth (formerly Leech)	Timothy McCarthy, Margaret Keen	Alexander Comberbach
1863-07-13	Grau, Catherine Agnes	1863-06-27	John Martin Grau & wife Mary Ann (formerly Rowley)	Ann Mary Tocque	Alexander Comberbach
1863-05-13	Utton, Frederick	1863-05-01	Philip & Ann Sophia Atton	– Trinder	Alexander Comberbach
1863-07-20 conditional	Utton, Ann Sophia	1829-05-20	–	–	Alexander Comberbach

Date of baptism	Person baptised	Date of birth	Parents	Godparents or sponsors	Priest officiating
1863-08-03 conditional	Higgins, Elizabeth	–	–	–	Alexander Comberbach
1863-08-15	Utton, Helen Martha	1859-02-22	Philip Utton & wife Ann Sophia (formerly Trinder)	Mary Barrett	Alexander Comberbach
1863-08-15	Utton, William	1861-04-22	Philip Utton & wife Ann Sophia (formerly Trinder)	Helen Williamson	Alexander Comberbach
1863-08-15 conditional	Foy, Mary	1855	–	Elizabeth Buggins	Alexander Comberbach
1863-09-27	Cureton, John Rowland Wynn	1863-08-31	William Cureton & wife Ann (formerly Ward)	Charles Ellis, Margaret Young	Alexander Comberbach
1863-10-21	Smith, John	1863-10-16	John Smith & wife Ann (formerly Connell)	Mary Ann Smith	Alexander Comberbach
1863-11-30 conditional	Collin, James	1817 approx.	–	–	Alexander Comberbach
1863-11-30 conditional	Collin, Florence Mary	1863-10-12	–	Elizabeth Brown	Alexander Comberbach
1863-12-13 conditional	Johnstone, John Mary	1841 approx.	–	–	Alexander Comberbach
1864-02-06	Taylor, Catherine	1864-02-04	William Taylor & wife Elizabeth (formerly Duckworth)	Lucy Taylor	Alexander Comberbach
1864-02-13 conditional	Horne, Harriet	1837-09-14	Joseph Shayler	–	Alexander Comberbach
1864-03-02	Massie, Mary	1863-11-01	William Massie & wife Catherine (formerly Dayli)	Mary Cunningham	Alexander Comberbach

THE REGISTERS   137

Date of baptism	Person baptised	Date of birth	Parents	Godparents or sponsors	Priest officiating
1864-03-14 conditional	Louise, John Aloysius, non–Catholic minister	1834 approx.	–	–	Alexander Comberbach
1864-03-14	Greenoway, Sarah Anna	1864-01-04	Martha Greenoway	Mary Cunningham	Alexander Comberbach
1864-05-24	Buggins, Mary Emma	1864-05-22	John Buggins & wife Emma (formerly Fogg)	Mary Buggins (proxy Mary Elizabeth Reave)	Alexander Comberbach
1864-06-07 conditional	Trevor Lloyd, Thomas	–	Robert Lloyd	–	Alexander Comberbach
1864-07-12 conditional	Rainbow, Anna	1790 approx.	–	–	Alexander Comberbach
1864-12-30 conditional	Scully, Sarah	1799 approx.	–	–	Alexander Comberbach
1864-10-17	Ridgely, Henry	1854-09-22	William Ridgely & wife Sarah (formerly Walker)	Arthur Bovill, Mary Barrett	Alexander Comberbach
1864-10-17	Ridgely, Frederick	1857-04-14	William Ridgely & wife Sarah (formerly Walker)	Arthur Bovill, Mary Barrett	Alexander Comberbach
1864-10-21	Mannion, Louise	1863-11-09	Michael Mannion & wife Frances (formerly Green)	Catherine Seeley	Alexander Comberbach
1864-10-26	Carter, Francis	1858-10-05	William Carter & wife Emma (formerly Hall)	John Buggins	Alexander Comberbach
1864-10-27 conditional	Carter, Emily	1860-04-23	William Carter & wife Emma (formerly Hall)	Elizabeth Brown	Alexander Comberbach
1864-11-21	Hettich, Mary Louise Josephine	1864-11-06	Karl Hettich & wife Josephine (formerly Fortwengler)	Herman Hettich, Elisabeth Fortwengler	Alexander Comberbach

Date of baptism	Person baptised	Date of birth	Parents	Godparents or sponsors	Priest officiating
1864-12-04	Kelly, Edward	1864-11-20	Michael Kelly & wife Bridget (formerly Mooran)	George Seeley, Mary Burck	Alexander Comberbach
1864-12-16	Smith, Thomas James	1864-11-22	Ambrose Smith & wife Frances (formerly Kimber)	Charles Smallwood, Mary Barrett	Alexander Comberbach
1864-12-22	Carroll, Charles Owen	1864-11-22	Joseph Carroll & wife Mary (formerly Porteus)	Karl Hettich, Mary Barrett	Alexander Comberbach
1864-12-22	Carroll, Frederick Melhan	1864-01-01	Joseph Carroll & wife Mary (formerly Porteus)	Karl Hettich, Mary Barrett	Alexander Comberbach
1864-12-24 conditional	Hitch, Wortham Joseph Ignatius Loyola	1832 approx.	–	–	Alexander Comberbach
1864-12-26	Liston, Belinda Sarah	1863-06-26	William Liston & wife Sarah (formerly George)	Frederick Chambers, Sarah Marriott	Alexander Comberbach
1865-01-01	Adams, Margaret Mary Elizabeth	1864-12-01	John Adams & wife Margaret (formerly Brennen)	Sarah Marriott	Alexander Comberbach
1865-01-09 private	Smith, Mary Monica	1864-12-29	George Smith & wife Mary (formerly Davey)	Robert Davey, G. Winifride Hanley	Alexander Comberbach
1865-02-20 completion	Smith, Mary Monica	1864-12-29	George Smith & wife Mary (formerly Davey)	Robert Davey, G. Winifride Hanley	Alexander Comberbach
1865-01-08	Cureton, William Arthur	1864-12-26	William Cureton & wife Ann (formerly Ward)	Henry Ridgeley, Margaret Young	Alexander Comberbach
1865-02-20 conditional	Hall, Mary Louise	–	–	–	Alexander Comberbach
1865-02-15 private	Stowell, Thomas	1865-01-24	Thomas Stowell & wife Catherine (formerly Foley)	Francis Raab, Sarah Kelly	Alexander Comberbach

Date of baptism	Person baptised	Date of birth	Parents	Godparents or sponsors	Priest officiating
1865-09-11 completion	Stowell, Thomas	1865-01-24	Thomas Stowell & wife Catherine (formerly Foley)	Francis Raab, Sarah Kelly	Alexander Comberbach
1865-03-15	Savin, Agnes Eleanor	1865-01-31	Isaac Savin & wife Sarah (formerly Turner)	Mary Barrett	Alexander Comberbach
1865-03-31	Gibbons, James	1864-10-14	John Gibbons & wife Elizabeth (formerly Kiernan)	Mary Ann Tocque	Alexander Comberbach
1865-04-15 conditional	Powell, Edward	–	–	–	Alexander Comberbach
1865-04-19 conditional	Gulliver, Thomas	–	–	–	Alexander Comberbach
1865-05-20	Hooper, James William	1865-04-25	James William Hooper & wife Christine Frances (formerly Irvine)	Karl Hettich, Mary Barrett	Alexander Comberbach
1865-05-25	Dixon, Ann O'Bryan	1865-05-04	Charles James Dixon & wife Sarah (formerly Sanders)	William Bradley, Joanna Dixon	Alexander Comberbach
1865-06-04 conditional	Phillips, George William	1848 approx.	–	–	Alexander Comberbach
1865-06-08 conditional	Young, Edward	–	–	–	Alexander Comberbach
1865-06-08 conditional	Young, Louisa	–	–	–	Alexander Comberbach
1865-06-08 conditional	Young, Elizabeth	–	–	–	Alexander Comberbach

ST IGNATIUS BAPTISMAL RECORDS, VOLUME 3

Date of baptism	Person baptised	Date of birth	Parents	Godparents or sponsors	Priest officiating
1865-06-16	Hill, William George	1865-05-14	John Hill & wife Ann (formerly Brennen)	Mary Barrett	Alexander Comberbach
1865-08-05 conditional	Young, Charles	–	–	–	Alexander Comberbach
1865-08-05 conditional	Young, Eva Mary	–	–	–	Alexander Comberbach
1865-08-05 conditional	Young, Francis George	–	–	–	Alexander Comberbach
1865-08-05 conditional	Young, Mary Matilda	–	–	–	Alexander Comberbach
1865-08-05	Perry, Ellen	1865-07-14	Henry Perry & wife Mary (formerly McHenry)	Emma Buggins	Alexander Comberbach
1865-09-02	Miles, Henry	1865-08-06	Henry Miles & wife Bridget (formerly Hagon)	Sarah Marriott	Alexander Comberbach
1865-09-21	Mannion, Mary	1865-08-09	Michael Mannion & wife Frances (formerly Green)	Florence Parker	Alexander Comberbach
1865-12-27 conditional	Sessions, Carol Mary	–	–	–	Alexander Comberbach
1866-01-08	Pendgrass, Michael	1865-09-17	Michael Pendgrass & wife Margaret (formerly Smith)	Francis Young, Mary Brown	Alexander Comberbach
1866-01-06 private completion	Carroll, Catherine	1865-11-08	Joseph Carroll & wife Mary (formerly Porteus)	Louisa Carroll	Alexander Comberbach

THE REGISTERS

Date of baptism	Person baptised	Date of birth	Parents	Godparents or sponsors	Priest officiating
1866-02-23	Smith, Gertrude Mary	1866-02-04	George Smith & wife Mary (formerly Davey)	Edward Davey (proxy Charles Smallwood), Sarah Davey (proxy Winefride Smith)	Alexander Comberbach
1866-03-05	Markham, Elizabeth	1863-11-10	Thomas Markham & wife Sarah (formerly Soundey)	Ellen Williamson	Alexander Comberbach
1866-04-16	Nutt, Mary Jane	1866-03-02	Joseph Nutt & wife Mary Ann (formerly Olington)	Mary Ann Whiting	Alexander Comberbach
1866-05-05	Daly, Ann	1866-03-03	Michael Daly & wife Mary Ann (formerly Janaway)	Mary Young	Alexander Comberbach
1866-05-13	Harrington, Eliza Ann	1866-05-10	Daniel Harrington & wife Elizabeth (formerly Leech)	Mary Winfield	Alexander Comberbach
1866-05-30 conditional	Mannion, Frances	–	–	–	Alexander Comberbach
1866-05-03 conditional	Camponovo, Elizabeth	–	–	–	Alexander Comberbach
1866-06-21	Ellis, Esther Mary	1863-12-15	William Ellis & wife Mary (formerly Elliot)	Mary Young	Alexander Comberbach
1866-07-06 conditional	Hedges, Ann	–	–	–	Alexander Comberbach
1866-07-29	Kelly, Catherine	1866-07-20	Michael Kelly & wife Bridget (formerly Mooran)	James Conroy, Sarah Kelly	Alexander Comberbach

Date of baptism	Person baptised	Date of birth	Parents	Godparents or sponsors	Priest officiating
1866-07-22	Bryan, Joseph[1]	1866-08-13	John Bryan and wife Mary (formerly Mullis)	–	Charles C. Russell
1866-09-14	Francis, Francis Albin	1866-07-05	Thomas Francis & wife Cecilia (formerly Albin)	Francis Lumpé, Mary Clayton (proxy Ellen Powell)	Alexander Comberbach
1866 conditional	Sims, Mary	–	–	–	Alexander Comberbach
1866-09-20	Arches, Harriet	1865-11-09	Henry Arches & wife Mary (formerly Kidney)	Mary Bradley	Alexander Comberbach
1866 conditional	Baston, John	–	–	–	Alexander Comberbach
1866-09-25	Hooper, Elizabeth	1866-09-08	John Hooper & wife Christine (formerly Irvine)	Mary Ann Whiting	Alexander Comberbach
1866-10-08	Fisher, Mary Ann	1866-07-23	John Fisher & wife Eliza (formerly Seymour)	Flora Parker	Alexander Comberbach
1866-11-11	Conroy, Bernard	1866-11-05	James Conroy & wife Mary (formerly Burk)	Thomas Carroll, Ann Burk	Alexander Comberbach
1866-12-19	Dowlinn, Catherine	1866-10-15	John Dowlinn & wife Susan (formerly Boggs)	Catherine Parker	Alexander Comberbach
1866-12-23	Bradley, William Francis Charles	1866-12-02	William Bradley & wife Mary (formerly Barrett)	Charles Dixon, Elizabeth Field	Alexander Comberbach
1867-01-16	Miles, Bridget	1866-12-15	Henry Miles & wife Bridget (formerly Hagon)	Catherine Parker	Alexander Comberbach

1 Baptism and birth dates apparently transposed.

THE REGISTERS

Date of baptism	Person baptised	Date of birth	Parents	Godparents or sponsors	Priest officiating
1867-02-18	Barrign, Abraham Ignatius, became a tramp	1867-02-04	Martin Barrign & wife Catherine (formerly Kennedy)	Alfred Williams, Catherine Parker	Alexander Comberbach
1867-02-26	Smith, Helen Teresa	1867-02-05	George Smith & wife Mary Teresa (formerly Davey)	Edward & Sarah Davey	Alexander Comberbach
1867-04-04	Savin, Henry	1867-02-23	Isaac Savin & wife Sarah Elizabeth (formerly Turner)	Alfred Williamson, Mary Ann Turner (proxy Mary Turner)	Alexander Comberbach
1867-04-04 conditional	Whiting, James	–	–	–	Alexander Comberbach
1867-04-10 conditional	Cooke, Margaret	–	–	–	Alexander Comberbach
1867-05-12	Hettich, Charles Joseph Frederick	1867-05-07	Karl Hettich & wife Josephine (formerly Fortwengler)	Nicholaus Fortwengler, Mary Kirner	Alexander Comberbach
1867-06-17	Mannion, Ann Sarah	1867-05-24	Michael Mannion & wife Frances (formerly Green)	Bridget Macguire	Alexander Comberbach
1867-07-21	Dixon, Charles William	1867-06-13	Charles James Valentine Dixon & wife Sarah (formerly Sanders)	William Henry & Mary Jane Dixon	Alexander Comberbach
1867-07-29	Carter, William	1865-03-26	William Carter & wife Emma (formerly Hall)	Arthur Winfield	Alexander Comberbach
1867-08-04	Finnegen, Eliza Louisa	1867-07-07	John Finnegen & wife Eliza (formerly Troulin)	Mary Finnegen	Alexander Comberbach

Date of baptism	Person baptised	Date of birth	Parents	Godparents or sponsors	Priest officiating
1867-08-10	Payne, William, became a tramp	1867-07-27	Albert Payne & wife Emma (formerly Anderson)	Catherine Parker	Alexander Comberbach
1867-11-29	Biovois, Mary Teresa Martha	1867-11-16	Victor Celestine & wife Ann (formerly Prew)	Karl Hettich, Helena Dayman (proxy Flavia Dayman)	Alexander Comberbach
1867-12-22 conditional	Bayliss, Henry	–	–	–	Alexander Comberbach
1868-01-05	Conroy, Catherine	1867-12-26	James Conroy & wife Mary (formerly Burk)	Peter Keating, Bridget Maguire	Alexander Comberbach
1868-01-07	Nutt, Amos John	1867-12-06	Joseph Nutt & wife Mary Ann (formerly Olington)	Arthur Winfield	Alexander Comberbach
1868-01-31	Brine, Mary Ann	1868-01-13	John Brine & wife Mary (formerly Mullis)	Mary Winfield	Alexander Comberbach
1868-02-02	Carroll, Henry Joseph	1868-01-16	Joseph Carroll & wife Mary (formerly Porteus)	Arthur Winfield, Catherine Parker	Alexander Comberbach
1868-02-05	Francis, Frances Beatrix	1867-12-29	Thomas Brook Turner Francis & wife Mary Cecilia (formerly Elbane)	Josephine Lumble (proxy Mary Teresa Cleton)	Alexander Comberbach
1868-02-16	Dixon, Thomas	1868-01-19	Matthew Dixon & wife Catherine (formerly Madey)	Arthur Winfield, Elizabeth Baker	Alexander Comberbach
1868-03-29	Howell, Catherine	1868-03-07	Thomas & Catherine Howell	A. Williamson, Catherine Parker	Alexander Comberbach
1868-03-24 conditional	Lovett, Elizabeth Mary	–	–	Arthur Winfield, Catherine Parker	Alexander Comberbach

THE REGISTERS 145

Date of baptism	Person baptised	Date of birth	Parents	Godparents or sponsors	Priest officiating
1868-04-12 conditional	Parker, Robert	–	–	–	Alexander Comberbach
1868-05-10	Quarterman, Mary Agnes	1868-04-18	Alfred Quarterman & wife Agnes (formerly Freeman)	Arthur Winfield, Winefride Smith	Alexander Comberbach
1868-05-18	Allin, William	1868-05-01	Charles Allin & wife Julia (formerly Sweeney)	Catherine Parker	Alexander Comberbach
1868-06-12 private	Carter, Rose Edith	1868-04-13	William Carter & wife Emma (formerly Hall)	Catherine Parker	Alexander Comberbach
1868-08-02 completion	Carter, Rose Edith	1868-04-13	William Carter & wife Emma (formerly Hall)	Catherine Parker	Alexander Comberbach
1868-07-25	Savin, Julia	1868-07-01	Isaac Savin & wife Sarah (formerly Turner)	Mary Savin	Alexander Comberbach
1868-08-02	McCarthy, Mary	1868-07-31	Daniel McCarthy & wife Bridget (formerly Shea)	Catherine Parker	Alexander Comberbach
1868-08-15	Smith, Joseph Mary	1868-08-05	George Smith & wife Mary Teresa (formerly Davey)	John Damen (proxy Charles Smallwood), Teresa Smith (proxy Winifreda Smith)	Alexander Comberbach
1868-08-23 conditional	Bates, Emma Mary	–	–	–	Alexander Comberbach
1868-08-26 conditional	Taylor, George	–	–	–	Alexander Comberbach
1868-09-02	Tansey, John	1868-08-23	John & Elizabeth Tansey	Michael Mannion	Alexander Comberbach
1868-10-19 conditional	Beckingham, Sarah Elizabeth	–	–	–	Alexander Comberbach

Date of baptism	Person baptised	Date of birth	Parents	Godparents or sponsors	Priest officiating
1868-10-28 conditional	Kalen, James William	–	–	–	Alexander Comberbach
1868-10-29 conditional	Bates, William Frederick Joseph	–	–	–	Alexander Comberbach
1868	Bradley	–	–	–	–
1868-12-29	Gibbs, Sidney Cuthbert Ravenshoe	1866-02-26	Sidney & Decima Gibbs	Joseph & Rose Mary Richardson	James Nary
1868-12-29	Gibbs, Mary	1867-05-31	Sidney & Decima Gibbs	Joseph & Rose Mary Richardson	James Nary
1869	Mingaye	–	–	–	–
1869 conditional	Drury	–	–	–	–
1869 conditional	Kelly	–	–	–	–
1869-05-09	Hooper	–	–	–	–
1869-05-09	Drury, Elizabeth Sarah	1868-01-26	–	Rose Mary Richardson	James Nary
1869-05-20	Francis, Juliet Isabella	1869-05-01	Thomas Brooke Turner Francis & wife Mary Cecilia (formerly Albin)	Juliet Albin	James Nary
1869-05-05	Mannion, Catherine	1869-05-05	Michael Mannion & wife Frances (formerly Green)	Francis Raab, Mary Ann Whiting	James Nary
1869-06-06	Conroy, Mary	1869-05-27	James Conroy & wife Mary (formerly Burke)	George Seely, Bridget Maguire	James Nary

Date of baptism	Person baptised	Date of birth	Parents	Godparents or sponsors	Priest officiating
1869-06-13	Dixon, Daniel	1869-05-20	Charles James Valentine Dixon & wife Sarah (formerly Sanders)	Daniel Dixon, Elizabeth Field	James Nary
1869-06-20	Hill, Charles James	1869-05-29	John Hill & wife Ann (formerly Brennan)	Esther Wakelin	James Nary
1869-07-15	Thomas, Julia	1869-06-27	Edward Thomas & wife Bridget (formerly Noon)	–	James Nary
1869-07-15 conditional	Bates, Agnes Mary	–	–	–	James Nary
1869-07-18	Hettich, Ernest Louis	1869-07-05	Karl Hettich & wife Josephine (formerly Fortwengler)	John Schaefer, Leopoldina Kirner	James Nary
1869 conditional	Rymer, Emma	–	–	–	James Nary
1869 conditional	Dodd, Mary	–	–	–	James Nary
1869-11-14	Brien, William James	1869-09-07	John Brien & wife Mary (formerly Mullis)	Matthew Wangler, Lucy Cummings	James Nary
1869-11-22	Nutt, Frederick Charles	1869-07-16	Joseph Nutt & wife Mary Ann (formerly Ollington)	Bridget Ollington	James Nary
1869-12-21	Carter, Rose Edith Elizabeth	1869-10-28	William Carter & wife Emma (formerly Hall)	Mary Josephine Byrne	James Nary
1869-12-26	Meredith, Marianne	1869-11-10	John Meredith & wife Sarah (formerly Godfrey)	Marianne Meredith	James Nary

Date of baptism	Person baptised	Date of birth	Parents	Godparents or sponsors	Priest officiating
1870-01-03	Selvy, Elizabeth Ann	1869-12-06	Cecilia Ann Selvy (formerly Hughes)	–	James Nary
1870-02-04	Berry, Ernest John	1870-01-10	John & Mary Berry	Ann Nora Slattery	James Nary
1870-03-06	Dickson, Sarah Margaret	1870-02-05	Matthew Dickson & wife Catherine (formerly Wright)	James & Harriet Wright	James Nary
1870-03-27 conditional	Kearsey, Charles Norman	–	–	–	James Nary
1870	Berry, Richard Thomas	–	–	–	–
1870-04-18	Quarterman, Edith Angelina	1870-03-11	Alfred Frederick Quarterman & wife Agnes (formerly Freeman)	Ann Bateman	James Nary
1870-07-07	Keen, Catherine	1870-06-10	Elizabeth Keen	Catherine Young	James Nary
1870-08-15	Tilley, Catherine Mary	1870-07-12	William Tilley & wife Catherine (formerly Jackson)	Thomas & Jane Jackson	James Nary
1870-08-28	Harrington, Henry	1870-08-20	Daniel Harrington & wife Elizabeth (formerly Leech)	Victor Biovois, Anne Nora Slattery	James Nary
1870 conditional	Button, Louis	–	–	–	–
1870-09-17	Shannon, Thomas	1870-07-13	Thomas & Elizabeth Shannon	Anne Nora Slattery	James Nary
1870-09-17 conditional	Orpwood, Elizabeth	–	–	–	James Nary

Date of baptism	Person baptised	Date of birth	Parents	Godparents or sponsors	Priest officiating
1870-10-23	Hettich, Adolf Frederick William	1870-10-08	Karl Hettich & wife Josephine (formerly Fortwengler)	John Schwerer, Crescentia Martin	James Nary
1870-10-30	Bradley, Mary Louisa	1870-10-06	William Bradley & wife Mary (formerly Barrett)	Arthur Winfield, Mary Finmore	James Nary
1870-11-07 conditional	Bishop, Elizabeth	–	–	–	James Nary
1870-12-24	Smith, Gertrude Elizabeth	1870-12-05	George Bernard Smith & wife Mary Teresa (formerly Davey)	George Davey, Frances Mary Machell	James Nary
1871-01-01	Dixon, John Edward Valentine	1870-12-02	Charles James Valentine Dixon & wife Sarah (formerly Sanders)	Robert & Helen Horseman	James Nary
1871-01-10	Turner, Philip Lorymer	1870-12-15	Job Turner & wife Cicely Eleanor (formerly Lorymer)	Philip Witham, Mary Ann Turner	James Nary
1871-03-19	Meredith, John	1871-02-04	John Meredith & wife Sarah (formerly Godfrey)	Anthony Leonard Kirner, Mary Ann Meredith	James Henry Corry
1869 private	Fitzherbert, Catherine	1869-01-31	William Fitzherbert & wife Catherine (formerly Hood)	–	–
1871-05-21 completion	Fitzherbert, Catherine	1869-01-31	William Fitzherbert & wife Catherine (formerly Hood)	James Henry Corry, Mary Doran	James Henry Corry
1871-07-09	Bannister, Jane Ann	1871-06-14	Henry Bannister & wife Mary Ann (formerly Newcome) of 25 Thames Street	William Horwood	James Henry Corry

Date of baptism	Person baptised	Date of birth	Parents	Godparents or sponsors	Priest officiating
1871-07-16	Savins, William Turner	1870-11-09	Isaac Savins & wife Sarah (formerly Turner) of Kidlington	James Henry Corry, Lucy Baldwin	James Henry Corry
1871-08-27	Scott, Miles	1865-07-05	William John Scott & wife Elizabeth Susan (formerly Witherden) of Thame	William Joseph Nash, Mary Ann Frances Austin	Thomas Meyrick
1871-08-27	Scott, Mary Priscilla	1867-12-08	William John Scott & wife Elizabeth Susan (formerly Witherden) of Thame	William Joseph Nash, Mary Ann Frances Austin	Thomas Meyrick
1871-08-27	Scott, William Joseph Charles	1870-09-10	William John Scott & wife Elizabeth Susan (formerly Witherden) of Thame	William Joseph Nash, Mary Ann Frances Austin	Thomas Meyrick
1871-10-20	Cullen, John Edward	1871-09-28	John Cullen & wife Elizabeth Jane (formerly Bishop)	Francis & Mary Beirne (proxies Lucy Baldwin)	James Henry Corry
1871-11-05	Gara, Catherine Mary	1871-08-11	James Gara & wife Elizabeth (formerly Wells) of Oxford	Anthony Leonard & Crescentia Kirner	James Henry Corry
1871-11-19	Flynn, Mary, a traveller who became a tramp	1871-11-12	Peter Flynn & wife Mary (formerly Early)	James Henry Corry, Lucy Baldwin	James Henry Corry
1872-01-08	Welsh, Elizabeth	1871-11-30	James Welsh & wife Elizabeth (formerly Smith) of Oxford	James Henry Corry, Lucy Baldwin	James Henry Corry
1872-01-17	Quartermain, Edward Arthur	1871-12-04	Alfred Frederick Quartermain & wife Agnes (formerly Freeman) of Great Milton	James Henry Corry, Lucy Baldwin	James Henry Corry

Date of baptism	Person baptised	Date of birth	Parents	Godparents or sponsors	Priest officiating
1872-04-01	Nutt, Edith	1871-12-29	Joseph Nutt & wife Mary Ann (formerly Ollington) of Oxford	James Henry Corry, Bridget Stevens	James Henry Corry
1872-05-14 private	Savins, Winefride Eliza	1872-03-18	Isaac Savins & wife Sarah Elizabeth (formerly Turner) of Kidlington	James Henry Corry, Mary Ann Turner	James Henry Corry
1872-08-07 completion	Savins, Winefride Eliza	1872-03-18	Isaac Savins & wife Sarah Elizabeth (formerly Turner) of Kidlington	James Henry Corry, Mary Ann Turner (proxy Lucy Baldwin)	James Henry Corry
1872-08-25	Bradley, Elizabeth Clara	1872-08-01	William Bradley & wife Mary (formerly Barrett) of Oxford	Leonard Kirner, Clara Robinson	James Henry Corry
1872-09-08	Smith, William Bernard	1872-08-25	George Smith & wife Mary Teresa (formerly Davey) of Oxford	Frederick Augustus & Louisa Smith	James Henry Corry
1872-10-13	Hettich, Matilda Constance Mary	1872-10-01	Karl Hettich & wife Josephine (formerly Fortwengler) of Oxford	John Swerer, Mary Schlink	James Henry Corry
1872-11-03	Moore, James William	1871-07-05	James Moore & wife Jane (formerly Sothcott) of Bridge Street	Michael & Jane Wood	James Henry Corry
1872-12-18	Nutt, Frederick Charles	1872-12-04	Joseph Nutt & wife Mary Anne (formerly Ollington) of Oxford	Mary Murphy	Francis Goldie

Date of baptism	Person baptised	Date of birth	Parents	Godparents or sponsors	Priest officiating
1872-12-29	Macmanus, John Stephen	1872-12-23	Thomas Macmanus & wife Mary (formerly Holmes) of Oxford	Martin Holmes, Mary Harrington	John Morris
1872-12-29	Dixon, Sarah Beatrice	1872-12-17	Charles James Valentine Dixon & wife Sarah (formerly Sanders) of Oxford	Robert Horsman, Sarah Collingridge	John Morris
1873-01-05	Bliss, Walter Thomas	1873-01-01	William Henry Bliss & wife Mary Jane (formerly Wray) of Oxford	Joseph Richardson, Isabella Holden	John Morris
1873-01-19	Cornish, James Lander	1872-10-16	Lydia Cornish	Joseph Richardson, Isabella Holden	John Morris
1873-01-31 conditional	Moore, Mary Catherine	–	Of Oxford	–	Francis Goldie
1873-02-16	Smith, Charles William	1873-02-03	Frederick Smith & wife Louisa (formerly Button) of Oxford	Ambrose & Julia Smith	Francis Goldie
1873-02-16	Conway, Sarah Ann	1872-10-31	Patrick Conway & wife Sarah (formerly Rogers) of Oxford	Richard Carroll (proxy Louis Self), Helen MacVeigh	John Morris
1873-02-28	O'Callaghan, Augustus John Barry	1873-02-16	John Barry O'Callaghan & wife Mary Catherine (formerly O'Callaghan) of London	Michael O'Hagan, Mary O'Callaghan (proxy – Holden)	Francis Goldie

Date of baptism	Person baptised	Date of birth	Parents	Godparents or sponsors	Priest officiating
1873-03-09	Morley, Alice	1873-01-18	Richard Morley & wife Elizabeth (formerly Loder) of Oxford	Edward & Mary Harrington	John Morris
1873-03-11	Morley, Mary	1870-09-15	Richard Morley & wife Elizabeth (formerly Loder) of Oxford	Thomas Whiting (proxy Daniel Harrington), – Whiting	Francis Goldie
1873-03-23	Mannion, Frances Elizabeth	1873-03-10	Michael Mannion & wife Frances (formerly Green) of Oxford	James Conroy, Mary Whiting	William Cotham
1873-04-03	Gara, William Andrew	1873-04-11	James Gara & wife Elizabeth (formerly Wells) of Oxford	Anthony & Crescentia Kirner	Francis Goldie
1873-04-11	Palmer, Thomas	1873-02-09	Thomas Palmer & wife Margaret (formerly Dunn) of Oxford	Thomas Powell, Mary Harrington	Francis Goldie
1873-08-03	Cullen, Arthur Charles	1873-07-11	John Cullen & wife Elizabeth Jane (formerly Bishop) of Oxford	Francis & Mary Beirne	John Morris
1873-08-17	O'Brien, Frederick	1873-07-15	John O'Brien & wife Mary (formerly Morris) of Oxford	John Harrington, Mary Ann Smith	Alexander Diomede
1873-10-26	Kirner, Mary Ottilia	1873-10-11	Anthony Leonard Kirner & wife Crescentia (formerly Wangler) of Oxford	Anthony Kirner, Josephine Hettich	William Johnson
1873-11-16	Telfer, Alfred Charles	1873-08-29	William Telfer & wife Mary (formerly Badger) of Oxford	Thomas John Powell & Elizabeth Powell	William Johnson

Date of baptism	Person baptised	Date of birth	Parents	Godparents or sponsors	Priest officiating
1873-11-30	Conway, Catherine Margaret	1873-10-22	Patrick Conway & wife Sarah (formerly Rogers)	Thomas & Mary McManus	William Johnson
1873-12-08	Savin, Isaac Ernest Laurence	1873-10-30	Isaac Savin & wife Sarah Elizabeth (formerly Turner)	Joseph Taylor, Mary Powell	William Johnson
1873-12-18	McFie, Ann Agnes	1873-10-05	John Stewart McFie & wife Ellen (formerly Dashey)	William Berry, Jane Murphy	William Johnson
1874-01-04	Casey, Mary	1872-11-07	John Casey & wife Margaret (formerly Histon)	Catherine Keating	William Johnson
1874-01-18	King, Henry Vincent	1873-10-25	Henry King & wife Elizabeth (formerly Hand)	Thomas Hill, Charlotte Mary Waring	William Johnson
1874-01-18 conditional	King, Agnes Mary	1871-09-08	Henry King & wife Elizabeth (formerly Hand)	Thomas Hill, Charlotte Mary Waring	William Johnson
1874-01-21	Allen, Walter Andoenus	1874-01-02	Charles Allen & wife Julia (formerly Sweeney)	William Dennis Powell, Elizabeth Harrington	William Johnson
1874-02-08	McManus, James	1874-02-03	Thomas McManus & wife Mary (formerly Holmes)	Patrick & Sarah Conway	William Johnson
1874-02-16	Bliss, Cuthbert Godfrey	1874-02-09	William Henry Bliss & wife Mary Jane (formerly Wray)	Henry Charles Reader, Ann Ward	William Johnson
1874-03-08	McLoughlin, Ellen Agnes	1874-02-14	Patrick McLoughlin & wife Elizabeth Jane (formerly Curtis)	William Henry Bliss, Marian Brown	William Johnson
1874-03-08 conditional	Braine, James	1865-05-??	George & Eliza Braine	Thomas Samuel Whiting	William Johnson
1874-03-08	Braine, Charles	1867	George & Eliza Braine	Thomas Samuel Whiting	William Johnson

Date of baptism	Person baptised	Date of birth	Parents	Godparents or sponsors	Priest officiating
1874-03-08	Braine, Henry	1869	George & Eliza Braine	Thomas Samuel Whiting	William Johnson
1874-03-15 conditional	Bliss, Margaret Harriet	1867	–	–	William Johnson
1874-04-26	Dixon, Henry Thomas	1874-04-06	Charles James Valentine Dixon & wife Sarah (formerly Sanders)	Daniel & Sarah Dixon	William Johnson
1874-06-04	Smith, Herbert Augustine	1874-05-19	Frederick Augustine Smith & wife Louisa (formerly Button)	George Bernard Smith, Mary Teresa Smith	William Johnson
1874-07-12	Bradley, Reginald Thomas	1874-06-20	William Bradley & wife Mary (formerly Barrett)	Robert Hill, Eliza Williamson	Thomas Meyrick
1874-07-26	Horseman, Cecily	1874-06-18	Robert Horseman & wife Isabella (formerly Kearsey)	Ambrose James Collingridge, Helen Teresa Horseman	William Johnson
1874-08-16	Venables, Edward	1874-08-13	William Venables & wife Charlotte (formerly Boyall)	Thomas Edwards, Mary Moran	George Kingdon
1874-09-20	Roche, James Francis Michael	1874-07-20	James Roche & wife Mary (formerly Caselle)	Jean-Baptiste Bégéron, Mary Agnes Roche	William Johnson
1874-10-09	Draper, Arthur Francis Walpole	1874-09-11	Joseph Draper & wife Mary Jane (formerly Goodall)	William Alcock, Emma Bunn	William Johnson
1874-10-19	Lawrence, Charles	1874-10-10	William Lawrence & wife Mary Ann (formerly Macarthy)	Joseph & Mary Ann Shelley	William Johnson
1874-10-25	Conroy, Margaret	1874-10-19	James Conroy & wife Emma (formerly Turner)	William & Charlotte Venables	William Johnson

Date of baptism	Person baptised	Date of birth	Parents	Godparents or sponsors	Priest officiating
1874-10-27	Turner, Mary	1874-10-04	William Turner & wife Julia (formerly Case)	Charles Hanley, Mary Ann Smith	William Johnson
1874-11-08 Abingdon	Herman, – (f.)	–	–	–	–
1874-11-17	Brien, Mary Margaret Ann	1874-10-30	Mary Brien	Mary Ann Brown, Margaret Brien	William Johnson
1874-12-25	Long, Joseph	1874-12-18	Thomas Long & wife Catherine (formerly Begley)	Jane Collins	William Johnson
1874-12-25	Long, John	1874-12-18	Thomas Long & wife Catherine (formerly Begley)	Jane Collins	William Johnson
1875-01-24	Braine, Francis	1875-01-??	George & Eliza Braine	Thomas Samuel Whiting, Mary Helen Hill	William Johnson
1875-01-24	Braine, Joseph	–	George & Eliza Braine	Thomas Samuel Whiting, Mary Helen Hill	William Johnson
1875-03-19	Bliss, James	1875-03-14	William Henry Bliss & wife Mary Jane (formerly Wray)	Daniel Parsons, Mary Eliza Bliss	William Johnson
1875-03-19	Bliss, Basil	1875-03-14	William Henry Bliss & wife Mary Jane (formerly Wray)	Daniel Parsons, Mary Eliza Bliss	William Johnson
1875-03-28	Mannion, Eliza	1875-03-14	Michael Mannion & wife Frances (formerly Green)	William & Ann Mannion	William Johnson
1875-04-05 conditional Nazareth Ho.	Williams, Jessy Matilda	1873-03-29	Frances Williams	–	William Johnson

Date of baptism	Person baptised	Date of birth	Parents	Godparents or sponsors	Priest officiating
1875-04-05 conditional Nazareth Ho.	Williams, Emily Catherine	1871	Frances Williams	–	William Johnson
1875-05-06	Forshaw, Florence Eveline	1867-10-31	William Forshaw & wife Emily (formerly Osborne)	Mary Turner	William Johnson
1875-05-06	Forshaw, Arthur William	1869-04-18	William Forshaw & wife Emily (formerly Osborne)	William Turner, Mary Jane Murphy	William Johnson
1875-05-06	Forshaw, Harry Lionel	1870-12-10	William Forshaw & wife Emily (formerly Osborne)	John Forshaw, Mary Jane Murphy	William Johnson
1875-05-06	Forshaw, Louis Gerald	1872-12-01	William Forshaw & wife Emily (formerly Osborne)	Mary Jane Murphy	William Johnson
1875-05-06	Forshaw, Percy Osborne	1874-10-09	William Forshaw & wife Emily (formerly Osborne)	Mary Jane Murphy	William Johnson
1875-06-06	King, Emily Gertrude	1875-04-27	Henry King & wife Elizabeth Anne (formerly Bull)	John William Embury, Miranda Mary Joslin	William Johnson
1875-08-01	Conway, Lydia Winefride	1875-06-06	Patrick Conway & wife Sarah (formerly Rogers)	James & Emma Conroy	William Johnson
1875-08-08	Kirner, Mary Lena	1875-06-14	Leonard Kirner & wife Crescentia (formerly Wangler)	Anthony Kirner, Mary Schwerer	William Johnson
1875-08-19 conditional Nazareth Ho.	Dawson, Violet Vivian Mary Josephine	1874-03-21	– Dawson	Mary Jennings	William Johnson

Date of baptism	Person baptised	Date of birth	Parents	Godparents or sponsors	Priest officiating
1875-08-19 Nazareth Ho.	Doran, Mary Louisa	1871-05-27	William Doran & wife Louise (formerly Sherring)	Louisa Abbott	William Johnson
1875-09-08 conditional	Worney, Mary Ann	–	–	Lucy Andrews	William Johnson
1875-09-08 conditional	Worney, Adelaide	1870-12-25	–	Ellen Macarthy	William Johnson
1875-09-19	Dixon, Henry James	1875-08-26	Charles James Valentine Dixon & wife Sarah (formerly Sanders)	William Henry Dixon, Olive Dixon	William Johnson
1875-11-18 Nazareth Ho.	Lovegrove, Clara Mary Martha	1875-02-07	Mary Lovegrove	Mary Ann Hennings	James Hoever
1875-11-13	Kelly, Catherine	1875-11-12	John Kelly & wife Ann (formerly Bushnell)	Elizabeth Kelly	Francis Goldie
1875-11-28	Venables, William Edward	1875-11-12	William Venables & wife Charlotte (formerly Boyall)	James & Emma Conroy	Thomas B. Parkinson
1875-11-17	Young, Frederick John Percy	1875-11-08	Francis & Elizabeth Young	William & Frances Mannion	Francis Goldie
1875-12-29	Walsh, John	1875-12-23	James Walsh & wife Elizabeth (formerly Carpenter)	Jane Clarke	Francis Goldie

This volume continues with baptismal records for the church of St Aloysius Gonzaga, 1876–8, not transcribed here.

ST MARY THE VIRGIN, BAMPTON, BAPTISMAL RECORDS 1856–60

During its brief existence, the chapel at Bampton, in the Diocese of Birmingham, was served from nearby Buckland, in the Diocese of Southwark, later Portsmouth. This register was therefore deposited in the St Ignatius/St Aloysius archives to ensure that it stayed in the correct diocese.

Date of baptism	Person baptised	Date of birth	Parents	Godparents or sponsors	Priest officiating
1856-12-24	Bull, William Charles	1856-11-20	William Bull & wife Sophia (formerly Gosling)	Francis Gauci Azzopardi, Ruth Watts	Francis Gauci Azzopardi
1857-02-23	Cuddon, Gertrude Anne	1857-02-21	William Cuddon & wife Anna Maria (formerly Rumbold)	Francis Lambert (proxy William Cuddon), Sarah Lambert (proxy Anna Rumball)	Francis Gauci Azzopardi
1858-07-11	Cuddon, George William	1858-07-11	William Cuddon & wife Anna Maria (formerly Rumball)	Edward Aloysius Williams, Teresa Frances Butler	Daniel Donovan
1859-01-03	Bull, Giles Joseph	1858-10-26	William Bull & wife Sophia (formerly Gosling)	George –, Susanna Gosling	Daniel Donovan
1860-03-19	Cuddon, William	1860-03-15	William Cuddon & wife Anna Maria (formerly Rumbell)	Thomas Cuddon, Mary Cuddon	Daniel Donovan

CONFIRMATIONS: 1753, 1758, 1763, 1810, 1855, 1856 & 1873

Confirmands usually have a sponsor, whose role is similar to that of a godparent or baptismal sponsor. The confirmand chooses a confirmation name, which is usually an additional forename, typically that of a saint who will be their personal patron; or it can be an existing forename.

1753: People confirmed at Waterperry by the Right Reverend John Hornyold, Vicar Apostolic of the Midland District, 20 May 1753

Confirmand	Confirmation name
Padwick, Mary	Anne
Symkins, Elizabeth	Mary
Harding, Lucy	Barbara
Million, Mary	Anne
Waterhouse, Elen	Mary
Waterhouse, Hannah	Margaret
Hodgekinson, Joseph	John
Hodgekinson, Richard	Francis
Waterhouse, Cornelius	Josepth
Floyd, Hannah	Mary
Watts, John	Thomas
Walker, Joseph	Richard
Walker, John	William
Partloo, Elizabeth	Winefred
Young, Mary	Catharine

1758: People confirmed at Waterperry by the Right Reverend John Hornyold, Vicar Apostolic of the Midland District, 16 May 1758

Confirmand	Confirmation name
Bertie, Lady Maria	Lucy
Bertie, Lady Sophia	Mary
Coolin, John	Antony
Franklin, Robert	John
Dodswell, Richard	Silvester
The following sent by Mr Richardson[2]	
Baker, James	Matthew

---

2   John Richardson, priest at Britwell.

Confirmand	Confirmation name
Baker, Antony	John
Davis, Mary	Agatha
Floyd, Anne	Mary
Baker, Mary	Martha
Bagnal, William	Matthew
Bagnal, Charles	Joseph
The following sent by Mr Wells[3]	
Millman, Anne	Mary

1763: People confirmed at Waterperry by the Right Reverend John Hornyold, Vicar Apostolic of the Midland District, 22 May 1763

Confirmand	Confirmation name
Sutton, Mary	Anne
The following sent by Mr Brown[4]	
Walker, Mary	Anne
Herring, Susanna	Teresa

1810: People confirmed at St Ignatius chapel, St Clement's, by the Right Reverend John Milner, Vicar Apostolic of the Midland District, 15 July 1810.[5]

Confirmand	Confirmation name
Cole, George	Joseph
Copus, Francis	John
Copus, Thomas	John
Bernard, Joseph	John
Gosford, William	John
Salamoni, Martha	Mary
Salamoni, Martha junior	Mary
Salamoni, Elizabeth	Margaret
Salamoni, Lucy	Mary
Guilby, Mary	Ann

3   Gilbert Wells, priest at Dorchester.
4   Possibly William Brown, formerly priest at Britwell.
5   Original in Archdiocese of Birmingham Archives, reproduced by kind permission of the Catholic Family History Society from their volume *The Bishops' Register of Confirmations in the Midland District of the Catholic Church in England, 1768–1811 & 1816* (1999).

Confirmand	Confirmation name
Guilby, Ann	Mary
Savage, Susanna	Jane
Hicky, Elizabeth	Mary
Mulhern, Mary	Mary
Mulhern, Hanna	Mary
Clarkson, Susanna	Mary
Hastings, Frances	Mary
Evans, Mary	Mary

1855: People confirmed at St Ignatius chapel, St Clement's, by the Most Reverend W.B. Ullathorne, Bishop of Birmingham, 6 November 1855

Confirmand	Confirmation name	Patron
Donovan, Michael	Joseph	Ambrose Smith
Smith, Frances	Mary	Mary Smith
Wakelin, Esther	Mary	Mary Smith
Watts, Ann	Mary	Mary Smith
Dixon, Catherine	Mary	Mary Smith
Dixon, Matthew	Joseph	Ambrose Smith
Holloway, George, son of George	Ambrose	Ambrose Smith
Holloway, Mark	John	Ambrose Smith
Holloway, Mary	Elizabeth	Mary Smith
Holloway, Mary Ann	Elizabeth	Mary Smith
Holloway, George, son of William	Ambrose	Ambrose Smith
Bennett, Richard	Joseph	Ambrose Smith
Parker, James	Francis	Ambrose Smith
Williamson, Eliza	Mary	Mary Smith
Tyson, Agnes	Mary	Mary Smith
De Brion, Henry	Francis Xavier	Ambrose Smith
Sparks, George	Joseph	Ambrose Smith
De Brion, Eliza	Mary	Mary Smith

1856: People confirmed at St Ignatius chapel, St Clement's, by the Most Reverend W.B. Ullathorne, Bishop of Birmingham 3 June 1856

Confirmand	Confirmation name	Patron
Young, Edward	Edward	Daniel Hanley
Young, Charles	Charles	Daniel Hanley
Young, Francis	Francis	Daniel Hanley
Anstey, Joseph	Joseph	Daniel Hanley
Wangler, Matthew	Matthew	Daniel Hanley
Trinder, William	William	Daniel Hanley
Horseman, Robert	Robert	Daniel Hanley
Markham, James	James	Daniel Hanley
Smith, Frederick	Frederick	Daniel Hanley
Lovett, James	James	Daniel Hanley
Macarthy, John	John	Daniel Hanley
Williamson, Alfred	Alfred	Daniel Hanley
Edges, Edward	Edward Augustine	Daniel Hanley
Powell, Edward	Edward Mary	Daniel Hanley
Pole, Robert	Robert William	Foy
Hooper, James G.	James G. Hooper	Daniel Hanley
Anstey, Rose	Rose Anna Ann	Agnes Nind
Camponovo, Elizabeth	Elizabeth Camponovo	Agnes Nind
Whiting, Mary Ann	Mary Ann Whiting	Agnes Nind
Horne, –	– Horne	Agnes Nind
Holloway, Harriet	Harriet Holloway	Agnes Nind
Smith, Frances Ann	Frances Ann Smith	Agnes Nind
Hanley, Julia	Julia Hanley	Agnes Nind
Hanley, Mary Ann	Mary Ann Hanley	Agnes Nind
Taylor, Mary	Mary Taylor	Agnes Nind
Parker, Catherine	Catherine Parker	Agnes Nind
Parker, Florence	Florence Parker	Agnes Nind
Finnaghan, Mary Margaret	Mary Margaret	Agnes Nind
Williamson, Elizabeth	Elizabeth Agatha	Agnes Nind
Hill, Mary	Mary Hill	Agnes Nind
Mary Foy	Mary Elisabeth	Agnes Nind
Seassions, Caroline	Caroline Mary	Agnes Nind
Brown, Elizabeth	Elizabeth Brown	Agnes Nind

Confirmand	Confirmation name	Patron
Brown, Bridget	Bridget Brown	Agnes Nind
Macarthy, Mary Ann	Mary Ann	Agnes Nind
Keane, Elizabeth	Elizabeth Keane	Agnes Nind
Keane, Louise	Louise Keane	Agnes Nind
Pieck, Catherine	Catherine Pieck	Agnes Nind

1873: People confirmed at St Ignatius chapel, St Clement's, by the Most Reverend W.B. Ullathorne, Bishop of Birmingham, 23 February 1873

Confirmand	Confirmation name	Patron
Terry, Richard	Joseph	George Smith
Fitzherbert, William	Mary Joseph Aloysius	George Smith
Harrington, Daniel	Mary Joseph Aloysius	George Smith
Smith, John	Joseph Ignatius Aloysius	George Smith
Nutt, Joseph	Mary John Aloysius	George Smith
Kearsey, Charles	Mary	George Smith
Whiting, James Alfred	Joseph	George Smith
Hill, Robert	Patrick	George Smith
Bates, Frederick	Augustine	George Smith
Kirner, Anthony	Joseph	George Smith
Whiting, Thomas	Mary Ignatius Augustine	George Smith
Harrington, John	Joseph John	George Smith
Embury, John William	Charles Mary	George Smith
Hill, Thomas	Joseph Ignatius	George Smith
Smith, Francis	Joseph Aloysius	George Smith
Harrington, Edward	Mary Joseph Aloysius	George Smith
Taylor, Joseph	Mary John Aloysius	George Smith
Berry, William	Joseph Patrick	George Smith
Burnham, Henry	Joseph	George Smith
Hill, John	Joseph Aloysius	George Smith
Mannion, William	Joseph John Aloysius	George Smith
O'Bryan, John	Joseph Aloysius	George Smith
Stowell, John	Joseph	George Smith
Powell, Elizabeth	Agnes Magdalen	– Hanley
Moore, Laura	Mary Agnes	– Hanley
Moore, Jane	Mary	– Hanley

Confirmand	Confirmation name	Patron
Moore, Catherine	Agnes Joseph	– Hanley
Josslin, Mary	Mary Ignatius	– Hanley
Moran, Ann	Mary Agnes	– Hanley
Moran, Maria Mary	Agnes Elizabeth	– Hanley
Smith, Ellen	Agnes Mary	– Hanley
Smith, Cecily	Catherine Ann	– Hanley
Smith, Mary	Mary Agnes	– Hanley
Bates, Mary	Joseph Theresa Cecilia	– Hanley
Bates, Emma	Elizabeth	– Hanley
Fitzherbert, Agnes	Theresa Magdalen Cecilia	– Hanley
Young, Helen	Mary Agnes	– Hanley
Mannion, Ann	Mary Joseph	– Hanley
Hill, Marion	Agnes Magdalen	– Hanley
Bryan, Mary	Mary Magdalen Clement	– Hanley
Robinson, Clara	Mary	– Hanley
McLaughlin, Elizabeth	Mary	– Hanley
Mackay, Ann	Winefride	– Hanley
Ashley, Emily	Mary	– Hanley
Nutt, Mary Anne	Elizabeth	– Hanley
Harrington, Mary	Agnes Magdalen	– Hanley
Harrington, Elizabeth	Mary	– Hanley

MARRIAGES AT WATERPERRY AND ST IGNATIUS: 1758, 1771, 1809 & 1854–75

Abbreviations: s/o = son of; d/o = daughter of

Date	Groom & parent(s)	Bride & parent(s)	Witnesses	Priest officiating
1758-06-06	Bagnall, Charles, s/o –	Nicks, Elizabeth, d/o –	–	–
1771-02-10	Maloni, James, s/o –	Pratt, Elizabeth, d/o –	–	–
1809-10-09	Copus, Thomas s/o –	Bradly, Jane d/o –	–	James Leslie[6]
1854-09-08	Last, William s/o –	Clarke, Mary Ann of Bury St Edmunds, d/o –	–	Francis Chadwick
1856-08-03	Harrington, Daniel, of Bantry, Ireland, s/o Michael Harrington	Leech King, Elizabeth of Oxford, d/o Charles Leech	Stanislaus Pfaff of Oxford, Anna Watts of Oxford	Francis Chadwick
1859-10-30	Murphy, John, of Trinity, Ireland, s/o John Murphy	Sparing, Ann, of Leeds	Michael McGough, Elizabeth Gillingham	Alexander Comberbach
1860	Young, Brown, s/o Charles Young	Flint, Margaret (widow, formerly Ward) d/o Thomas Ward	Henry Waklin, Ann Ward	Alexander Comberbach
1862-01-16	Biovois, Victor, s/o Charles Biovois	Prew, Ann, d/o James Prew	James Howtens, Adeli Fortel	Alexander Comberbach
1862-01-20	McHugh, Christopher Henry, of Galway, Ireland, s/o Henry McHugh	Wheeler, Clare of Oxford, d/o William Wheeler	William & Susan Wheeler	Alexander Comberbach
1862-05-29	Hanley, William Henry, s/o Daniel Hanley	Smith, Eliza Winefride, d/o Ambrose Smith	Charlotte Morris, Frederick Smith	Alexander Comberbach

6 This marriage is found among the baptisms in the previous volume.

THE REGISTERS

Date	Groom & parent(s)	Bride & parent(s)	Witnesses	Priest officiating
1862-10-20	Cureton, William, s/o Benjamin Cureton	Ward, Ann, d/o Thomas Ward	Margaret Young, Thomas Ward	Alexander Comberbach
1864-01-18	Wehrly, Theodore, s/o Theodore Wehrly	Hettich, Stephanie, d/o Valentine Hettich	Karl & Joseph Herman Hettich	Alexander Comberbach
1864-02-14	Wormington, Charles, s/o William Worthington	Collin, Rose, d/o James Collin	Thomas Adams, Caroline Collin	Alexander Comberbach
1864-04-19	Le Boutillier, Philip, from Canada, s/o John Le Boutillier	Thorp, Susan Mary, d/o John Thorp	George Balleine, Henry Thorp	Alexander Comberbach
1865-02-15	Whiting, James Alfred, s/o Thomas Whiting	Tocque, Mary Ann Howes, d/o George Tocque	James Martin, Mary Rattledge	Alexander Comberbach
1865-04-24	Mingaye, Augustine Joseph, of Oxford, alias Richardson, s/o Joseph Richardson	Goodship, Emma, of Oxford, d/o Edwin Goodship	Daniel Hanley, Mary Ann Whiting	Alexander Comberbach
1865-09-12	Bradley, William, s/o John Bradley	Barrett, Mary, d/o James Barrett	Charles Forrest, Louisa Bradley	Alexander Comberbach
1867-06-07	Rouxel, Paul Antoine Charles Marie, s/o Paul Jean Marie Rouxel	Perquit, Felicité Josephine, d/o Alexandre Perquit	James & Mary Whiting	Alexander Comberbach
1868-06-23	Evans, Robert Claude, s/o James Clarence Evans	Hoy, Ellen Mary, d/o Jane Baslow Hoy	William Henry Warwick, Helen Gardner	Alexander Comberbach
1868-10-04	Rogers, Cheold, s/o John Rogers	Buons, Ann, d/o Michael Buons	John Lee, Julia Heulett	Alexander Comberbach
1870-09-18	Gara, James, s/o Andrew Gara	Orpwood, Elizabeth, d/o George Orpwood	Daniel Harrington, Eliza Ash	James Nary

Date	Groom & parent(s)	Bride & parent(s)	Witnesses	Priest officiating
1870-10-05	Smith, Frederick Augustine, s/o Ambrose Smith	Button, Louisa, d/o William Button	George Smith, Jane Blake	James Nary
1870-10-25	Davey, Edward, s/o George Davey	Turner, Teresa, d/o Job Turner	Job Turner, – Hanley	James Nary
1870-10-24	Cullen, John Blisby, s/o John Cullen	Bishop, Elizabeth Jane, d/o William Bishop	Thomas & Elizabeth Powell	J.P. O'Toole
1870-11-26	Kirner, Anthony Leonard, s/o Dominic Kirner	Wangler, Crescentia, d/o Kasper Wangler	Raphael Kirner, Eliza Ash	James Nary
1870-12-01	Simpson, Thomas, s/o Job Simpson	Morris, Sarah, d/o Thomas Morris	Daniel & Eleanor Hanley	James Nary
1871-10-24	Stevens, Henry, s/o John & Ann Stevens	Ollington, Bridget, d/o James & Margaret Ollington	Joseph Miles, Lucy Baldwin	James Henry Corry
1871-11-27	O'Keefe, Philip, s/o John & Mary O'Keefe	Gearon, Catherine, d/o John & Mary Gearon	Jane & Mary Gearon	James Henry Corry
1872-02-14	Conway, Patrick, s/o Michael & Mary Ann Conway	Daly, Sarah, d/o Joseph & Lydia Daly	Henry Stevens, Lucy Baldwin	James Henry Corry
1873-05-15	Holloway, Mark, s/o George & Charlotte Holloway	Fry, Mary, d/o Thomas & Mary Fry	Ambrose & Henrietta Holloway	Francis Goldie
1873-11-25	Conroy, James, s/o Patrick Conroy	Turner, Emma, d/o James Cowley	George Seeley of Oxford, Eliza Cowley of Oxford	William Johnson
1874-01-04	Horseman, Robert, of Marston, s/o Robert Horseman	Kearsey, Isabella Jemima, d/o David Kearsey	Ellen Horseman, Edwin Haynes	William Johnson
1875-12-01	Flynn, James, of Oxford, s/o John Flynn	O'Callaghan, Mary of Oxford, d/o Thaddeus O'Callaghan	William Venables, Mary Bradley	Thomas B. Parkinson

Two further marriages, both at St Aloysius, are recorded in this volume.

DEATHS AT WATERPERRY AND FURTHER AFIELD, 1700–79

Date	Name	Age	Burial date	Burial place
1700-09-26	Greeneawaye, Jeane	–	–	–
1700-08-??	Saunders, Mrs	–	–	–
1701-04-24	Eyston, George	–	–	–
1701-03-31	Day, Dame	–	–	–
1701-05-09	Matthews, Jeane, alias Hobby	–	–	–
1701-10-10	Brinkhurst, Mr	–	–	–
1702-05-27	Warren, Henry	–	–	–
1703-04-14	Powell, Mary	–	–	–
1703-04-17	White, Winefred (sister of Mary Powell)	–	–	–
1703-10-18	Allcock, John	–	–	–
1704-03-07	Martin, Mr	–	–	–
1705-06-21	Chamberlain, Anne	–	–	–
1706-06-21	Wignor, William	–	–	–
1709-11-03	Crompton, Thomas	–	–	–
1710-07-17	Brinckhurst, Mary, the younger	–	–	–
1713-07-18	Dormer, Lord	–	–	–
1713-07-25	Grimesditch, Mrs	–	–	–
1714-10-02	Kilby, Alicia	–	–	–
1714-10-17	Kilby, Jeane, daughter of Alicia Kilby	–	–	–

Date	Name	Age	Burial date	Burial place
1715-05-06	Belson, Mary	–	–	–
1715-10-09	Davy, Edward	–	–	–
1716-02-08	Webb, Agnes	–	–	–
1716-03-15	Grimesditch, Captain John	–	–	–
1716-04-21	Belson, Bridget	–	–	–
1716-05-22	Kimber, Thomas	–	–	–
1718-02-11	Christmass, Thomas	–	–	–
1719-01-26	Collingwood, Charles[7]	–	–	–
1719-06-06	Wollmer, Francis	–	–	–
1721-08-09	Belson, Maurice	–	–	–
1721-11-05	Eyston, Charles	–	–	–
1722-10-23	Padwick, Daniel	–	–	–
1726-07-20	Brinckhurst, John	–	–	–
1727-05-11	Bartlett, Mary	–	–	–
1727-11-17	Powell, Anne	–	–	–
1727-10-17	Curson, Sir John	–	–	–
1728-06-20	Christmass, Em. junior	–	–	–
1729-10-17	Abby, Thomas	–	–	–
1729-10-08	Malham, Mary	–	–	–
1730-05-03	Philips, James	–	–	–

7   Jesuit chaplain to the Powells at Sandford-on-Thames.

THE REGISTERS

Date	Name	Age	Burial date	Burial place
1736-01-10	Coles, Thomas	–	–	–
1736-03-01	Hooker, Margaret	–	–	–
1736-05-17	Springwell, John	–	–	–
1730-08-12	Powel[l], John	–	–	–
1738-04-05 at Kiddington	Gibson, Francis	–	–	–
1739-03-08	Latham, Richard	–	–	–
1741-06-02	Ingelby, Peter[8]	–	–	–
1742-08-26	Philips, Thomas	–	–	–
1744-03-23	Curson, Robert	–	–	–
1743-06-02	Christmass, Simon	–	–	–
1744-04-21	Winlow, Susan	–	–	–
1746-03-31	Clarck, James	–	–	–
1746-10-12	Curson, Lady, senior	–	–	–
1747-04-03	Perst, Anne	–	–	–
1747-07-10	Waterhouse, Francis	–	–	–
1747-08-28	Burrel, Thomas	–	–	–
1748-03-22	Stephens, Mary	–	–	–
1748-11-19	Hodskinson, Francis	–	–	–

8   Surname spelled variously, former chaplain to John Powell at Sandford-on-Thames and possibly chaplain to Sir Francis Curson.

Date	Name	Age	Burial date	Burial place
1750-01-26	Walker, Mary, senior	–	–	–
1748-10-22	Hooker, William	–	–	–
1750-05-01	Burrel, Mary	–	–	–
1750-05-29	Curson, Sir Francis	–	1750-06-07	Waterperry
1750-10-??	Walker, Nanny	–	–	–
1751-02-07	Hodsginson, James	–	–	–
1751-04-19	Lucas, John	–	–	–
1753-01-02	Hodskinson, Anne	–	–	–
1753-11-23	Whiteing, Mrs	–	–	–
1754-07-01	Waterhouse, James	–	–	–
1755-10-19 at Tusmore	Newton, William	–	–	–
1756-10-19 at London	Provel, Philip Carteret	–	–	–
1756-03-29 at Stonor	Stonnor, Bishop	–	–	–
1756-04-05 at Hendred	Ward, John	–	–	–
1756-09-25	Kimberly, James (stable boy)	–	–	–
1756-11-29	Hunt, Mary	–	–	–
1758-03-23	Barnes, James	–	1758-03-26	–
1760-03-29 at Oakley	Pim, Mary	–	–	–

Date	Name	Age	Burial date	Burial place
1762-10-06	Hodgekinson, John	–	–	–
1763-01-24 at Wheatley	Lawrence, Richard	–	–	–
1763-05-12 at Waterperry	Lee, Apollonia	–	–	–
1763-10-21 at Brill	Bikerstaff, Thomas	–	–	–
1763-10-02 at Noke	Parsloo, Frances	–	–	–
1764-04-02	Curson, Lady	–	1764-04-07	Waterperry
1764-05-09 at Waterperry	Waterhouse, Winefred	–	–	–
1764-09-18	Bagnall, Anne Ellen	–	–	–
1768-10-11	Yateman, Anne	–	–	–
1768-09-13 at Brussels	Woolfe, Charles of Haseley	–	–	–
1769-10-30	Hooker, Marguerite	–	–	–
1770-04-04	Waterhouse, Ann	–	–	–
1770-07-11	Nelson, William, former chaplain at Waterperry House	58	–	St Mary's CoE parish church, Waterperry
1771-01-08	Hodgkinson, William	–	1771-01-09	–
1771-01-16	Teynham, Lady	–	–	–

Date	Name	Age	Burial date	Burial place
1771-02-01 at Wheatley	Laurence, Margaret	82	–	–
1772-09-25 at Wheatley	Paddock, Mary	–	–	Wheatley
1776-08-03	Brinckhurst-Curson, Catharine	76	–	–
1777-10-09	Waterhouse, John	77	–	–
1778-11-08 at Barton	Butt, Thomas	48	–	–
1778-11-30 at Furz-hall, Essex	Cusack, Frances	66	–	–
1778-03-20 at Marston	Capè, Francis	74	–	–
1779-02-15 approx. at Oxford	Blackwell, Mrs	–	–	–

No further death entries in this first volume, apart from the first seven below, which are the earliest for the chapel of St Ignatius.

DEATHS AND BURIALS IN THE REGISTERS OF THE CHAPEL OF ST IGNATIUS, 1798, 1807, 1819 and 1854–75

Date of death	Name of deceased	Age	From	Burial date	Cemetery or other burial place	Last rites	Priest officiating
–	Platt, Charles, son of Robert & Mary Platt	–	–	–	St Ignatius, confessional	–	–
–	Platt, Sarah, daughter of Robert & Mary Platt	–	–	–	St Ignatius, confessional	–	–
1798-02-21	Dwyer, Francis, gardener to William Fermor Esq.	–	Ireland	1798-10-24	St Ignatius burying ground, first burial	–	–
–	Hothersall, Revd William, assistant priest at St Ignatius	–	–	–	St Ignatius, in quire towards garden	–	–
–	Leslie, Revd Charles, builder of St Ignatius and first priest in charge	–	–	–	St Ignatius, in quire near pulpit	–	–
1807	OConnell, Mrs	–	–	–	St Ignatius, in chapel	–	–
1807	Machenry, Mrs	–	–	–	St Ignatius, in burying ground	–	–

The following entry of death is in the first volume of baptisms at St. Ignatius.

Date of death	Name of deceased	Age	From	Burial date	Cemetery or other burial place	Last rites	Priest officiating
1819-10-22	Reade, Sir Richard	–	Ireland	1819-10-22	St Ignatius chapel	√	Robert Newsham

DEATHS AT ST IGNATIUS 1854–77 (PART OF THE VOLUME ENTITLED BAPTISMS, CONFIRMATIONS, MARRIAGES AND DEATHS AT ST. IGNATIUS 1854–77)

No other death or burial records for St Ignatius are known prior to those listed below.

Date of death	Name of deceased	Age	From	Burial date	Cemetery or other burial place	Last rites	Priest officiating
1854-05-17	Bryan, John	22	Ireland	–	Headington workhouse	√	Francis Chadwick
1854-10-04	Dorsett, Hannah	29	Kidlington	1854-10-06	Jericho	√	Francis Chadwick
1854-10-16	Lacy, Catherine	–	Ireland	1854-10-17	Jericho	√	Francis Chadwick
1854-10-24	Dixon, Ellen	–	Oxford	1854-10-26	Oxford workhouse	√	Francis Chadwick
1854-12-27	Mahieu, Amand	–	–	–	Sandford	–	Francis Chadwick
1855-02-14	Jarvis, Edward	–	Oxford	–	–	√	Francis Chadwick
1855-03-14	Tyson, Francis	2	Oxford	–	–	–	Francis Chadwick
1855-03-23	Bennett, James	–	Oxford	–	–	–	Francis Chadwick
1855-05-12	Tyson, Hugh	–	Oxford	1855-05-14	–	√	Francis Chadwick
1855-09-28	Richardson, Ann	–	Oxford	–	–	√	Francis Chadwick
1856-02-17	Haynes, Joseph James	1	Marston	–	–	–	Francis Chadwick
1856-06-05	Markham, John	–	Oxford	1856-06-11	St Clement's	√	Francis Chadwick
1856-05-22	Smith, Helen	21	Oxford	–	Jericho	√	Francis Chadwick
1856-07-01	Pfaff, Fidel	22	Friburg	1856-07-04	St Clement's	√	Francis Chadwick
1856-07-19	Smith, Ann	–	Kidlington	1856-07-22	Kidlington	√	Francis Chadwick
1856-08-14	Holloway, Thomas	18	Garsington	1856-08-18	Garsington	√	Francis Chadwick
1856-08-25	Sullivan, Thomas	3	Oxford	1856-08-27	Jericho	–	Francis Chadwick

THE REGISTERS

Date of death	Name of deceased	Age	From	Burial date	Cemetery or other burial place	Last rites	Priest officiating
1857-01-29	Burel, Eliza	30	[Le] Havre	1857-01-31	Jericho	√	Francis Chadwick
1857-02-08	Wainwright, Ann	58	Oxford	1857-02-14	Radford	√	Francis Chadwick
1857-03-05	Chadwick, Francis (priest)	56	Oxford	1857-03-09	St Ignatius cemetery	√	William Johnson
There are no entries for the next 32 months: possibly four pp. missing
1859-11-19	Curtis, John	82	Charlton	1859-11-23	Hethe, near Bicester	√	Alexander Comberbach
1860-01-23	Hanley, Mary	42	Oxford	1859-01-27	Abingdon	√	Alexander Comberbach
1860-01-26	Tyson, L. (f.)	37	Oxford	1860-01-29	Jericho	√	Alexander Comberbach
1860-02-19	Hanley, James Alexander	36 days	Oxford	1860-02-22	Abingdon	–	Alexander Comberbach
1860-06-28	O'Hagan, Michael	–	Oxford	1860-07-01	Jericho	√	Alexander Comberbach
1860-06-28	Von Stockum, Frederick Oswald Joseph	55	Düsseldorf	1860-08-17	Jericho	√	Alexander Comberbach
1860-11-16	Morgan, William	45	Isle of Man	1860-11-20	Jericho	√	Alexander Comberbach
1861-01-12	Jarvis, Alice	78	Oxford	1861-01-16	Jericho	√	Alexander Comberbach
1861-01-13	Grafton, Francis Henry	11 months	Oxford	1861-01-16	St Giles', Oxford	–	Alexander Comberbach

Date of death	Name of deceased	Age	From	Burial date	Cemetery or other burial place	Last rites	Priest officiating
1861-01-28	Twycross, Isaac	84	Oxford	1861-01-31	St Clement's	√	Alexander Comberbach
1861-02-26	Williamson, Eliza	43	Oxford	1861-03-06	St Clement's	√	Alexander Comberbach
1861-06-12	Holloway, Ann	7	Garsington	1861-06-17	Abingdon	√	Alexander Comberbach
1861-06-15	Holloway, William	7	Garsington	1861-06-17	Abingdon	√	Alexander Comberbach
1861-09-13	Nelly, L. (m.)	47	Banbury	1861-09-13	Jericho	√	Alexander Comberbach
1861-09-06	Wangler, Lucas	42	Enderzaten[9]	1861-09-10	Abingdon	√	Alexander Comberbach
1861-10-18	Madewright, Mary	55	–	1861-10-23	St Thomas's, Oxford	√	Alexander Comberbach
1861-12-13	Grafton, Charles	51	Oxford	1861-12-13	St Giles', Oxford	√	Alexander Comberbach
1862-01-10	Crips, Mary Ann	59	Deddington	1862-01-14	Jericho	√	Alexander Comberbach
1861	Pfaff, Joseph	41	Neesbach[10]	–	–	–	Alexander Comberbach

9 Hinterzarten, near Freiburg, Germany.
10 Nussbach, near Oberkirch, Germany.

Date of death	Name of deceased	Age	From	Burial date	Cemetery or other burial place	Last rites	Priest officiating
1862-05-18	Lovatt. Mary	15	Wheatley	1862-05-22	Wheatley	√	Alexander Comberbach
1862-08-13	Curtis, Augustus John	53	Charlton-on-Otmoor	1862-08-17	Hethe, near Bicester	–	Alexander Comberbach
1862-10-30	Markham, Thomas	78	Oxford	1862-11-04	St Thomas's, Oxford	√	Alexander Comberbach
1862-04-30	Hemmins, William John	8	Oxford	1862-05-06	St Clement's	√	Alexander Comberbach
1862-11-30	Gillingham, Elizabeth	58	Oxford	1862-12-05	Abingdon	√	Alexander Comberbach
1862-12-18	Fidler, Elizabeth	74	Witney	1862-12-22	Witney	√	Alexander Comberbach
1863-03-02	Beale, John Arthur	31	Oxford	1863-03-09	Abingdon	√	Alexander Comberbach
1863-03-14	Humphris, William	79	Witney	1863-03-18	–	–	Alexander Comberbach
1863-04-21	West, Daniel	44	Woolhampton	1863-04-24	Littlemore	√	Alexander Comberbach
1863-08-28	Utton, Ann Sophia	34	Headington	1863-09-02	Headington	√	Alexander Comberbach
1863-11-23	Lovett, Elizabeth	47	Wheatley	1863-11-26	Wheatley	√	Alexander Comberbach
1864-02-08	Slate, Adelaide	70	Oxford	1864-01-12	Jericho	√	Alexander Comberbach

Date of death	Name of deceased	Age	From	Burial date	Cemetery or other burial place	Last rites	Priest officiating
1864-02-08	Taylor, Catherine	4 days	Oxford	1864-02-10	St Aldate's, Oxford	–	Alexander Comberbach
1864-04-17	Roach, John	22	Cork	1864-04-20	St Thomas's, Oxford	√	Alexander Comberbach
1864-05-24	Lovett, Thomas	15	Headington	1864-05-27	Headington	√	Alexander Comberbach
1864-06-28	Cossar, George	50	Oxford	1864-06-30	Hethe, near Bicester	√	Alexander Comberbach
1864-07-09	Jeffery, William	50	Old Wardour	1864-07-13	Old Wardour	√	Alexander Comberbach
1864-08-26	Collin, James	47	Oxford	1864-08-28	Jericho	√	Alexander Comberbach
1864-09-16	Paddey, John	33	Woolhampton	1864-09-19	St Thomas's, Oxford	–	Alexander Comberbach
1864-10-09	Hickey, Thomas	68	Oxford	1864-10-13	Osney	√	Alexander Comberbach
1864-10-12	Scully, Thomas	68	Cork	1864-10-18	St Ebbe's, Oxford	√	Alexander Comberbach
1864-10-16	Smith, Ambrose	73	Oxford	1864-10-20	Abingdon	√	Alexander Comberbach
1864-11-13	Foy, William	93	Oxford	1864-11-17	St Clement's	√	Alexander Comberbach
1864-11-17	Lamb, Patrick	63	Oxford	1864-11-20	St Clement's	√	Alexander Comberbach

Date of death	Name of deceased	Age	From	Burial date	Cemetery or other burial place	Last rites	Priest officiating
1864-12-27	Hooper, Mary	3	Oxford	1865-01-01	St Clement's	√	Alexander Comberbach
1865-01-27	McHale, John	24	– soldier	1865-01-31	Jericho	√	Alexander Comberbach
1865-04-19	MacCarthy, Mary Ann	13	Banbury	1865-04-26	Jericho	√	Alexander Comberbach
1865-05-17	Tinder, Ann	77	Oxford	1865-05-20	Headington	√	Alexander Comberbach
1865-05-31	Coleman, Ann	65	Oxford	1865-06-05	Summertown	√	Alexander Comberbach
1865-06-30	Tyson, Catherine	24	Oxford	1865-07-04	St Clement's	√	Alexander Comberbach
1865-08-19	Hancock, Thomas	58	Banbury	1865-08-26	Banbury	√	Alexander Comberbach
1865-10-31	Hanley, Teresa	15	Oxford	1865-11-04	Abingdon	√	Alexander Comberbach
1865-10-24	Savoury, Mary	42	Oxford	1865-10-28	–	√	Alexander Comberbach
1866-02-09	Seeley, Catherine	45	Oxford	1866-02-13	Abingdon	√	Alexander Comberbach
1866	Smith, Gertrude Mary	–	Oxford	1866	Abingdon	–	Alexander Comberbach
1866-04-16	Grafton, Mary Frances	83	Oxford	1866-04-21	St Giles', Oxford	√	Alexander Comberbach

Date of death	Name of deceased	Age	From	Burial date	Cemetery or other burial place	Last rites	Priest officiating
1866-05-20	Daly, Ann	2 months	Oxford	1866-05-23	St Thomas's, Oxford	–	Alexander Comberbach
1866-05-28	Gulliver, Thomas	68	Woodstock	1866-05-31	St Clement's	√	Alexander Comberbach
1866-06-14	Baston, Teresa	28	East Hendred	1866-06-17	St Thomas's, Oxford	√	Alexander Comberbach
1866-06-24	Pendergrass, Michael	23	Ireland	1866-06-28	St Thomas's, Oxford	√	Alexander Comberbach
1866-07-07	Dagnall, Winefride	60	East Hendred	1866-07-12	Littlemore	√	Alexander Comberbach
1866-09-30	Ragen, Edward	30	Northampton	1866-10-02	St Thomas's, Oxford	–	Alexander Comberbach
1866-11-08	Sims, Mary	43	Oxford	1866-11-12	St Clement's	√	Alexander Comberbach
1866-12-03	Smiley, William	23	Dublin	1866-12-07	St Clement's	√	Alexander Comberbach
1866-12-20	Baston, John	31	Oxford	1866-12-23	St Thomas's, Oxford	√	Alexander Comberbach
1867-03-04	Ahern, John	50	Ireland	1867-03-09	Jericho	√	Alexander Comberbach
1867-05-12	McMahon, Patrick	28	Ireland	1867-05-17	St Clement's	√	Alexander Comberbach
1867-05-31	Hemmins, Mary	37	Oxford	1867-06-05	St Clement's	√	Alexander Comberbach

THE REGISTERS

Date of death	Name of deceased	Age	From	Burial date	Cemetery or other burial place	Last rites	Priest officiating
1867-05-29	Savin, Henry	3 months	–	1867-06-03	–	–	Alexander Comberbach
1867-03-27	Parker, Mary	60	Oxford	1867-03-30	Holywell	–	Alexander Comberbach
1868-02-10	Sheea, Owen	–	–	1868-02-14	St Thomas's, Oxford	–	Alexander Comberbach
1868-03-04	Roche, Agnes	74	Cork [Ireland]	1868-03-09	Cowley	√	Alexander Comberbach
1868-03-08	Grafton, Mary Ann	47	–	1868-03-12	St Giles', Oxford	–	Alexander Comberbach
1868-05-06	Anstey, Rose Ann	70	Oxford	1868-05-09	Cowley	√	Alexander Comberbach
1868-06-05	Cooke, Margaret	64	Oxford	–	St Thomas's, Oxford	–	Alexander Comberbach
1868-09-13	Taylor, George	62	Oxford	1868-09-18	St Clement's	√	Alexander Comberbach
There are no entries for the next 33 months: possibly four pp. missing						
1871-06-16	Dockery, Thomas	45?	St Ebbe's St, Oxford	1871-06-20	'the public cemetery'	√	James Henry Corry
1871-07-01	Foy, Michael	76	St Clement's	1871-07-04	'the public cemetery'	√	James Henry Corry
1871-08-14	Collingridge, John	80	Marston	1871-08-19	Marston	√	James Henry Corry
1871-08-17	Mullen, Anthony	23	St Thomas's, Oxford	1871-08-21	'the public cemetery'	–	James Henry Corry
1871-09-09	Bliss, Jane Monk	78	Oxford	1871-09-15	Abingdon RC	√	James Henry Corry

Date of death	Name of deceased	Age	From	Burial date	Cemetery or other burial place	Last rites	Priest officiating
1871-12-13	Foy, William	44	Oxford	1871-12-16	'the public cemetery'	√	James Henry Corry
1871-12-18	Bateman, Eliza	–	Marston	1871-12-21	Marston	√	James Henry Corry
1872-04-23	Smallwood, Charles	24	Oxford	1871-04-26	Abingdon RC	–	James Henry Corry
1872-06-25	Dayman, Flavia	73	Oxford	1872-06-28	Abingdon RC	√	James Henry Corry
1872-11-17	Ellis, Charles	65	Oxford	1872-11-21	'the public cemetery'	–	John Morris
1872-12-23	O'Brien, Jane	55	Freeland	–	Freeland	–	John Morris
1873-02-02	May, Ellen	75	Market Harborough	1873-02-05	St Thomas's, Oxford	√	John Morris
1873-02-06	Hedges, David	57	Oxford	1873-02-11	Abingdon RC	√	John Morris
1873-02-15	Bliss, Walter Thomas	6 weeks	Oxford	1873-02-19	Abingdon RC	–	John Morris
1873-02-21	Smith, William Bernard	6 months	Oxford	1873-02-25	Abingdon RC	–	John Morris
1873-03-22	Wright, Christopher	73	Mullingar	–	–	–	–
1873-03-27	Adams, Thomas	–	Oxford	–	–	–	–
1873-09-16	Kelly, James	–	–	–	–	–	–
1873-09-28	Perret, Mary	–	Oxford	1873-10-02	Dorchester RC	√	John Morris
1873-10-02	Burnhill, Catherine	84	Oxford	1873-10-06	Abingdon RC	√	William Johnson
1873-11-??	Hanley, Winefride	84	Walton Street, Oxford	1873-11-13	Abingdon RC	√	William Johnson
1873-12-18	Miles, Catherine	40	Caroline Street, St Clement's	1873-12-21	Abingdon RC	√	William Johnson

Date of death	Name of deceased	Age	From	Burial date	Cemetery or other burial place	Last rites	Priest officiating
1874-01-03	Kettle, Elizabeth	–	Jericho	1874-01-06	Jericho	√	William Johnson
1874-05-05	Berry, William	–	Jericho	1874-05-09	St Thomas's, Oxford	–	William Johnson
1874-04-30	Hettich, Karl	40	St Clement's	1874-05-02	St Clement's	–	William Johnson
1874-08-12	Walford, Mary Ann	78	St Giles' Road West, Oxford	1874-08-15	Jericho	√	William Johnson
1874-08-23	Field, Elizabeth	63	Holywell	1874-08-26	Abingdon RC	√	William Johnson
1874-09-19	Gearon, John	69	St Giles, Oxford	1874-09-23	Jericho	√	William Johnson
1874-11-17	Camponovo, Amyda	69	Cowley Union[11]	1874-11-22	St Thomas's, Oxford	√	William Johnson
1874-12-24	Kavanagh, William	–	Macelerfeelt[12]	1874-12-29	Shipton-on-Cherwell	–	William Johnson
1874-12-23	Kennedy, Thomas	–	Cowley	–	Shipton-on-Cherwell	–	William Johnson
1874-12-24	Sullivan, Michael	80	Wheatley	1874-12-28	Wheatley	–	William Johnson
1875-01-10	Smith, Mary Teresa	–	Beaumont Street, Oxford	1875-01-15	Abingdon RC	√	William Johnson
1875-01-13	Saltmarsh, Amy (Amata)	91	Woodstock	1875-01-16	Woodstock	√	William Johnson
1875-01-24	Gane, Eliza	35	Headington	1875-01-26	Headington	√	William Johnson
1875-03-29	Smith, Mary	74	Walton Street, Oxford	1875-04-03	Headington	√	William Johnson

11 The Union workhouse.
12 Magherafelt, Ireland.

Date of death	Name of deceased	Age	From	Burial date	Cemetery or other burial place	Last rites	Priest officiating
1875-07-01	Veal, John	–	Littlemore asylum	1875-07-05	Littlemore	√	William Johnson
1875-11-05	Mannion, Mary	10	St Catherine Street, Oxford	1875-11-10	St Clement's	√	James Hoever

Further entries in this volume continue to March 1877, but are not included here because they were made after the transfer to St Aloysius.

CONVERSIONS 1872–75

RIP = Rest in Peace, indicating a deathbed conversion.
Nazareth House = a Catholic alternative to the workhouse, opened in 1875 and run by the Sisters of Nazareth.
Formerly = former surname, usually a maiden name but sometimes a former married name.
As the church of St Aloysius Gonzaga was opened in 1875, some or all of the later conversions listed here may have occurred there.

Date of conditional baptism	Name of convert	Date of birth	Parents	Spouse	Priest officiating
1872-10-13	Ashley, Emily, of Oxford	–	Thomas Seddington & wife Ann (formerly Hesell)	Henry John Ashley	John Morris
1872-11-10	Ashley, Edward Henry	1867-03-05	Henry John Ashley & wife Emily (formerly Seddington)	–	John Morris
1872-11-10	Ashley, Henry John	1869-10-11	Henry John Ashley & wife Emily (formerly Seddington)	–	John Morris
1872-11-04	Eagles, Ann, of Thame	1810-08-30	Thomas Eagles & wife Mary (formerly Bowman)	Widow of Alexander Kirby, usually known as Burnham, her first husband's surname	John Morris
1872-12-08	Moore, John Finton Sothcott	1870-01-23	James Moore & wife Jane (formerly Sothcott)	–	John Morris
1872-12-23	Whiting, Thomas Samuel, of Northampton	1859-01-25 Daventry	Samuel Whiting & wife Mary (formerly Foster)	–	John Morris
1873-01-31	Moore, Mary Catherine	–	James Moore & wife Jane (formerly Sothcott)	–	Francis Goldie
1873-01-31	Moore, Laura Frances	–	James Moore & wife Jane (formerly Sothcott)	–	Francis Goldie

Date of conditional baptism	Name of convert	Date of birth	Parents	Spouse	Priest officiating
1873-02-19	Embury, John William Francis	1856-08-23	William Shepherd Embury & wife Catherine Adelaide (formerly Parr)	–	John Morris
1873-02-21	Moore, Jane Wade	1839-04-22	William Sothcott & wife Elizabeth (formerly Dyer)	James Moore	John Morris
1873-02-28	Wright, George Henry Bateson, of Queen's College	1853-05-06 Biggleswade, Bedfordshire	George Bache Wright & wife Mary Griffith (formerly Baird)	–	John Morris
1873-04-12	Griffin, Jane Mary Imelda Scholastica, of Oxford	1854-02-26	Joseph Griffin & wife Martha (formerly Wheeler)	–	Francis Goldie
1873-04-15	Savin, Isaac Joseph (RIP)	–	–	–	Francis Goldie
1873-06-21	Taylor, Matilda	–	–	–	Francis Goldie
1873-09-12	Kettle, Mary (RIP)	–	–	–	Francis Goldie
1873-09-22	Burrows, Jane Mary Kirby	1850-02-27	–	–	Alexander Diomedi
1873-09-28	Young, Aloise	1872-11-13	–	–	Alexander Diomedi
1873-12-20	Burrows, Henry	1864 approx.	–	–	William Johnson
1873-12-22 Radcliffe Infirmary	Lewis, Thomas	1826 approx.	–	–	William Johnson
1874-02-25 Woodstock	Saltmarsh, Amy	1780 approx.	–	–	William Johnson
1874-03-15 Oxford	Walford, Mary Ann	1796 approx.	–	–	John Walford, Scholar
1874-03-27	Betterriss, Clara Jane	1866 approx.	–	–	William Johnson

THE REGISTERS

Date of conditional baptism	Name of convert	Date of birth	Parents	Spouse	Priest officiating
1874-03-28	Williams, Ellen Eliza	–	–	–	William Johnson
1874-04-05	Holloway, Mary	–	–	–	William Johnson
1874-04-26	Poole, Charles Henry	1850 approx.	–	–	William Johnson
1874-04-30	Pope, Frederick Andrew	1855 approx.	–	–	William Johnson
1874-05-14	Turner, Julia	–	–	–	William Johnson
1874-09-22	Conroy, Emma	1839 approx.	–	–	William Johnson
1874-12-29	Seely, Emma	–	–	–	William Johnson
1875-01-30	Ackerman, Walter	1852 approx.	–	–	William Johnson
1875-03-17	Manning, Martha	1854 approx.	–	–	William Johnson
1875-04-16	Veal, John	1820 approx.	–	–	William Johnson
1875-06-11	Edmunds, George	1861 approx.	–	–	William Johnson
1875-06-17	Ashley, Henry	1835 approx.	–	–	William Johnson
1875-08-28	Gerning, Sarah	1851 approx.	–	–	William Johnson
1875-09-10	Atkins, Adeline Jane	1850 approx.	–	–	William Johnson
1875-11-12	Lovegrove, Clara Mary, Nazareth Ho.	1875-02-07	Mary Lovegrove	–	James Hoever
1875-12-13	Mabbatt, Frederick Alfred	1855 approx.	–	–	Thomas B. Parkinson
1875-12-28	Wizard, Elizabeth	1864-06-14	William Wizard & wife Elizabeth (formerly Denney)	–	Francis Goldie
1875-12-28	Wizard, Hannah	1870-01-20	William Wizard & wife Elizabeth (formerly Denney)	–	Francis Goldie

Appendix A:
Priests of the Oxford Mission 1700–1875

Mostly Jesuits

(Ex-Jesuits – later 'Gentlemen of Stonyhurst' – during the official suppression of the English Society of Jesus by the Vatican, 1773–1829)

1683–1702	Henry Pelham alias Warren, SJ
1701–18	Charles Collingwood, SJ (Sandford)
1724	Thomas Whitgrave, SJ
1724–38	Francis Gibson, SJ (Kiddington)
1724–?	Peter Inghilby, SJ (Sandford)
1728–53?	Henry Stanley, SJ (Waterperry)
1729–50	William Brown (Britwell)
1740–61	Thomas Brooke, SJ (Tusmore)
1751–65	John Richardson, SJ (Britwell)
1752–61?	Francis Pole (Waterperry)
1752–8	Gilbert Wells, SJ (Dorchester)
1755–69	John Bernard Warmoll, OSB (Brize Norton)
1765–88	George Bruning (Britwell)
1765	? Woods
1770	Charles Blount (signs at Britwell)
?–1770	William Nelson (Waterperry)
1772–3	Bernard Daniel Young, OSB (Waterperry)
1773–4	John Jerome Butler, OSB (Waterperry and at Tusmore in 1786)
1773–4	Anselm John Geary, OSB (Waterperry)
1773	James Lane (signs at Britwell)
1771–88	Bernard Cassidy, alias Stafford, SJ (various locations including Warkworth, Dorchester and Thame Park)
1775	Francis Green, SJ (Waterperry and Tusmore)
1775	James Lewis (Waterperry and Tusmore)
1777–9	John (or Joseph) Closette, SJ (Waterperry)
1780–85	Peter Jenkins, SJ (Waterperry)
1782	Blaise Money (Britwell)
1785	Peter Walker alias Westby (a chance visitor at Waterperry?)

1789   James Taylor (at Heythrop in 1795)
1792   James Charles Hunter (Britwell)
1789–1803   Charles Leslie, SJ (Tusmore, Waterperry and St Clement's
1798   Mgr Thoumin des Valpons, Vicar General of Dol (at Overy)

Poor Clares' Franciscan Chaplains at Britwell

1799–1800   Thomas Pacificus Kington, OSF
1800–1803   Isaac Anselm Milward, OSF
1803–1809   Paschal Harrison, OSF
1809–1811   Edward Andrew Weetman, OSF
1811–1812   Joseph Tate, OSF

Jesuits

1799–1803   William Hothersall, SJ (St Clement's)
1806–12   James Leslie, SJ (St Clement's)
1812–18   John Connolly, SJ (St Clement's)
1818–49   Robert Newsham, SJ (St Clement's and from 1823 Dorchester)
1823   William Ibbotson, SJ (Dorchester)
1849–59   Robert Newsham, SJ (Dorchester)
1849–53   Henry Brigham, SJ (St Clement's)
1854–57   Francis Chadwick, SJ (St Clement's)
1857   Francis Jarrett, SJ (St Clement's)
1857–9   Charles Blackett, SJ (St Clement's)

Priests of the Diocese of Birmingham

1860–7   Alexander Comberbach
1860   F. Englebert, OSFC
1861   Rafaele Gorga
1866   Charles Russell
1867   Ambrose St John, CO
1868–71   James Nary
1870   J.P. O'Toole

Jesuits

1871–2   James Henry Corry, SJ
1871   Thomas Meyrick, SJ
1872–3   John Morris, SJ, Francis Goldie, SJ
1873–5   William Johnson, SJ
1873   William Cotham, SJ, Alexander Diomede, SJ

1874	George Kingdon, SJ
1875	Francis Goldie, SJ, Thomas Parkinson, SJ, James Hoever, SJ, H. Venturi, SJ, Thomas Meyrick, SJ

This list is derived primarily from a document kindly provided by the late Fr Jerome Bertram of the Oxford Oratory.

Appendix B:
The Catholic Mission at Bampton

The parish and market town of Bampton lies on the River Thames in west Oxfordshire. The Earls of Shrewsbury held property there from the fourteenth century onwards, including Bampton Castle. The castle gatehouse survived and in 1856 Bertram Arthur Talbot (1832–56), Earl of Shrewsbury, established an oratory chapel dedicated to the Virgin Mary in the upper part of the gatehouse.[1]

On the opposite bank of the Thames from Bampton lies Buckland, the most recusant village in Berkshire in the late seventeenth century.[2] At the time the chapel at Bampton was established, Buckland still had a strong Catholic presence under the patronage of the Throckmorton family, who had recently built a new Catholic church in the village, designed by Charles Hansom, brother of Joseph the architect of St Aloysius, Oxford.[3] The Catholic priest at Buckland during the short existence of the Bampton chapel was Franco Guaci Azzopardi, a Maltese. In a letter to the historian Mrs Stapleton, Edward Williams of Buckland recalled, 'I helped to fashion a beautiful Oratory in the old Bampton Castle (Lord Shrewsbury's estate there.)'

Tadpole Bridge, built across the Thames in the late eighteenth century, made travel between the Buckland and Bampton much easier than hitherto. Azzopardi agreed to say Mass at Bampton on alternate Sundays. He first celebrated Mass at Bampton on 16 June 1856 and the chapel was officially licensed ten days later. However, just a month after that first Mass, the Earl of Shrewsbury died at Lisbon, aged 23. Franco Azzopardi continued serving the chapel until 23 August 1857, when the last recorded Mass was celebrated there. His successor, Henry Clark, closed the chapel and sent its fittings to the chapel of St Ignatius at St Clement's. They were later used at Witney.[4]

However, as the register shows, baptisms continued at Bampton until March 1860. There were five in all: two by Franco Azzopardi and three by Daniel Donovan, who succeeded Henry Clark at Buckland in the summer of 1858 and stayed there

1   *VCH Oxon.* xiii, pp. 6, 25, 57.
2   Now in Oxfordshire.
3   Charles Hansom was also the uncle of Joseph Stanislaus Hansom, who made the earlier partial transcription of these registers.
4   Stapleton, pp. 172–3.

until late 1860. After 1857 Mass was not available again in Bampton until the 1930s and then only in hired rooms. Since 1976, thanks to the generous ecumenical spirit of the Church of England, the Catholic Mass has been celebrated in the Anglican parish church of St Mary the Virgin.

Select bibliography

◆

Primary sources

Archives of the Oxford Oratory: Sacramental records of the domestic chapel at Waterperry House, the chapel of St Ignatius at St Clement's, the church of St Aloysius Gonzaga, Oxford, and the chapel of St Mary the Virgin, Bampton:

Book 1
Confirmations: 20 May 1753, 16 May 1758, 22 May 1763
Deaths: 26 September 1700 to February 1807
Baptisms: 12 June 1701 to 30 June 1800
Marriages: 6 June 1758 to 10 February 1771

Book 2 (bound together with Book 1)
Baptisms: 4 November 1800 to 2 December 1855
Marriage: 9 October 1809

Composite volume
Baptisms: 30 March 1854 to 8 June 1865
Confirmations: 30 March 1854 to 23 February 1873
Marriages: 30 March 1854 to 7 June 1876
Deaths: 30 March 1854 to 20 March 1877

Baptisms
29 June 1865 to 16 January 1878

Converts
13 October 1772 to 6 January 1909

Baptisms at the Chapel of St Mary the Virgin, Bampton
4 November 1856 to 19 March 1860

Archives of the Oxford Oratory: 'Priests of St Aloysius' (undated list)

The Bishops' Register of Confirmations in the Midland District of the Catholic Church in England, 1768–1811 and 1816 (Catholic Family History Society, Occasional Publication 3, 1999)

Secondary sources

Aveling, J.C.H., *The Handle and the Axe* (Colchester, 1976)
Bassett, B., *The English Jesuits: from Campion to Martindale* (London, 1967)
Beeson, C.F.C., *Clockmaking in Oxfordshire* (Oxford, 1989)
Bellenger, D.A., *The French Exiled Clergy* (Bath, 1986)
Berington, J., *The State and Behaviour of English Catholics, from the Reformation to the Year 1781* (London, 1781)
Bertram, J., *St Aloysius' Parish, Oxford: The Third English Oratory* (Birmingham, 1993)
Bettenson, H., *Documents of the Christian Church* (Oxford, 1967)
Bossy, J., *The English Catholic Community, 1570–1850* (London, 1975)
Brooks, A. and J. Sherwood, *The Buildings of England: Oxfordshire North and West* (New Haven and London, 2017)
Burton, E.H., *The Life and Times of Bishop Challoner* (London, 1909)
Challoner, Bishop R., *Memoirs of Missionary Priests and other Catholics of Both Sexes that have Suffered Death in England on Religious Accounts* (Philadelphia, 1839)
Clapinson, M. (ed.), *Bishop Fell and Nonconformity* (ORS 52, 1980)
Clark, A. (ed.), *The Life and Times of Anthony Wood* (Oxford Hist. Soc. 5 vols 1891–1900)
Clark, J.C.D., *English Society 1688–1832: Ideology, Social Structure and Political Practice During the Ancien Regime* (Cambridge, 1985)
Davey, E.C., *Memoirs of an Oxfordshire Old Catholic Family* (London, 1897)
Davidson, A., 'Roman Catholicism in Oxfordshire from the late Elizabethan period to the Civil War, 1580–1640' (unpubl. Bristol PhD thesis, 1970)
Duffy, E., 'Englishmen in vaine: Roman Catholic allegiance to George I', *Studies in Church History*, xviii (1982), pp. 345–65
Edge, J., 'The Catholic registers of Britwell Prior or Brightwell, Oxfordshire, 1765–88', in CRS Records Series 13, *Miscellanea VIII* (1913), pp. 292–8
Foley, H., *Records of the English Province of the Society of Jesus* (8 vols. London, 1875–80)
Fraser, A., *The King and the Catholics: The Fight for Rights, 1829* (London, 2018)
Gibson, D. (ed.), *A Parson in the Vale of White Horse: George Woodward's Letters from East Hendred, 1753–61* (Gloucester, 1982)
Gibson, W., *James II and the Trial of the Seven Bishops* (Basingstoke, 2009)
Glickman, G., *The English Catholic Community, 1688–1745: Politics, Culture and Ideology* (Woodbridge, 2009)
Hadland, T., *Thames Valley Papists: From Reformation to Emancipation* (2nd edn Mapledurham, 2004)
Hansom, J.S., 'Catholic registers of the domestic chapel at Waterperry manor house, Oxon, and St Clement's church, Oxford, 1701?–1834', in CRS Records Series 7, *Miscellanea VI* (1909), pp. 388–422
Hassall, W.O., 'Papists in early eighteenth-century Oxfordshire', *Oxoniensia*, 13 (1948), pp. 76–82
Hilton, J.A. (ed.), *Bishop Leyburn's Confirmation Register of 1687* (Wigan, 1987)
Hodges, M., 'Roman Catholic recusants 1558–1800', in K. Tiller and G. Darkes (eds), *An Historical Atlas of Oxfordshire* (ORS 67, 2010), pp. 84–5
Hodgetts, M., *Secret Hiding-places* (Dublin, 1989)
—, *Midlands Catholic Buildings* (Birmingham, 1990)

Jordan, S. 'Gentry Catholicism in the Thames Valley, 1660–1780', *Recusant History*, 27 (2004), pp. 217–43
Leslie, C., *Pedigree of the Family of Leslie of Balquhain* (Bakewell, 1861)
Lewycky, N. and A. Morton (eds), *Getting Along? Religious Identities and Confessional Relations in Early Modern England* (Farnham, 2012)
McLynn, F., *Charles Edward Stuart: A Tragedy in Many Acts* (London, 1988)
Mathew, D., *Catholicism in England: Portrait of a Minority, its Culture and Tradition* (London, 1936)
Marshall, P. and G. Scott (eds), *Catholic Gentry in English Society: The Throckmortons of Coughton from Reformation to Emancipation* (Farnham, 2009)
Martindale, C.C., *Catholics in Oxford* (priv. print, 1925)
Norman, E., *Roman Catholicism in England: From the Elizabethan Settlement to the Second Vatican Council* (Oxford, 1985)
Oates, J., 'The rise and fall of Jacobitism in Oxford', *Oxoniensia*, 68 (2003), pp. 89–111
Petti, A.G. (ed.), *Recusant Documents from the Ellesmere Manuscripts* (CRS Records Series 60, 1968)
Pincus, S.C.A., *1688: The First Modern Revolution* (New Haven, 2009)
Rannie, D.W. (ed.), *Remarks and Collections of Thomas Hearne*, viii (Oxford Hist. Soc. 51, 1907)
Rowlands, M.B. (ed.), *English Catholics of Parish and Town, 1558–1778* (CRS Monograph Series 5, 1999)
Schaaf, B., *Schwarzwalduhren* (Karlsruhe, 2008)
Sherwood, J. and N. Pevsner, *The Buildings of Oxfordshire* (Harmondsworth, 1974)
Stapleton, Mrs B., *A History of the Post-Reformation Catholic Missions in Oxfordshire* (London, 1906)
Stonor, R.J., *Stonor: A Catholic Sanctuary in the Chilterns* (Newport, 1952)
Tiller, K. (ed.), *Church and Chapel in Oxfordshire 1851* (ORS 55, 1987)
—, 'Religion and community: Dorchester to 1920', in K. Tiller (ed.), *Dorchester Abbey: Church and People 635–2005* (Stonesfield, 2005), pp. 61–83
—, 'Priests and people: Changing relationships in south Oxfordshire, 1780–1920', in Berkshire Local History Association, *People, Places and Context: Essays in Local History in honour of Joan Dils* (Purley, 2016), pp. 27–42
—, 'Oxford diocese, Bishop Wilberforce and the 1851 religious census', *Oxoniensia*, 83 (2018), pp. 93–100
Tiller, K. and G. Darkes (eds), *An Historical Atlas of Oxfordshire* (ORS 67, 2010)
Vallance, E., *The Glorious Revolution* (London, 2007)
Walsham, A., *Church Papists: Catholicism, Conformity and Confessional Polemic in Early Modern England* (Woodbridge, 1993)
—, *Charitable Hatred: Tolerance and Intolerance in England, 1500–1700* (Manchester, 2006)
Whiteman, A. (ed.), *The Compton Census of 1676: A Critical Edition* (British Academy Records of Social and Economic History, n.s. 10, 1986)
Williams, J.A., *Catholic Recusancy in Wiltshire, 1660–1791* (CRS Monograph Series 1, 1968)
Worrall, E.S. (ed.), *Returns of Papists 1767*, ii (CRS Occasional Publications 2, 1989)
Wright, A.S.N., *The History of Buckland* (Oxford, 1966)

https://taking-stock.org.uk (an architectural and historical review of Catholic churches and chapels in England and Wales)

Index to the Introduction

Act of Settlement   4
Advowson ownership ban   21, 34
Albino, Blasio Antonio   63–4
Albino, Vincent   63
Allen, William   30
Anglicanism, penalties for non-conformity   17
Anne, Queen   22
Arnold, Rich   34
Atterbury Plot   23
Azzopardi, Franco Guaci   69

Badger, mason   30
Bampton   52
Banbury RC congregation in 1851   16
Baptism, Anglican   18
Baptism, RC   17
Barrett, Bryan   8
Beale, Arthur   51
Beek, George   60
Belson, Thomas   33
Benediction   53, 72
Berington, Joseph   7, 11
Bertie, Anna Maria, Countess of Abingdon   53
Bertie, Willoughby, Earl of Abingdon   53
Bertin, Georges   59
Bill of Rights   4
Birmingham RC Diocese   44
Blount family of Mapledurham   29
Blount, Joseph   37
Blount, Michael Henry   10
Blount, Richard   32

Bona Morte, Congregation of   53, 73
Boulter family of Haseley Court   38
Bounty hunters   9, 22, 25
Bradly, Jane   60
Breton priests   13
Brigham, Henry   44, 62
Brinkhurst, Catharine   53
Britwell, villages served by its mission   38
Britwell Prior   14, 36–8, 39
Brown, William   38, 53
Bruning, George   37, 38
Brunswick Clubs   10
Bryan, John   67
Burcot   39
Burel, Eliza   68
Burial, Anglican   18
Burial, RC   18
Burial Act   44
Burial ground closure   62
Burke, Edmund   8
Bute, Marquess of   45, 65

Camoys, third Lord   10
Camponovo, Amyda   69
Camponovo, Elizabeth   69
Catholic chapels permitted   9
Catholic Committee   7
Catholic Emancipation Act   10, 15, 25
Catholic Relief Act, 1778   8, 9, 25
Catholic Relief Act, 1791   9, 25
Catholic school ban   9
Census of Papists, 1676   20

Census of Papists, 1706   22
Census of Papists, 1767   34, 48, 68, 74
Chadwick, Francis   62, 67, 68
Challoner, Richard   7, 8, 9
Chapels legalised   25
Charles II   6, 20, 21
Chipping Norton RC congregation in 1851   16
Church papists   2
Cisalpine views   6, 7
Clarendon Code   19
Clarke, Mary Ann   65
Cleeve, Lucas   61
Clifton Hampden   39
Collin, Florence Mary   64
Collingridge family of north Oxfordshire   60, 71
Collingridge, Bishop Peter   61
Collingridge, Ignatius   61
Collingridge, John   68
Collingwood, Charles   36
Collingwood, George   36
Comberbach, Alexander   51, 52, 64, 65, 67
Compton, Henry   20
Compton Census. *See* Census of Papists, 1676
Conolly, John William   44, 60, 71
Conversions   52, 74
Copus, Thomas   60
Corporation Act   19
Corry, James Henry   45, 66, 67, 68
Cruse, Mary   62
Curson family of Waterperry   32–5, 53
Curson, Bridget   57
Curson, Sir Francis, third baronet   33, 35, 41, 53, 54, 71
Curson, Henry   57
Curson, Sir John, second baronet   33, 70–1
Curson, Sir Peter, priest, fourth baronet   33

Curson, Sir Thomas, first baronet   33
Curtis, John   68

Dashwood, Sir James   5
Davey family of Overy, Dorchester   39–40, 71
Davey, Edward   66
Davey, Helen   39
Davey, John   19, 40
Davey, Lucy   60
Davey, Sarah (née Haskey)   39, 59
Davey, William   13, 39, 59, 60
Davidson, Alan   29
Davis, Henry   71
Day family of Dorchester district   39
Day, John Nicholas   32
Day, Mary   62
Day, Thomas   62
Declarations of Indulgence   3, 20, 21
Desvalpons, Monsignor Michel   39–40
Devlin, Daniel   62
Devlin, Elizabeth   62
Devlin, James   62
Devlin, Margaret   62
Dixon, Ellen   67
Dolphin Inn, St Giles, Oxford   29
Domville, Compton Charles   61
Donovan, Daniel   69
Donovan, Mary   62
Dorchester. *See also* Overy
Dorchester, St Birinus RC Church   40
Dorchester Abbey   13
Dorchester RC congregation in 1851   16
Douai-Rheims Bible   8
Douglas, Adaline Domville   61
Douglas, Julie Isabelle Gianetta   61
Douglas, Sholto   61
Dryden, John   21

Eagan, James Charles   69, 75
Ecclesial Titles Act   15

INDEX TO THE INTRODUCTION

Elizabeth I   2
English College, Douai   3, 7
English College, Rome   44
Englishness of Catholic gentry   7
Eyston family of East Hendred   19

Facer, Martha Hannah   66
Fairfax, F.   32
Fell, John   20
Fermor family of north Oxfordshire   60
Flaminian Gate pastoral letter   15
Flynn, James   66
Fortwengler, Josephine   64
French clergy, exiled   13–14

Gage, Thomas, first Viscount   11
Ganter, Joseph   66
Gargaro, Domenico   64
Garnet, Henry   2
Gasgoigne, Sir Thomas   11
Geographical reach of the Oxford mission   75
George I   22
George II   23
George III   5
George IV   10
Gerard, John   33
Gladstone, W.E.   10
Glickman, Gabriel   5
Glorious Revolution   3, 21
Goldie, Francis   66
Gordon, Lord George   9
Gordon Riots   9
Gorga, Raphael   64
Greene, Adam   32

Hansom, Charles Francis   51
Hansom, Edward Joseph   51
Hansom, Joseph Aloysius   50
Hansom, Joseph Stanislaus   50
Harding family of Holywell   31
Harding, Lucy   53

Hardwicke Marriage Act   23–4
Harleyford conference   2
Harleyford Manor   2
Hart, James   57
Hart, Joseph   57
Hart, Mary   57
Haseley, Great and Little   38–9
Haseley Court   38
Haynes, Edwin   66
Hearne, Thomas   29
Hethe RC congregation in 1851   16
Hettich, Josephine   64
Hettich, Karl   64, 68–9
Hettich, Mary Louise Josephine   64
Heueritsi, Adam   61
Heueritsi, Summala   61
Heueritsi, Totia   61
Heythrop RC congregation, 1851   16
Hierarchy, restoration   14–15, 44
Hoever, James   67
Holywell Manor   29–32, 41
Hornyold, Bishop   53
Horse ownership ban   21
Horseman family of Great Haseley   38
Horseman, Helen   66
Hothersall, William   42–4, 59
Howard, Geo   34
Huddleston family of Haseley Court   38
Huguenot refugees   3
Hunter (alias Weldon), James Charles   37

Ibbotson, William   40
Immigration of Catholics   12, 70
Inghilby, Peter   36

Jacobite risings   5, 23
Jacobitism   4, 8
James II   3, 4, 6, 21
Jeffery, William   68
Jesuits, suppression of   13, 61

Johnson, Hannah   57
Johnson, Joseph   57
Johnson, William   66, 67, 69

Kavanagh (Cavannah), William   69
Kelly, Bridget   59
Kennedy, Thomas   69
Kerampuilh, Count and Countess of   57
Kimber family of Holywell   31
Kimber, Thomas   32
Kimberley, James   70
Kingscote, Adeline Georgiana Isabella   61
Kirner, Anthony Leonard   66
Kirtlington Park   5

Lacey, William   32
Land tax   6, 10, 11, 22, 25
Landed property holding   9, 16, 21–2, 25
Last, William   65
Latchford   38
Le Boutillier, Philip   65
Legal status of RCs   16–25
Lenthall family of Latchford   38
Leslie, Charles   13, 35, 39, 40–4, 57, 58, 60, 62, 71
Leslie, Countess   44
Leslie, James   44
Leyburn, John   3, 4
Locations of the Oxford Mission   29–46
Louise, John Aloysius   64
Lucas, Jon   34

Mahieu, Amand   67
Maloni, James   24
Mansfield, Lord   24
Marriage, Anglican   23–4
Marriage, RC   17
Marshall, Peter   14
McHugo, Henry   65

Military service as officer   9, 16, 25
Milner, Dr John   64–5
Milton, near Abingdon   8
Mitre Inn, Oxford   4, 29
Morgan, Lucy   60
Morgan, William   68
Morris, John   67
Mortality   75
Mortuaire, Jean-Baptiste   13

Napier (Napper) family of Holywell   30–1
Napier, George   31–2, 36
Napier, William   30, 36
Nary, James   44, 65–6
Nazareth House   72
Nelson, William   71
Neville family of Holt   31
Newington. *See* Britwell Prior
Newman, John Henry   44
Newsham, Robert   40, 44, 60, 61, 62, 67
Norfolk, Dukes of   5, 23
Norman priests   13

O'Callaghan, Mary   66
O'Toole, J.P.   66
Oates, Titus   20
Oaths of allegiance and supremacy   6, 8, 9, 10, 19, 21, 22, 23, 25
Oglethorpe, John   37
Ollington, Bridget   66
Overy, Dorchester   13, 39–40
Overy Farm   39
Overy House   39
Oxford, St Clement's district   40–6
Oxford Diocesan Synod, 1850   15
Oxford Movement   15–16
Oxford RC congregation in 1851   16, 74
Oxford RC meeting places   29

Paddey, John   68

INDEX TO THE INTRODUCTION

Padwick family of Waterperry   70
Padwick, Ann   34
Padwick, Dan   34
Padwick, Mary, wife of Dan   34
Padwick, Mary   53
Papist (term)   2
Parkinson, Thomas B.   66, 67
Peel, Robert   10
Pelham (alias Warren), Henry   32
Penal code, compliance   73
Petre, Sir George   61
Petre, George Glynn   61
Petre, Lord   8
Pfaff, Fidel   67–8
Pfaff, Joseph   68
Pfaff, Stanislaus   65, 67–8
Phillips, George William   64
Phillips, Thomas   56
Platt, Peter Stephen   59
Pole, Francis   50, 57
Poor Clares of Aire   13–14, 37
Popery Act   22
Popish Plot   20
Popish recusants convicted (legal term)   16
Powell family of Sandford-on-Thames   30, 31
Powell, Catherine   36
Powell, Edmund   36
Powell, Edmund   36
Powell, John   36
Powell, Mary   55
Powell, Winefred   36
Pratt, Elizabeth   24
Prayers for Hanoverian monarchy   8
Presentation of Benefices Act   34
Price, Henry   34
Priestley, Joseph   7
Prince family of Dorchester district   39
Professions, preclusion of RCs   16, 22, 25
Protesting Catholic Dissenters   7

Public office, preclusion of RCs   16

Radford RC congregation in 1851   16
Rag Plot   5
Reade, Sir Richard   60, 66–7
Reading, King's Arms   13
Recusant, meaning   2
Registration Act   23
Religious census 1851   16
Richardson, John   38, 53
Rites of passage, Catholic   17–19
Roper (became Curson, later Roper-Curzon), Henry Francis   35
Rouxel, A.   59
Russell, Lord John   15
Rycote   38
Ryder, Mrs Elizabeth   34

St Aloysius Gonzaga RC Church, Oxford   16, 46
St Clement's district. *See* Oxford, St Clement's district
St Ignatius RC Chapel at St Clement's, Oxford   12, 16, 40–6
Saisy, Marie Julie Anne   58
Sandford-on-Thames   36
Sardinian embassy chapel   7
Savage, Susanna   60
Savile, Sir George   8
Schoelard, Victoire   61
Senechal, Pierre Michel François   67
Seven bishops' petition   3
Sheldon, William   8
Shepherd, John   58, 59
Shepherd, William Stonor's curate   18
Simeon, Sir Edward   37
Simeon, Edward, priest   37
Simeon, John   37
Smith, Isabel   63
Smith, John   61
Smith, John and Elizabeth   61
Smith, Mary   63
Smith, Mary Monica   64

Social class   70
Southwell, Robert   2
Stapleton, Mrs Bryan   36, 50, 66–7
Star Inn, Oxford   29
Stevens, Henry   66
Stonor, Thomas   10
Stonor, William   18
Stonor RC congregation in 1851   16
Stuart, Charles Edward   5, 8, 11
Surrey, Earl of   11
Swinburnes of Capheaton   5

Talbot, Charlotte   59
Talbot, Earls of Shrewsbury   16
Talbot, John   59
Talbot, Susan Harriet Anne   59
Tarbuck, Catherine   63
Tarbuck, Charles   63
Temple Cowley   30–1
Test Acts   19, 20, 21, 22, 23
Thame, Mansion House   13
Thoumin des Valpons, Michel   13
Throckmorton, Sir Robert   7
Timbs, Martha   59
Timbs, Mary   59
Tocque, Mary Ann   64
Toleration Act, 1689   18
Travel restrictions   21, 22
Triquet, Julien François Rene   59
Truckines, Jesuit priest   32
Turner, Teresa   66
Twycross, Robert   34

Ullathorne, William Bernard   19, 65
Ultramontane influences   14
Urban Catholicism, growth   11–12

Veal, John   69
Vicars Apostolic   3, 7, 13, 14, 22–3, 42, 61, 64

Von Stockum, Frederick Oswald Joseph   68

Walpole, Edward   33
Walsham, Alexandra   6
Wangler, Crescentia   66
Wangler, Lucas   66, 68
Wangler, Marcus   66
Waterhouse, Winny   57
Waterperry   2, 24, 32–5
Weapon ownership ban   21, 22
Weld family   5
Weld, Edward   37
Weld, James   37
Weld, Mary, nun   37
Weld, Thomas Simeon   13, 37
Wellington, Duke of   10
Wells, Gilbert   39, 53
Wesley, John   7
West, Daniel   68
Weston, William   2
White, Sarah   59
White, Winefred   55
Wilberforce, Samuel   15
William III (William of Orange)   3, 21
William and Mary   4, 21
Wilmore, Eliz   34
Wiseman, Nicholas   15
Wolfe, Charles   55
Wolfe, Henry Drummond Charles   61
Wolfe, John   38
Wood, Anthony   31, 33, 36
Woodward, George   19
Woodward, Mary Margaret   34

Young, Arthur   39
Young, Edward   64
Young, Elizabeth   64
Young, Louisa   64

Index to the Registers

Abby, Thomas   170
Ackerman, Walter
Adams, Anne   104
Adams, Frances   134
Adams, Margaret Mary Elizabeth   138
Adams, Thomas   104, 184
Ahern, John   182
Albino, Vincent   133
Aldworth, William   123
Allcock, John   169
Allen, Walter Andoenus   154
Allin, William   145
Allison, William   93
Angleri, Antonio Giovanni Battista Alexandro Joseph   109
Anstey, Joseph   163
Anstey, Rose   163
Anstey, Rose Ann   183
Arches, Harriet   142
Archibald, Sarah   103
Arrow, Henry   100
Ashley, Edward Henry   187
Ashley, Emily   165, 187
Ashley, Henry
Ashley, Henry John   187
Atkins, Adeline Jane
Atkins, Edmund   109
Auger, John   98
Austin, Elizabeth   98

Backford, James   91
Badcock, Mary   98
Bagnal, Anne Ellen   83

Bagnal, Appolonia   82
Bagnal, Charles   161
Bagnal, William   161
Bagnal, Winifrid   82
Bagnall, Anne Ellen   173
Bagnall, Charles   166
Baker, Antony   161
Baker, James   160
Baker, Mary   161
Banclery, Vincent John Gilbert   113
Bannister, Jane Ann   149
Barnes, Elizabeth   118
Barnes, Emma   118
Barnes, James   172
Barnhill, –   117
Barrett, Mary   167
Barrign, Abraham Ignatius   143
Bartlett, Mary   170
Baston, Ann   98
Baston, John   142, 182
Baston, Lydia   99
Baston, Teresa   182
Bateman, Eliza   184
Bates, Agnes Mary   147
Bates, Emma   165
Bates, Emma Mary   145
Bates, Frederick   164
Bates, Mary   165
Bates, William Frederick Joseph   146
Bayliss, Henry   144
Beale, John Arthur   179
Becket, Katharine Rachael   120
Beckingham, Sarah Elizabeth   145
Beechey, Martha   97

Beek, George   90
Beek, James Charles   90
Bell, Benjamin   106
Belson, Bridget   170
Belson, Mary   170
Belson, Maurice   170
Bennett, James   176
Bennett, Richard   162
Bergin, John Charles   130
Bernard, George   104
Bernard, Joseph   161
Berry, Ernest John   148
Berry, Mary Ann   135
Berry, Richard Thomas   148
Berry, William   132, 164, 185
Bertie, Lady Maria   160
Bertie, Lady Sophia   160
Betterriss, Clara Jane   188
Bianco, Angelina   111
Bickerstaff, John   79
Bikerstaff, Thomas   173
Biovois, Mary Teresa Martha   144
Biovois, Victor   166
Biovois, Victor Celestin   134
Bishop, Elizabeth   149
Bishop, Elizabeth Jane   168
Blackwell, Mrs   174
Blake, Mary Anne   105
Bliss, Basil   156
Bliss, Cuthbert Godfrey   154
Bliss, James   156
Bliss, Jane Monk   183
Bliss, Margaret Harriet   155
Bliss, Walter Thomas   152, 184
Bloxham, –   101
Bloxham, Susanna   98
Bradley, –   146
Bradley, Elizabeth Clara   151
Bradley, Mary Louisa   149
Bradley, Reginald Thomas   155
Bradley, William   167
Bradley, William Francis Charles   142
Bradly, Jane   166

Brain, Mr   94
Brain, Mrs   94
Braine, Charles   154
Braine, Francis   156
Braine, Henry   155
Braine, James   154
Braine, Joseph   156
Brewerton, John   90
Brien, Mary Margaret Ann   156
Brien, William James   147
Brinckhurst, John   170
Brinckhurst, Mary   169
Brinckhurst-Curson, Catharine   174
Brine, Mary Ann   144
Brinkhurst, Mr   169
Brooks, Elizabeth   114
Brooks, Jane   114
Brooks, Mary Ann   114
Brooks, Sarah   114
Brown, Bridget   164
Brown, Elizabeth   105, 163
Brown, Emma   109
Brown, James   130
Brown, John   109
Brown, Louise   104
Brown, Mary Elizabeth   114
Brown, Robert   123
Bryan, John   176
Bryan, Joseph   142
Bryan, Mary   165
Buggins, Mary Emma   137
Bull, Elizabeth   119
Bull, Giles Joseph   159
Bull, William Charles   159
Bultely, Elizabeth   119
Buons, Ann   167
Burel, Eliza   177
Burnham, Henry   164
Burnhill, Catherine   184
Burrel, Mary   172
Burrel, Thomas   171
Burrows, Henry   188
Burrows, Jane Mary Kirby   188

INDEX TO THE REGISTERS

Butt, Thomas   174
Button, Louis   148
Button, Louisa   168
Byrnes, Elizabeth Sara   101

Cambell, Jane   134
Camponovo, Amyda   185
Camponovo, Elizabeth   141, 163
Capè, Francis   174
Carr, Elizabeth   91
Carr, Martha   91
Carroll, Catherine   140
Carroll, Charles Owen   138
Carroll, Frederick Melhan   138
Carroll, Henry Joseph   144
Carter, Andrew Edwin   130
Carter, Emily   137
Carter, Francis   125, 137
Carter, Phebe   121
Carter, Rose Edith   145
Carter, Rose Edith Elizabeth   147
Carter, Sibbia   121
Carter, William   122, 143
Casey, Mary   154
Castle, Charlott   121
Cecil, William   106
Chadwick, Francis   177
Chamberlain, Anne   169
Chapman, Thomas   112
Charleton, William   92
Chopping, Sarah Richardson   115
Christmass, Anna   78
Christmass, Em., jnr   170
Christmass, Simon   78, 171
Christmass, Susan   80
Christmass, Thomas   170
Christmass, William   79
Clancy, Bridget   89
Clarck, James   171
Clare, Ann   124
Clare, David   124
Clare, Emily   124
Clare, Jacob   123

Clare, James   124
Clare, Mary   123
Clare, Mary Ann   124
Clark, Anne   79, 83
Clark, Charles   81
Clark, David   84
Clark, John   79
Clark, Mary   79
Clark, Sarah   79
Clark, William   84, 114
Clarke, Catharine   80
Clarke, Francis   80
Clarke, George   80
Clarke, James   79
Clarke, Mary Ann   166
Clarke, Sam   80
Clarke, William   80
Clarkson, Susanna   162
Cole, George   161
Cole, Mary   90
Cole, Robert   91
Coleman, Ann   181
Coleman, John   120
Coles, Thomas   171
Collin, Florence Mary   136
Collin, James   136, 180
Collin, Rose   167
Collingridge, Ignatius   104
Collingridge, Jemima   106
Collingridge, John   183
Collingwood, Charles   170
Collyer, Phoebe   97
Conley, Christopher   134
Connell, Thomas   132
Conroy, Bernard   142
Conroy, Catherine   144
Conroy, Emma
Conroy, James   168
Conroy, Margaret   155
Conroy, Mary   146
Conway, Catherine Margaret   154
Conway, John   90
Conway, Lydia Winefride   157

Conway, Patrick 168
Conway, Philip 90
Conway, Sarah Ann 152
Cooke, Margaret 143, 183
Coolin, John 160
Cooney, John 90
Cooney, Susanna 90
Copus, Arabella 95
Copus, Francis 161
Copus, Joanna Elizabeth 91
Copus, John 92
Copus, John William 93
Copus, Maria Elizabeth 91
Copus, Peter 93
Copus, Thomas 161, 166
Copus, William 92
Cornish, James Lander 152
Corry, John 92
Cossar, George 180
Courtis, Augustus John 91
Cox, Mary Ann 133
Cox, William Patrick 133
Cripps, Mary Ann 120
Cripps, Sarah 120
Cripps, Temperance Ann 120
Crips, Mary Ann 178
Crompton, Thomas 169
Croney, Cornelius 108
Cuddon, George William 159
Cuddon, Gertrude Anne 159
Cuddon, William 159
Cullen, Arthur Charles 153
Cullen, John Blisby 168
Cullen, John Edward 150
Cureton, John Rowland Wynn 136
Cureton, William 167
Cureton, William Arthur 138
Curl, Thomas 110
Curril, Rachael 114
Curson, Caroline 85
Curson, Ellen 88
Curson, Francis 85
Curson, Sir Francis 172

Curson, George Henry 86
Curson, Sir John 170
Curson, Julia 85
Curson, Lady 173
Curson, Lady, snr 171
Curson, Robert 171
Curson, Thomas 84
Curtis, Augustus John 179
Curtis, John 177
Cusack, Frances 174

Dagnall, Winefride 182
Daley, Sidney 130
Daly, Ann 141, 182
Daly, Cornelius 129
Daly, Mary 131
Daly, Mary Ann 108
Daly, Sarah 168
Davey, Edward 168
Davey, Edward Charles 107
Davey, Frances Mary 110
Davey, George 97
Davey, Henry 98
Davey, John 103
Davey, Joseph 86, 88, 89
Davey, Mary Elizabeth 102
Davey, Mary Theresa 108
Davey, Robert 95, 105
Davey, Vincent 86
Davey, William 93, 101
Davidson, Maria Louisa 107
Davies, William 116
Davis, Frances Sophia 106
Davis, Henry 92
Davis, Lydia 124
Davis, Mary 161
Davy, Edward 170
Dawson, Violet Vivian Mary Josephine 157
Day, Dame 169
Dayman, Flavia 184
De Brion, Eliza 162
De Brion, Henry 162

INDEX TO THE REGISTERS

de Cardi, Gertrude   113
de Cardi, Mark Oliver   113
de Cardi, Nicolette   113
de Cardi, Peter Louis   113
de Cardi, Philip Antony   113
de Crusse, Bridget   98
de Mascarène, Frederick Emanuel   111
Delaney, John   112
Dennis, William   133
Dennison, John   122
Dennison, Mary Ann   124
Develin, Mary Anne   125
Devlin, Daniel   129
Devlin, Elizabeth   127
Devlin, Margaret   131
Dickson, Sarah Margaret   148
Dinnison, William   118
Dixon, Ann O'Bryan   139
Dixon, Catherine   132, 162
Dixon, Charles William   143
Dixon, Daniel   147
Dixon, Ellen   127, 176
Dixon, Henry James   158
Dixon, Henry Thomas   155
Dixon, James   135
Dixon, John Edward Valentine   149
Dixon, Matthew   129, 162
Dixon, Sarah Beatrice   152
Dixon, Thomas   144
Dockery, Thomas   183
Dodd, Mary   147
Dodswell, Richard   160
Donovan, John   125
Donovan, Michael   162
Doran, Mary Louisa   158
Dorsett, Hannah   176
Dougharty, Sarah   84
Douglas, Adaline Domville   107
Dowlinn, Catherine   142
Downey, Rosamund   90
Draper, Arthur Francis Walpole   155
Driscoll, Dennis   110

Driscoll, Mary   110
Drothery, Mary   82
Drury, –   146
Drury, Elizabeth Sarah   146
Duffy, Elizabeth   130
Dwyer, Francis   175

Eagles, Ann   187
East, Charlotte   86
East, Elizabeth   89
East, William Justin   122
Edges, Edward   163
Edmunds, George
Ellis, Charles   123, 184
Ellis, Esther Mary   141
Embury, John William   164
Embury, John William Francis   188
England, Mary Anna   119
Evans, Francis   102
Evans, Mary   162
Evans, Robert Claude   167
Eyston, Charles   170
Eyston, George   169

Fidler, Elizabeth   179
Field, Elizabeth   185
Finmore, Maria Agnes   114
Finnaghan, Mary Margaret   163
Finnakin, William   123
Finnegen, Eliza Louisa   143
Finnighan, Mary Ann   134
Fisher, Mary Ann   142
Fisher, Sarah Esther   135
Fitzgibbon, Ann   104
Fitzgibbon, Ellen   111
Fitzgibbon, Helena   107
Fitzgibbon, John   106, 108
Fitzgibbon, William   109
Fitzgibbons, William   102
Fitzherbert, Agnes   165
Fitzherbert, Catherine   149
Fitzherbert, William   164
Flint, Margaret   166

212 INDEX TO THE REGISTERS

Floyd, Anne   161
Floyd, Hannah   160
Flynn, James   168
Flynn, Mary   150
Forshaw, Arthur William   157
Forshaw, Florence Eveline   157
Forshaw, Harry Lionel   157
Forshaw, Louis Gerald   157
Forshaw, Percy Osborne   157
Foy, Ann   99, 106
Foy, David   93, 112
Foy, Elizabeth   92, 93, 101
Foy, John   111
Foy, Margarita   91
Foy, Mary   105, 136, 163
Foy, Michael   183
Foy, Sarah   108
Foy, William   102, 180, 184
Francis, Frances Beatrix   144
Francis, Francis Albin   142
Francis, Juliet Isabella   146
Frankham, Harriet Mary   129
Franklin, Robert   160
Fry, Mary   168

Gane, Eliza   185
Gara, Catherine Mary   150
Gara, James   167
Gara, William Andrew   153
Gardiner, Harriet   118
Gaverick, Caroline   92
Gearon, Catherine   168
Gearon, John   185
Geoghegan, Thomas   96
Gerning, Sarah
Gibbons, James   139
Gibbs, Mary   146
Gibbs, Sidney Cuthbert Ravenshoe   146
Gibson, Francis   171
Gillingham, Elizabeth   179
Godfrey, Matilda May   105
Goldby, Martha   91

Goldby, Mary Elizabeth   91
Gooch, Alban   115
Gooch, Hanna   115
Gooch, Herbert   115
Gooch, Hugh   115
Gooch, John   114, 115
Gooch, Robert   115
Gooch, Samuel   115
Gooch, William   115
Goodship, Emma   167
Goom, Elizabeth   97
Gosford, William   161
Grafton, Charles   178
Grafton, Charles Hardman   128
Grafton, Francis Henry   131, 177
Grafton, Henry Albert   133
Grafton, Mary Angela   129
Grafton, Mary Ann   183
Grafton, Mary Frances   181
Grau, Catherine Agnes   135
Green (alias Kelly), James   97
Green, Charles Samson (adult)   117
Green, Charles Samson   118
Green, James   83
Green, Mary Ann   119
Green, Sarah Rose Hanna   122
Green, William   84
Greeneawaye, Jeane   169
Greenoway, Sarah Anna   137
Griffin, Jane Mary Imelda Scholastica   188
Grimesditch, John   170
Grimesditch, Lord   169
Grogan, Thomas   135
Grove, Mary   118
Guilby, Ann   162
Guilby, Mary   161
Gulliver, Thomas   139, 182

Hall, Mary Louise   138
Halloway, Anne   125
Halloway, Harriet   125
Halloway, Marcia   109

Halloway, William   110
Hancock, Thomas   181
Hanley, Ann   94
Hanley, Charles   112
Hanley, Charles Ambrose   126
Hanley, Daniel   94
Hanley, Edmund Augustus   128
Hanley, Elizabeth   94
Hanley, George Daniel   129
Hanley, Hannah H.   112
Hanley, James Alexander   131, 177
Hanley, Julia   163
Hanley, Julia Frances   126
Hanley, Maria Teresa   125
Hanley, Mary   177
Hanley, Mary Ann   127, 163
Hanley, Sarah   94
Hanley, Teresa   181
Hanley, William Henry   110, 166
Hanley, Winefride   184
Hanlon, James   92
Harding, Lucy   160
Harrington, Daniel   135, 164, 166
Harrington, Edward   132, 164
Harrington, Eliza Ann   141
Harrington, Elizabeth   165
Harrington, Henry   148
Harrington, John   129, 164
Harrington, Mary   130, 165
Harris, Alfred   108
Harris, Andrew   110
Harris, Walter John   111
Hart, Henry   89
Hart, James   85
Harwood, Elizabeth   122
Harwood, Richard Hall   122
Hastings, Frances   162
Hastings, Louisa Catherine   126
Haynes, Joseph James   128, 176
Haynes, Thomas Murray   126
Hedges, Ann   141
Hedges, David   184
Hemmins, Elizabeth Mary   127

Hemmins, Mary   182
Hemmins, Teresa   130
Hemmins, William John   128, 179
Herman, –   156
Herring, Susanna   161
Hettich, Adolf Frederick William   149
Hettich, Charles Joseph Frederick   143
Hettich, Ernest Louis   147
Hettich, Karl   185
Hettich, Mary Louise Josephine   137
Hettich, Matilda Constance Mary   151
Hettich, Stephanie   167
Heueritsi, James   107
Hickey, John Thomas   125
Hickey, Mary Jane   121
Hickey, Michael   98
Hickey, Sarah   104
Hickey, Thomas   180
Hickie, Katherine   126
Hicky, Elizabeth   136, 162
Higgins, Sarah   95
Higgins, William   99
Hill, Charles James   147
Hill, John   164
Hill, John Patrick   130
Hill, Marion   165
Hill, Marion Josephine   135
Hill, Mary   163
Hill, Mary Helen   128
Hill, Robert   164
Hill, Thomas   132, 164
Hill, William George   140
Hinton, Angelina   116
Hinton, John   116
Hinton, Mercy   116
Hinton, William   116
Hitch, Wortham Joseph Ignatius Loyola   138
Hitchman, James   96
Hodgekinson, Anne   82

Hodgekinson, John   82, 173
Hodgekinson, Joseph   160
Hodgekinson, Richard   160
Hodgkinson, William   173
Hodgskinson, Joseph   83
Hodsginson, James   172
Hodskinson, Anna   80
Hodskinson, Anne   172
Hodskinson, Francis   80, 171
Hodskinson, James   79, 82
Hodskinson, Joseph   80
Hodskinson, Mary   81
Hodskinson, Richard   80
Hodskinson, William   80
Holloway, Agnes   121
Holloway, Ann   122, 178
Holloway, Anthony Joseph   131
Holloway, George   114, 162
Holloway, Harriet   163
Holloway, James   114
Holloway, John   116
Holloway, Mark   119, 162, 168
Holloway, Mary   117, 162
Holloway, Mary Ann   162
Holloway, Mary Anne   118
Holloway, Thomas   111
Holloway, Thomas   176
Holloway, William   178
Holyoak, Ann   98
Holyoak, Eliza Emilia   101
Holyoak, James   100
Holyoak, John   96, 100
Holyoak, Mary   96
Holyolk, Ann   95
Holyolk, James   94
Holyolk, John   95
Holyolk, Maria   95
Holyolk, Sarah   95
Hooker, Margaret   171
Hooker, Marguerite   173
Hooker, William   172
Hooper,   146
Hooper, Elizabeth   142

Hooper, James G.   163
Hooper, James William   139
Hooper, Mary   181
Hope, Mary   122
Hope, Mary Jane   122
Hopkins, George   89
Hopkins, Mary Ann   89
Horne, –   163
Horne, Harriet   136
Horseman, Cecily   155
Horseman, Robert   163, 168
Hothersall, William   175
Howard, Anne   78
Howard, Catharine   78
Howard, George   78
Howard, John   78
Howard, Martha   78
Howard, Mary   78
Howard, Sarah   78
Howell, Catharine   97
Howell, Catherine   144
Howell, Jane   121
Howell, Mary Ann   97
Howell, Samuel   97
Howes, Susan   79
Hoy, Ellen Mary   167
Humphris, William   179
Hunt, Mary   172
Hussey, Sarah   117

Ikky, Thomas   131
Ikky, Winefride   131
Ingelby, Peter   171

Jackson, Peregrine   94
January, Emery   110
January, Lucy Catharine   111
Jarvis, Alice   177
Jarvis, Edward   119
Jarvis, Edward   176
Jeffery, William   180
Johnson, Joseph   85
Johnson, Sarah   106

Johnson, Thomas   87
Johnson, William   88
Johnston, George Spokes   112
Johnston, John   107
Johnston, Mary   105
Johnston, Thomas Roberts Spokes   112
Johnstone, John Mary   136
Jones, Ann   121
Jones, Davey   121
Jones, Mary   121
Josslin, Mary   165

Kalen, James William   146
Kavanagh, William   185
Keane, Elizabeth   164
Keane, Louise   164
Kear, Eliza   111
Kear, Elizabeth   111
Kearsey, Charles   164
Kearsey, Charles Norman   148
Kearsey, Isabella Jemima   168
Keen, Catherine   148
Kelly, –   146
Kelly, Bridget   86
Kelly, Catherine   141, 158
Kelly, Edward   138
Kelly, Henry   96
Kelly, James   184
Kelly, Mary   97
Kennedy, Thomas   185
Kenrick, Mary Ann   119
Kerr, Mary   85
Kerr, Thomas   85
Kerr, William   86
Kettle, Elizabeth   185
Kettle, Mary   188
Kilby, Alicia   169
Kilby, Jeane   169
Kilby, Mrs   169
Killian, Rose Ann   131
Kimber, Thomas   170
Kimberly, James   172

King, Agnes Mary   154
King, Ann   122
King, Emily Gertrude   157
King, Henry Vincent   154
King, Mahala   121
King, Sophia   122
King, Thirsa   121
Kirner, Anthony   164
Kirner, Anthony Leonard   168
Kirner, Mary Lena   157
Kirner, Mary Ottilia   153

Lacy, Catherine   176
Lacy, Daniel   126
Lamb, Charles   117
Lamb, Elizabeth   106
Lamb, Henry   117
Lamb, James   108
Lamb, Jane   110
Lamb, John   115
Lamb, Mary Ann   111
Lamb, Patrick   180
Lamb, Sarah   106, 112
Lamb, Teresa   123
Lamb, Thomas   120
Lamb, William Stephen   109
Last, William   166
Latham, Richard   171
Laurence, Frances   78
Laurence, Jane   79
Laurence, Jos   78
Laurence, Margaret   79, 174
Laurence, Mary   78
Lawrence, Charles   155
Lawrence, Richard   173
Lawrence, Richard, jnr   79
Le Boutillier, Philip   167
Leader, Mary Anne   118
Lee, Apollonia   173
Lee, Sarah   86
Leech King, Elizabeth   166
Leslie, Charles   175
Lewis, Thomas   188

Liston, Belinda Sarah   138
Long, John   156
Long, Joseph   156
Louise, John Aloysius   137
Lovatt, Mary   179
Lovegrove, Clara Mary
Lovegrove, Clara Mary Martha   158
Lovett, Elizabeth   179
Lovett, Elizabeth Mary   144
Lovett, James   163
Lovett, Thomas   180
Lucas, John   172
Lyden, Mary Ann Magdalen Mingay   119

Mabbatt, Frederick Alfred
Macarthy, John   163
Macarthy, Mary Ann   164
MacCarthy, Mary Ann   181
MacHenry, Ann   88
Machenry, Mrs   175
Mackay, Ann   165
Macmanus, John Stephen   152
Madewright, Mary   178
Mahieu, Amand   176
Malham, Mary   170
Maloni, James   166
Maloni, Joseph   83
Manning, Martha
Mannion, Ann   133, 165
Mannion, Ann Sarah   143
Mannion, Catherine   146
Mannion, Eliza   156
Mannion, Frances   141
Mannion, Frances Elizabeth   153
Mannion, Louise   137
Mannion, Mary   140, 186
Mannion, William   134, 164
Marcum, Thomas   95
Marden, Thomas   117
Markam, Betsy   119
Markham, Elizabeth   141

Markham, Frederick William John   134
Markham, James   104, 163
Markham, John   100, 176
Markham, Thomas   179
Markum, Thomas Joseph   96
Martin, Mr   169
Massie, Mary   136
Matthews, Jeane   169
May, Ellen   184
Maycock, Mary   109
Mcafie, Maria   96
McCarthy, Jeremy   107
McCarthy, Mary   145
McCarty, Donald   118
McFie, Ann Agnes   154
McGowan, Frances   113
McGowan, Margaret   122
McGowen, Frances   118
McGowen, Maria   116
McGowen, Mary   112
McHale, John   181
McHugh, Christopher Henry   166
McLaughlin, Elizabeth   165
McLoughlin, Ellen Agnes   154
McMahon, Patrick   182
McManus, James   154
McMullen, William   123
Mellet, William Henry   116
Meredith, John   149
Meredith, Marianne   147
Milburn, John   94
Miles, Bridget   142
Miles, Catherine   184
Miles, Elizabeth   122
Miles, Henry   140
Million, James   80
Million, John   81
Million, Mary   81, 160
Millman, Anne   161
Mingaye, –   146
Mingaye, Augustine Joseph   167
Monis, Ann Elizabeth   107

Moore, Catherine   165
Moore, James William   151
Moore, Jane   164
Moore, Jane Wade   188
Moore, John Finton Sothcott   187
Moore, Laura   164
Moore, Laura Frances   187
Moore, Mary Catherine   152, 187
Moran, Ann   165
Moran, Maria Mary   165
Morgan, William   177
Morley, Alice   153
Morley, Mary   153
Morris, Ann   109
Morris, Charles   119
Morris, Charlotte   111
Morris, Sarah   110, 168
Morris, Thomas   112
Mulhern, George   103
Mulhern, Hanna   162
Mulhern, John Thomas   99
Mulhern, Mary   162
Mulhern, Mary Ann   101
Mulhern, Michael Stephen   102
Mullen, Anthony   183
Mullen, John   88
Murphy, Catherine Mary   132
Murphy, John   166
Murray, Thomas   125

Nelly, L.   178
Nelson, William   173
Neville, Charles   116
Newton, William   172
Nicks, Elizabeth   166
Nolen, John Francis   132
Nutt, Amos John   144
Nutt, Edith   151
Nutt, Frederick Charles   147, 151
Nutt, Joseph   164
Nutt, Maria Anna   131
Nutt, Mary Anne   165
Nutt, Mary Jane   141

O'Brien, Frederick   153
O'Brien, Jane   184
O'Bryan, John   164
O'Callaghan, Augustus John Barry   152
O'Callaghan, Mary   168
O'Connell, Mrs   175
O'Hagan, Michael   177
O'Keefe, Philip   168
O'Shea, Ann   129
O'Shea, Bridget   131
O'Shea, John Baptist   133
Oger, Mary Gertrude   128
Ollington, Bridget   168
Orpwood, Elizabeth   148, 167
Ortelli, Angela Lucy   116
Ortelli, Angelian Lucy Pasealina   119
Ortelli, Maria Lucy Paulina   121
Ortelli, Paul John   123
Owen, John Thomas   134

Paddey, John   180
Paddock, Mary   174
Padwick, Daniel   79, 170
Padwick, John   78, 79
Padwick, Mary   78, 79, 160
Palmer, Thomas   153
Parker, Catherine   163
Parker, Florence   163
Parker, Florence Mary Jermyns   126
Parker, James   162
Parker, James Joseph Mills   120
Parker, John Robert Howell   114
Parker, Kate Agnes Lester   124
Parker, Mary   183
Parker, Robert   145
Parsloo, Frances   173
Partloo, Elizabeth   160
Payne, William   144
Peake, Edwin   102
Pendergrass, Michael   182
Pendgrass, Michael   140
Penny, William Goodenough   118

Perquit, Felicité Josephine   167
Perret, Mary   184
Perry, Ellen   140
Perst, Anne   171
Petre, George Glynn   108
Pfaff, Fidel   176
Pfaff, Joseph   178
Phelan, –   108
Phelan, John   105
Phelan, Thomas   109
Philips, Ed   78
Philips, Elizabeth   78
Philips, Henry   78
Philips, James   78, 170
Philips, Samuel   78
Philips, Thomas   171
Phillips, George William   139
Pieck, Catherine   164
Pim, Mary   172
Platt, Alathea   84
Platt, Ann Frances   89
Platt, Charles   84, 175
Platt, John   90
Platt, Mary   86
Platt, Peter Stephen   88
Platt, Robert   85, 86
Platt, Sarah   175
Platt, Sarah   88
Plumb, Emma   121
Pole, Robert   163
Poole, Charles Henry
Pope, Frederick Andrew
Poulton, Henry   110
Poulton, James P. Hans   117
Poulton, Jane   110
Poulton, Mary Ann   96
Poulton, Nicholas   100
Powel, John   171
Powell, Anne   170
Powell, Edward   139, 163
Powell, Elizabeth   164
Powell, Mary   169
Pratt, Elizabeth   166

Preston, Hannah   103
Prew, Ann   166
Prior, John   112
Pritchett, Thomas Henry   98
Provel, Philip Carteret   172

Quartermain, Edward Arthur   150
Quarterman, Edith Angelina   148
Quarterman, Mary Agnes   145
Quin, Peter   89

Ragen, Edward   182
Rainbow, Anna   137
Rany, Mary   108
Read, Michael   124
Reade, Sir Richard   175
Rentz, Henry   108
Richardson, Ann   111, 176
Richardson, Augustin Joseph Mingaye   121
Richardson, Gertrude Agnes Annie   119
Richardson, Rosa Maria Mingaye   124
Ridgely, Frederick   137
Ridgely, Henry   137
Riley, Henry   134
Roach, John   180
Robinson, Clara   165
Robinson, John   120
Roche, Agnes   183
Roche, James Francis Michael   155
Rodwell, Clementina   101
Rodwell, Julia   103
Rouxel, Paul Antoine Charles Marie   167
Russell, James   124
Ryan, Helen   93
Rymer, Emma   147

Saisy, Marie Julie Anne   86
Salamoni, Elizabeth   161
Salamoni, Lucy   161

Salamoni, Martha   161
Salamoni, Martha, jnr   161
Salmoni, Mark   95
Salomini, Frances   93
Salomini, William   92
Salomone, George   91
Salomone, Martha   88
Salomone, Mary Ann   88
Salomone, Thomas   91
Saltmarsh, Amy   185
Saltmarsh, Amy   188
Saunders, Mrs   169
Savage, Susanna   162
Savin, Agnes Eleanor   139
Savin, Charles Joseph   130
Savin, Henry   143, 183
Savin, Isaac Ernest Laurence   154
Savin, Isaac Joseph   188
Savin, Julia   145
Savin, Mary Elizabeth   132
Savin, Teresa Mary   135
Savins, William Turner   150
Savins, Winefride Eliza   151
Savory, Mary Ann   128
Savoury, Mary   181
Scott, Mary Priscilla   150
Scott, Miles   150
Scott, William Joseph Charles   150
Scully, Sarah   137
Scully, Thomas   180
Seager, Osmund   117
Seassions, Caroline   163
Seeley, Catherine   181
Seely, Emma   189
Seillier, Alexander Miles   134
Selvy, Elizabeth Ann   148
Sessions, Carol Mary   140
Shannon, Thomas   148
Shaw, Michael   94
Shea, Joseph   129
Sheea, Owen   183
Sheen, Mary   87
Shepherd, John   87

Sheppard, Johanna   89
Shevelin, Mary Ann   116
Shevlan, Catharine Elizabeth   120
Short, Thomas   88
Shorter, Ann   93
Simpson, Thomas   168
Sims, Mary   142, 182
Sirett, Mary Ann   113
Slate, Adelaide   179
Smallwood, Charles   184
Smiley, William   182
Smith, –   89
Smith, Agnes Catherine   106
Smith, Alfred   101
Smith, Ambrose   180
Smith, Ambrose Frederick   126
Smith, Ambrose Henry   99
Smith, Ann   176
Smith, Cecilia Frances   129
Smith, Cecily   165
Smith, Charles   101
Smith, Charles William   152
Smith, Edward   107, 127
Smith, Eliza   100
Smith, Eliza Winefred   111
Smith, Eliza Winefride   166
Smith, Elizabeth   87, 101
Smith, Ellen   165
Smith, Ellen Elizabeth   130
Smith, Frances   84, 98, 162
Smith, Frances Ann   163
Smith, Frances Georgia   128
Smith, Francis   164
Smith, Frederic Augustus   110
Smith, Frederick   163
Smith, Frederick Augustine   168
Smith, George Frederick   104
Smith, Gertrude Elizabeth   149
Smith, Gertrude Mary   141, 181
Smith, Helen   176
Smith, Helen Teresa   143
Smith, Helen Theresa   108
Smith, Herbert Augustine   155

Smith, Isabel   133
Smith, James   102, 104
Smith, John   94, 136, 164
Smith, John Alfred   133
Smith, Joseph   96
Smith, Joseph Mary   145
Smith, Julia Lucy   114
Smith, Margaret   84
Smith, Mary   165, 185
Smith, Mary Ann   97
Smith, Mary Anne   126
Smith, Mary Clotilda   132
Smith, Mary Frances   103
Smith, Mary Louisa   109
Smith, Mary Monica   138
Smith, Mary Teresa   185
Smith, Rebecca   97
Smith, Richard   121
Smith, Sarah   119
Smith, Thomas   105
Smith, Thomas James   138
Smith, William   85, 118
Smith, William Bernard   151, 184
Snow, John   123
Sparing, Ann   166
Sparks, George   162
Sparshatt, John   95
Springwell, John   171
Stanley, Mary Anne   117
Steen, Teddy   109
Stephens, Mary   171
Stephens, Michael   79
Stevens, Henry   168
Stonnor, Bishop   172
Stowell, John   164
Stowell, Thomas   138, 139
Sullivan, Michael   185
Sullivan, Thomas   128, 176
Sutton, Mary   161
Sweeny, Thomas   105
Symkins, Elizabeth   160
Symkins, James   81
Symkins, Philip   82

Symkins, Thomas   81
Sympkins, Catharine   82
Sympkins, Francis   82

Talbot, Charlotte   89
Tansey, John   145
Tarant, Sarah   122
Tarbuck, Charles   134
Tayler, Helen   96
Tayler, Mary   99
Taylor, Catherine   136, 180
Taylor, Charles   101
Taylor, George   145, 183
Taylor, Henry   132
Taylor, John   96
Taylor, Joseph   133, 164
Taylor, Martha   134
Taylor, Mary   102, 163
Taylor, Matilda   188
Taylor, William   102
Teague, Alexander   100
Teague, Diana Elizabeth   100
Teague, George Vivers   100
Teague, Joanna Tilly   100
Teague, Mary Syndercomb   100
Telfer, Alfred Charles   153
Terry, Elizabeth   105
Terry, Emma   104
Terry, Frances   112
Terry, Richard   164
Teynham, Lady   173
Thick, Ann   109
Thick, Charles   114, 115
Thick, Christina   108
Thick, John   111
Thomas, Julia   147
Thorp, Susan Mary   167
Tilleman, Jane   83
Tilley, Catherine Mary   148
Timbs, Martha   88
Tinder, Ann   181
Tison, Catharine   113

Tobin, Edward   114
Tocque, Mary Ann   135
Tocque, Mary Ann Howes   167
Tod, Robert Joseph Whitelock   113
Tool, Anna   93
Trevor Lloyd, Thomas   137
Trinder, William   163
Turner, Eliza Mary   117
Turner, Emma   168
Turner, Julia
Turner, Mary   156
Turner, Philip Lorymer   149
Turner, Sarah Elizabeth   115
Turner, Teresa   168
Turner, Teresa Mary   114
Twycross, Isaac   119, 178
Tyler, Emma   106
Tyson, –   125
Tyson, Agnes   117, 162
Tyson, Catherine   181
Tyson, Francis   126, 176
Tyson, Hugh   110, 115, 176
Tyson, L.   177
Tyson, William   127

Utton, Ann Sophia   135, 179
Utton, Frederick   135
Utton, Helen Martha   136
Utton, William   136

Veal, John   186, 189
Venables, Edward   155
Venables, William Edward   158
Verni, Catharine   83
Verni, Mary   81
Viner, William   93
von Stockum, Frederick Oswald
    Joseph   177

Wainwright, Ann   177
Wakelin, Esther   162
Walford, Mary Ann   185, 188
Walker, Anne   79

Walker, John   160
Walker, Joseph   160
Walker, Mary   79, 161
Walker, Mary, snr   172
Walker, Nanny   172
Wallace, William   129
Walsh, John   158
Walton, Frederick Benjamin   120
Wangler, Crescentia   168
Wangler, Lucas   178
Wangler, Matthew   163
Ward, Ann   167
Ward, John   172
Warren, Henry   169
Waterhouse, Alice   80
Waterhouse, Ann   173
Waterhouse, Anne   79
Waterhouse, Barbara Ann   83
Waterhouse, Cornelius   80, 160
Waterhouse, Elen   160
Waterhouse, Francis   80, 83, 171
Waterhouse, Hannah   80, 160
Waterhouse, James   81, 172
Waterhouse, James   82
Waterhouse, John   79, 174
Waterhouse, Mary   81, 84
Waterhouse, Samuel   80
Waterhouse, Winefred   173
Waterhouse, Winny   81
Watson, Maria Elizabeth   123
Watts, Ann   162
Watts, John   160
Watts, William   105
Webb, Agnes   170
Wehrly, Theodore   167
Welland, Elizabeth   125
Wells, Alicia   92
Welsh, Elizabeth   150
Welsh, John   103
West, Daniel   179
Wheeler, Clara   133
Wheeler, Clare   166
Wheeler, Elizabeth   107

Wheeler, Frances   103
Wheeler, John   97
Wheeler, Mary   99
Wheeler, William   105
Whelan, Mary Ann   130
Whelan, Thomas Edward   131
Whitaker, Ann   94
White, Sarah   87
White, Winefred   169
Whiteing, Mrs   172
Whiting, –   107
Whiting, James   143
Whiting, James Alfred   164, 167
Whiting, Mary Ann   163
Whiting, Thomas   164
Whiting, Thomas Samuel   187
Wiblin, Ann   120, 121
Wignor, William   169
Wilkins, Elizabeth   122
Williams, Ellen Eliza
Williams, Emily Catherine   157
Williams, Jessy Matilda   156
Williamson, Alfred   163
Williamson, Alfred John   127
Williamson, Charles   125
Williamson, Eliza   162, 178
Williamson, Eliza Lucy   117
Williamson, Elizabeth   163
Williamson, Ellen Elizabeth   123
Williamson, George Alexander   103
Williamson, John   103
Winlow, Susan   171
Winter, Susan   79
Wizard, Elizabeth   189
Wizard, Hannah   189
Wollmer, Francis   170

Wood, Jane   116
Wood, Margaret   111
Wood, Rose   109
Woodley, Gemima   125
Woodley, Sarah   124
Woodmason, Ann   120
Woodward, Sarah   92
Woolfe, Charles   173
Wormington, Charles   167
Worney, Adelaide   158
Worney, Mary Ann   158
Wright, Christopher   184
Wright, George Henry Bateson   188

Yateman, Anne   173
Yates, Abraham   104
Yates, Amelia   102
Yates, Ann   99
Yates, Elizabeth   98, 99
Yates, Frances   101
Yates, John   102
Yates, Mary Anne   106
Yates, Thomas   102
Young, Aloise   188
Young, Brown   166
Young, Charles   140, 163
Young, Edward   139, 163
Young, Elizabeth   139
Young, Eva Mary   140
Young, Francis   163
Young, Francis George   140
Young, Frederick John Percy   158
Young, Helen   165
Young, Louisa   139
Young, Mary   160
Young, Mary Matilda   140